URBAN POWER

Princeton Studies in Global and Comparative Sociology
Andreas Wimmer, *Series Editor*

Urban Power

Democracy and
Inequality in
São Paulo and
Johannesburg

Benjamin H. Bradlow

PRINCETON UNIVERSITY PRESS
PRINCETON AND OXFORD

Published by Princeton University Press
41 William Street, Princeton, New Jersey 08540
99 Banbury Road, Oxford OX2 6JX

press.princeton.edu

ISBN 9780691237114
ISBN (pbk.) 9780691237121
ISBN (e-book) 9780691237107

British Library Cataloging-in-Publication Data is available

Editorial: Meagan Levinson and Erik Beranek
Production Editorial: Jaden Young
Jacket/Cover Design: Marcella Macalalag
Production: Lauren Reese
Publicity: William Pagdatoon
Copyeditor: Elisabeth A. Graves

Cover Credit: Marcella Macalalag

This book has been composed in Adobe Text and Gotham

10 9 8 7 6 5 4 3 2 1

To Fenna

In memory of Louisa Bradlow Carman

CONTENTS

Figures

Tables

LIST OF ACRONYMS

ABC	Santo André, São Bernardo do Campo, São Caetano do Sul
ANC	African National Congress
ARSESP	Agência Reguladora de Serviços Públicos do Estado de São Paulo (Regulatory Agency of Public Services São Paulo)
BLA	Black Local Authority
BRT	bus rapid transit
CBD	central business district
CEB	*comunidade eclesiais de base* (ecclesiastical base community)
CID	city improvement district
CIMS	Capital Investment Management System
CMTC	Companhia Metropolitana de Transportes Coletivos (Municipal Company for Collective Transport)
COSATU	Congress of South African Trade Unions
CWMC	Central Witwatersrand Metropolitan Chamber
FLM	Frente da Luta por Moradia (Front for the Housing Struggle)
FMSAI	Fundo Municipal de Saneamento Ambiental e Infraestrutura (Municipal Fund for Environmental Sanitation and Infrastructure)
FUNDURB	Municipal Fund for Urban Development
MAS	Movement towards Socialism
MCMV	Minha Casa, Minha Vida (My House, My Life)
MNRU	Movimento Nacional pela Reforma Urbana (National Movement for Urban Reform)
MOE	municipal-owned entity
MPL	Movimento Passe Livre (Free Tariff Movement)
MTST	Movimento dos Trabalhadores Sem Teto (Homeless Workers Movement)

PSDB   Social Democratic Party of Brazil

PT   Workers' Party

RDP   Reconstruction and Development Program

SABESP   Companhia de Saneamento Básico do Estado de São Paulo (Basic Sanitation Company of the State of São Paulo)

SAPOA   South African Property Owners Association

SDI   Shack/Slum Dwellers International

SECOVI   Sindicato das Empresas de Compra, Venda e Administração de Imóveis (Syndicate of Purchases, Sales, and Administration of Property of São Paulo)

SPTN   Strategic Public Transport Network

UDF   United Democratic Front

UISP   Upgrading of Informal Settlements Program

UMM   União dos Movimentos de Moradia (Federation of Housing Movements)

ZEIS   Zonas Especiais de Interesse Social (Special Zones of Social Interest)

Mayors of São Paulo, 1989–2016

1989	Luiza Erundina	Workers' Party	Left
1993	Paulo Maluf	Progressive Party	Right
1997	Celso Pitta	Progressive Party	Right
2001	Marta Suplicy	Workers' Party	Left
2005	José Serra	Social Democratic Party	Center-right
2006	Gilberto Kassab	Democrats	Center-right
2013	Fernando Haddad	Workers' Party	Left

Mayors of Johannesburg, 1995–2016

1995	Isaac Mogase	African National Congress	Left
2000	Amos Masondo	African National Congress	Left
2011	Parks Tau	African National Congress	Left

ACKNOWLEDGMENTS

Like many first scholarly books, this project was incubated as a doctoral dissertation. Upon my arrival at Brown University in the fall of 2014, Patrick Heller immediately seized on my desire to pursue an ambitious comparative, fieldwork-based project. He first suggested that I consider comparing South Africa with Brazil, a country about which I knew almost nothing and which speaks a language of which I knew not a word. In other words, he's the one who got me into this mess. Given the conservative inclinations of many academic social scientists, I can imagine that some may say that he was committing professional malpractice. It is a rare privilege to have an advisor who never wavered (at least outwardly!) in the belief that I could pursue a project that required a new language and the cultivation of a network of contacts across multiple continents. Every conversation about this project with Patrick left me with new energy and excitement about the work, even when he was brutally honest about the need for improvements.

Nitsan Chorev advised this project almost as long as Patrick, and she did so with a consistent capacity to provide feedback that is, in the best sense, always skeptical but never cynical. She has pushed me to a clarity of thought and writing that has taught me what it means to speak of a "comparative sensibility" as a researcher.

I first encountered many of the ideas that inspired this project in Peter Evans's work, and it was an honor to have him help guide it. He gave me the confidence to pursue ambitious theoretical arguments. And his enthusiasm for both Brazil and South Africa encouraged me that I had the cases with which to make these arguments.

Other faculty in Brown's sociology department whose conversations and advice enriched this work include Scott Frickel, Nicole Gonzalez Van Cleve, José Itzigsohn, John Logan, Josh Pacewicz, Andrew Schrank, Mike White, and Leah VanWey. Outside of the sociology department, I found additional faculty who were eager to engage with my work. In the political science, economics, and anthropology departments, I am grateful for conversations with Mark Blyth, Rick Locke, Dan Smith, Barbara Stallings, Bryce Steinberg, and Rebecca Weitz-Shapiro. I want to particularly thank the historian Jim Green, who created a fascinating and vibrant community of Brazilianist scholarship, events, and discussion at Brown. I cannot imagine developing my facility in understanding and discussing Brazilian politics and society without the great institution of Brazilian studies that he has built at Brown.

The Massachusetts Institute of Technology's Department of Urban Studies and Planning has incubated some of the most important sociological work on the state, cities, and development in the past half century. It is where, as a master's student, I first discovered many of the ideas that shape this book and learned to value the insights of field-based original research and practice. I am particularly grateful to Gabriella Carolini and Jason Jackson for their comments and encouragement about this book, as well as for invitations to present work in progress. Conversations with Diane Davis at MIT and later at Harvard University's Graduate School of Design were deeply influential.

I spent the last year of writing the first draft of this manuscript—that is, the dissertation—as a Visiting Democracy Fellow at the Ash Center at Harvard's Kennedy School and was grateful for the insights of Fernando Bizarro, Marshall Ganz, Quinton Mayne, Fritz Sager, and Guillermo Toral. I developed a subsequent draft as a Postdoctoral Fellow in the Weatherhead Scholars Program at Harvard's Weatherhead Center for International Affairs. During that time, Michèle Lamont and her Research Cluster on Comparative Inequality and Inclusion provided a very stimulating home. Michèle has since become a mentor, for which I am immensely grateful. I am also grateful for comments and discussions about this work with Bruno Carvalho, Alisha Holland, and Alice Xu.

The Weatherhead Center supported a workshop of the book manuscript in April 2021 that was immeasurably helpful in the revision of this work. I am grateful to Gianpaolo Baiocchi, Archon Fung, Marco Garrido, Josh Pacewicz, and Liza Weinstein for such careful reading and reflections and for being both unflinching and generous in their comments.

My colleagues at Princeton have been immensely supportive as I have finalized this work. Mitch Duneier first gave me a boost of confidence to pursue this work from the time when I was still deep in the midst of fieldwork in 2017. I am grateful for his incisive insights into the implications of my work and for his support since that time. João Biehl, Miguel Centeno, Adam Goldstein, Tod Hamilton, Alison Isenberg, Sanyu Mojola, Alejandro Portes, John Robinson, and Fred Wherry have given me a helpful final push to clarify my arguments and to be confident in putting them forward to the widest possible audience.

I gratefully acknowledge the financial support of the American Council of Learned Societies, the National Science Foundation, the Fulbright Program, the Brazilian Studies Association, the Harvard Mellon Urban Initiative, and a range of entities at Brown University: the Graduate Program in Development, the Institute at Brown for Environment and Society, and the Office of

Global Engagement. In particular, the support from Harvard's Mellon Initiative enabled me to work with Asher Kaplan to design the maps in chapter 2. Parts of this book draw on arguments that I first began to develop in peer-reviewed journal articles, including "Urban Social Movements and Local State Capacity," published in 2024 in *World Development*; "Embeddedness and Cohesion: Regimes of Urban Public Goods Distribution," published in 2022 in *Theory and Society*; and "Weapons of the Strong: Elite Resistance and the Neo-Apartheid City," published in 2021 in *City and Community*.

The editorial team at Princeton University Press has been immensely supportive throughout this process. Meagan Levinson understood this project from our first conversation. Rachael Levay, Eric Crahan, and Erik Beranek have helped bring this to the finish line. I am grateful to the anonymous reviewers of both the proposal and the full manuscript. I want to especially thank Michael Jauchen, who, as an independent developmental editor for this manuscript, not only improved the text greatly but taught me enduring lessons about writing and storytelling. My undergraduate thesis advisor, the historian Bruce Dorsey, taught me how to write analytically about original research. And my high school literature teacher Gill Cook taught me how to write analytically. I often recalled their feedback and encouragement as I finalized this text.

I was very lucky to meet an incredibly wide range of informants during my fieldwork in Brazil and South Africa. I am grateful to every movement activist, public official, and private-sector actor who made the time to talk, to think reflectively about their own experiences, to invite me to meetings, and to share documents for this project. A full list of informants who participated in taped interviews appears in appendix B.

In São Paulo, the Center for Metropolitan Studies (CEM) at the University of São Paulo was truly an intellectual home. The research group led by Eduardo Marques, and populated by an incredible group of young researchers, influenced my thinking about the city in deep and profound ways. I was uniformly welcomed by all, from faculty to postdoctoral, doctoral, and master's-level researchers, and pushed to seek out new reading, informants, and ways of interpreting the city's political history. Across its work on data collection, theoretical development, and policy engagement, CEM serves as a unique and world-class example of an urban research institution. There, I was especially grateful for sharing conversations, drinks, and food with Rogério Barbosa, Carla Bezerra, Marcos Campos, Gabriel Feltran, Adrian Gurza Lavalle, Telma Hoyler, Eduardo Marques, Guilherme Minarelli, Magaly Pulhez, and Matt Richmond. Beyond CEM, the community of urban researchers in São Paulo is incredibly rich and diverse. I was especially grateful to Alex Abiko, Renato Cymbalista, Kazuo Nakano, Raquel Rolnik, and Luciana Royer for their time and multiple conversations. A number of others involved in the politics of social movements, elected office, and bureaucratic agencies opened doors for me and shared their thoughts, their experiences, and, in many cases, their friendship. Of particular note are Higor Carvalho, Evaniza Rodrigues, Helô Regina, Ana Claudia Rossbach, Paulo Teixeira and his family, and Graça Xavier. Sean Purdy has housed a number of U.S.-based scholars over the years, and I was very lucky to share beers and conversations with him while renting a room in his apartment in Bela Vista. Thais Carrança, Sam Cowie, Alex Hochuli, and Euan Marshall were excellent raconteurs and thinkers to befriend. I was also grateful for the friendship of early-career U.S.-based Brazilianist scholars I first met in São Paulo, especially Daniel Aldana Cohen, Carter Koppelman, Liz McKenna, Manuel Rosaldo, Becky Tarlau, Cos Tollerson, and my fellow South African comrade in Brazil, Ben Fogel.

In Johannesburg, I felt part of an equally motivating group of scholars associated with the Public Affairs Research Institute, which hosted my research visits, as well as the Gauteng City-Region Observatory and the South African Research Chairs Initiative Chair in Spatial Planning at the University of Witwatersrand. My sincere thanks go to Richard Ballard, Mbongiseni Bhutelezi, Ryan Brunette, Sian Butcher, Sarah Charlton, Ivor Chipkin, Rom Dittgen, Federica Duca, Phil Harrison, Alan Mabin, Aidan Mosselson, Joel Pearson, Mosa Phadi, Margot Rubin, Kate Tissington, and Matthew Wilhelm-Solomon for fascinating conversations over seminars, coffees, beers, and food. Old friends Dave Cornwell, Alex Dubb, Murray Hunter, Katie Huston, Michael Kransdorff, Adi Kumar, Kulani Nkuna, Dani Rodin, Simon Shear, and Ilham Rawoot were always good company.

A scholarly community of Brazilianist, South Africanist, and global urbanist academics and journalists has enriched this work through many conversations at conferences, as well as in regular correspondence via email, WhatsApp, and Twitter. In addition to those already mentioned, I want to thank Adam Aboobaker, Sneha Annavarapu, Josh Budlender, Yuri Gama, Sean Jacobs, Zach Levenson, Simeon Newman, Andre Pagliarini, Marcel Paret, Gay Seidman, Micah Reddy, Niall Reddy, Xuefei Ren, William Shoki, Dennis Webster, and Joel Wolfe. My collaborators in article-writing over the past few years have kept me accountable and inspired: Tomás Gold, Ali Kadivar, Alex Kentikelenis, Stefano Polloni, Adaner Usmani, and Will Violette. I am also grateful to former and current graduate students and postdocs at Brown whose discussions and friendship were critical ingredients to this work: Subadevan, Ani Adhikari, Sa'ed Atshan, Emily Avera, Amanda Ball, Ben Bellman, Marcelo Bohrt, Aimee Bourassa, Liz Brennan, Karida Brown, Rui Carvalho, Laura Garbes, Diana Graizbord, Rici Hammer, Sara Hefny, Dennis Hogan, Rehan Jamil, prabh kehal, Johnnie Lotesta, Syeda Masood, Dan McDonald, Izzy Notter, Carilee Osborne, Chantel Pheiffer, and Marcus Walton.

Throughout my work on this book, I was lucky enough to be involved in communities of friends in the Boston and Philadelphia regions, who sustained me with music, food, drink, and companionship. Thanks go to Leo Bittleston,

Dan Beyer, Blake Roberts Crall, James Roberts Crall, Ben Ewen-Campen, Jonah Eaton, Alex Feinstein, Eliza Hale, Cliff Hall, Tev Kelman, Joe Kille, Waverly Kille, Jacob Kramer, Emiliano Rodriguez, Kelly Rodriguez, Pennie Taylor, and Alex Wheeler. Old friend Adam Dalva came through with some generous edits of the preface and appendix as I was finalizing the text.

I was lucky to have had an extended group of political organizing comrades in Somerville, where I lived for most of the writing of this book. Of those not already mentioned, I especially want to thank Bill Cavellini, Mike Firestone, Michele Hansen, and the late Van Hardy.

I have been aware for some time now that my parents are the inspiration for this work. Their search for home has framed lives of love and worldly, humanistic values that have made the best parts of me as both a person and a scholar. I also thank my brother, Adam, for his steadfast companionship.

My wife, Fenna, has been my best cheerleader and critic, before and throughout this work. Her enthusiasm for a project that would require long periods spent apart made this plausible to begin with. Her readings of various parts of this project were insightful and gave me the encouragement that I could follow through. More times than I can count, her belief in me has made it possible to complete this work and to continue to think big. I learn every day from the example that she sets in her own scholarship. Her love gives me purpose, inspiration, and joy.

During the writing of this book, Miriam Daphne and Frank Abraham joined our lives. Though raising two young children while writing a book has its challenges, their delight and curiosity have provided unique motivation. They are a constant reminder of what is important in life. In addition to the contributions already mentioned, Fenna took on key childcare responsibilities at critical moments, without which I would never have completed this work. For similar reasons, I also want to thank Miriam and Frank's day care and kindergarten teachers.

Finally, I am sorry that Walter Fieuw left this world long before he should have. I remember his infectious enthusiasm about this book-in-progress the last time we spoke on the phone. I would have loved to share a draft with him (and a few pints, *nogal*). I know he would have read it closely and provided comments that would have made it better than what it is.

Inside the car, a man was screaming. The words came out fast, in a language I could not understand. Shacks of corrugated iron butted up against the side of the road; a thin stream of raw sewage ran down the street where the car was driving. I had been there for a couple of hours and, by that point, had become acclimated to the smell.

I was standing with a group of about ten people wearing blue T-shirts. They calmly observed the man. Even as a number of passersby crowded more closely around, only the man in the car seemed agitated. It was early April 2009, in Johannesburg's Alexandra township, one of the oldest black neighborhoods in the city. Door-to-door campaigning for South Africa's upcoming national election was in full swing.

I had recently arrived in the country, which I had visited regularly throughout my life. South Africa had been home to generations of my family since the late nineteenth century, when my ancestors migrated from villages in the Jewish "Pale of Settlement" in czarist Russia—present-day Lithuania, Poland, and Ukraine. My parents left South Africa for the United States in the late 1970s, fleeing conscription into the Apartheid military and hoping for professional opportunity. Now, they had returned to live and work in Johannesburg, the city of their birth. I was freshly graduated from college in the United States and looking for work as a journalist to cover the election.

I had lucked into an entry-level position with a daily newspaper in Johannesburg. During an orientation meeting for new journalists, one editor underscored that we should think of our readership as solidly middle class. When I proposed tagging along with canvassers of the main political parties contesting the election to write about how the election looked from the poor and working-class neighborhoods of Johannesburg, I received some skeptical raised eyebrows from my editors. But as long as I kept up with my other assignments, I was welcome to give it a shot.

The 2009 election was when anger over the unrealized promises of democracy in South Africa began to be articulated in the country's electoral politics. The Democratic Alliance—the party whose rainbow logo was emblazoned on the blue T-shirts of those men and women in Alexandra—was the first to respond to my cold calls. They proposed that I join them in the historic black township on a Saturday morning. Their party was historically associated with wealthier, white voters, and the man shouting in the car was unhappy that black residents of one of the oldest neighborhoods in the city would be out campaigning for the Democratic Alliance.

Over the course of that month, the ruling African National Congress (ANC) and the Congress of the People, which had split from the ANC a few months before, would also invite me to accompany them in door-to-door canvassing in neighborhoods across the city. I joined the ANC in the large Soweto township in the southern part of the city, in a neighborhood called Klipspruit. This was an area with paved roads and reliable basic services such as electricity, water, and sanitation, the result of the ANC government's investments in the neighborhood since the end of Apartheid in 1994. The Congress of the People, the ANC breakaway, invited me along as they campaigned in an informal settlement north of Johannesburg called Kanana Extension. There, a disorganized patchwork of shacks marked the landscape, and sewage seeped through the light brown dirt paths that wound between the homes made of thin metal sheets. Party activists highlighted the poor conditions of the neighborhood as they campaigned.

It was in these places that I started searching for a story that was not only about a single election, a single city, or even a single country. It is a story about how the politics of democracy, the social dynamics of inequality, and the distributional consequences of what urban planners call the "built environment" are indivisible across the globe.

The inequalities of urban life amid pervasive informal settlement are perhaps the biggest challenge that local governments in most of the world face today. The quintessential image of contemporary urbanization across the globe is the one I encountered in Alexandra and Kanana Extension back in 2009. As the historian Mike Davis (2006) predicted a few years before I began working in Johannesburg, we are hurtling toward a future "planet of slums."

But this future has started to arrive unevenly and is certainly not preordained. This book is about why some cities become better equipped than others to reduce inequalities in the urban built environment—for example, housing, sanitation, and collective transportation. It is also a story of the promise of democracy and how it translates into the everyday reality of governing.

After the 2009 election, I continued to get to know informal settlements, first while I covered stories as a journalist in Johannesburg, then as a researcher with an international nongovernmental organization called Slum Dwellers International. This latter position led me to encounters in informal settlements in countries across Africa, Asia, and Latin America. I witnessed and documented how community organizations in these settlements tried to negotiate with local governments for improvements to housing and the basic infrastructure in their communities.

Through these experiences, I first learned of the figure of the "urban planner"—a profession about which I knew not a thing. I began to see how this figure—sometimes in government, sometimes in private real estate development, sometimes in an activist space—was mediating many of the key relationships that mattered. Urban planning links the social realities of the built environment to government policies that attempt to alter that built environment.

As I met both activists and local government officials in cities across the Global South, I realized that they faced similar problems despite the wide range of resources at their disposal. And I do not just mean money, though that is certainly always important. The real preoccupations of governing frequently concerned the resources of what social scientists often call "governance." Would informal settlement residents oppose or enable a policy? Would a policy be seen as legitimate across departments, both within local government and at higher levels, such as a state or province or a national government?

The kinds of conversations among government officials and grassroots activists that I observed as a young practitioner are, ultimately, what led me to write this book. They guided me to meet the kinds of people who matter for reducing inequalities in rapidly urbanizing cities. They also helped me to understand the questions I should ask.

And they helped me to understand the importance of comparison. This book is written with what Albert Hirschman (1971) once called a "bias for hope." In this book, I seek to understand why, even under the most difficult of conditions, improvements in urban distribution are sometimes possible. I do so not by comparing one case to an imagined ideal but, rather, by aiming to generate deep understandings of two cities, so that, when taken together, they might help us to understand many other cities.

The task of researching even one city, armed with the history and sensitivity to context that are the hallmark of useful qualitative fieldwork, is no simple task. I conceived this book with the ambition of researching two cities. More than that would likely be too unwieldy for a single researcher. With this book, I hope to convince readers that comparing two cities can provide useful lessons for thinking about variation in contemporary patterns of urbanization and inequality well beyond the two that I focus on here. And I will make that case by presenting evidence collected through a commitment to field-based research in those two cities: Johannesburg and São Paulo.

By the time I returned to Johannesburg in 2015 to begin the research for this book, it was clear that so much that matters in how policy gets both made and implemented has not been documented. I had to be on the ground, speaking with the activists, bureaucrats, politicians, and private-sector actors who were collectively writing the city's story of governing inequality in a new democracy. I had a good sense of which kinds of local government agencies, movements, and private developers might be important to interview. I had met some of them before.

But I also knew that in order to really understand why some cities are more effective than others in reducing inequalities, I would have to compare Johannesburg with somewhere else. In the pages that follow, I will describe why I chose São Paulo, another global megacity with deep inequalities in the distribution of housing, sanitation, and transportation. I will show how São Paulo started its democratic era, in the late 1980s, from a strikingly similar position as Johannesburg in terms of political mobilization and the material distribution of public goods across the space of the city. But São Paulo would later make the kinds of improvements in distributing public goods, especially in comparison with Johannesburg, that could help me draw out broader lessons not based on abstract hypotheticals but taken from realities on the ground. As my field research expanded across sixteen months between 2015 and 2018, I developed similar networks of social movement leaders, government officials, and private-sector actors in both São Paulo and Johannesburg. Two hundred twenty-five semistructured interviews—and countless other informal encounters and observations—make up the bulk of the original evidentiary base that I present here.

What historically minded, field-based, comparative research can do is help us understand the social roots of political and institutional action. This is the approach that I take in this book. The comparison contained here aims to show what a "bias for hope" in changing the formal and informal institutions that govern urban life looks like when we start with a view from the most excluded parts of cities: slums, in English; *favelas*, in Brazilian Portuguese; and *mjondolos*, in isiZulu. The arguments that I make are my attempt to explain why some cities manage to include these neighborhoods while others reproduce their exclusion. These are the places that characterize humanity's urban present and future. And they are among our definitive crucibles for building a more just world.

Princeton, New Jersey, United States
November 19, 2023

URBAN POWER

1

Theorizing Power, Public Goods, and the City

In 1996, Mariza Dutra Alves and her husband split up. Without her husband's income, finding a place to live within the municipal limits of São Paulo, Brazil, one of the world's largest and most unequal cities, suddenly felt out of reach. She moved in with her parents in Suzano, a municipality in the eastern part of the larger São Paulo metropolitan region, which is home to some twenty million people.

There, she found work as a domestic cleaner in Cidade Lider, a working-class district in the city's sprawling eastern periphery. In a private car with no traffic, the drive from Suzano to Cidade Lider would take about an hour. By intermunicipal public bus, the journey was two times as long. For the wealthy residents who occupy the city's core, a district like Cidade Lider, with its simple, low-rise shop fronts, winding roads, and informal shack settlements, feels like a world away.

But for Mariza, it was an entrée into the city's economic opportunities. Basic necessities were her concern. "Because I was working so far from my children, I would return home extremely late," she told me twenty-one years after the breakup. "Just to give you an idea, I left home at 4:30 in the morning, only to return at nine o'clock at night."[1]

Mariza hoped to make enough money to one day get a place to live that she could call her own. She befriended someone who lived in an informal shack that was close to the houses she cleaned. Her new friend was a participant in a self-build housing project in São Paulo, known in Portuguese as a *mutirão* (pronounced "moo-chee-rau"). The project was organized through a cooperative formed under the umbrella of one of the oldest housing movements in the city, called the União dos Movimentos de Moradia.

When I interviewed her, Mariza remembered how she was apprehensive at first about attending one of the cooperative's meetings. She told herself that she didn't have the time, that she didn't know what to do at a meeting, that she didn't understand why there needed to be a movement in the first place.

"Why did people have to occupy land given that there was a right to housing in the constitution?" she recalled asking herself.

But by October 1998, Mariza had become convinced that it was time to join the movement. And she was ready to act. She began speaking with a group of people who were similarly desperate for a foothold in the city to plan a collective occupation in Mooca, a working-class district in the north and east of the municipality. The group hoped to use the occupation to force somebody—anybody—to act.

For twenty days, they slept under wood and tarps. Finally, the group was granted government land in the far eastern district of Itaim Paulista. There, members could begin to construct a neighborhood of their own, eventually totaling 420 homes in all.

Mariza had begun a life of occupying and organizing. This would become a life of forcing the hand of government to act and then working to ensure that action led to results on the ground.

―――

The past half century has witnessed a great global migration to cities, particularly across poor and middle-income countries in the Global South. For the one out of every seven humans who lives in an urban slum today,[2] cities are sites of struggle. The proliferation of slums—where the basics of city life are largely unavailable—as a dominant mode of urban life underscores how the creation of cities is inherently divided and unequal. Many of these areas lack decent shelter without a threat of eviction. A toilet. A way to move between work and home. The distribution of these goods characterizes the rationed inequalities of our urban world.

Now, in a warming world, slums are both the first refuge of climate migrants within the Global South and the zones of deepest vulnerability to climate impacts (Rigaud et al. 2018; Vince 2022). In 2014, the Intergovernmental Panel on Climate Change published its *Fifth Assessment Report* (2014). These reports are the authoritative synthesis of the global research consensus on interdisciplinary climate science. The *Fifth Assessment Report* was the first to have a stand-alone chapter on cities and urbanization.

Across the text of this Intergovernmental Panel on Climate Change report, slums are frequently mentioned as sites of two core problems for governing climate resilience. First, inequalities in urban public goods define an urban built environment unable to cope with climate-induced migration and disaster risk. Of particular importance here are the defining inequalities in the distribution of housing, sanitation, and transportation. And second, the lack of responsive governing arrangements prevents resilient urban systems.

The people who manage the formal life of cities—primarily bureaucrats and politicians who work in local government—often cite the frustrating impotence of the bureaucracy associated with their work. They might say that formal hierarchies or interagency competition constrain their scope to act. But they also enjoy a profound sense of empowerment because the institutions they populate clearly matter for changing the lives of the people who live in their cities.

The people who live in the slums of cities experience different deficits of influence: to be heard, to get ahead, to live what Amartya Sen has famously described as "lives they value—and have reason to value" (1999, 8). Yet they have also discovered their own forms of power: in movements, organizations, and largely informal arrangements that make the contingencies of urban life bearable and meaningful.

Like Mariza, urban residents across the globe frequently take it upon themselves to develop housing and municipal services when their governments have been slow to act or have failed them completely. Usually, these actions are a form of resistance to the reproduction and spread of exclusion that characterizes contemporary patterns of urbanization. These actions sometimes concatenate into broader social movements.

And when these actions turn into movements, they sometimes generate a broader process—usually in local government—to include the most excluded parts of these cities in the array of public goods that make urban life livable and full of opportunity. This book is about the push and pull of grassroots activists like Mariza, the movements they form, and the politicians, bureaucrats, and private actors they encountered—and continue to encounter. It is the story of, on the one hand, those who have organized to gain the attention and will of government and, on the other, the process of working to make the government capable of delivering on that will. In other words, it is about what it takes to see the will to power for rights in the city realized in the built environment of cities: urban power.

To state the question that motivates this study: *Why are some cities more effective than others at reducing inequality?* This book will answer that question through an in-depth comparison of two global "megacities": São Paulo in Brazil and Johannesburg in South Africa. In doing so, it will propose and test an argument about the governance of urban inequality that speaks to a wider range of cities across the globe, particularly—though not exclusively—in the rapidly urbanizing Global South.

This book will argue that what differentiates cities that can begin to include their most excluded places from those that cannot is what I call "urban power." I define *urban power* as the coordination of the formal and informal social relations that produce governing institutions that manage the distribution of public goods across the space of the city. The ties between local government and a sphere of social movements in civil society—*embeddedness*—and coordinating capacity internal to the state—*cohesion*—are what make urban power effective in building toward a more equal city.

"Urban power" is about the processual configurations of power that enable the distribution of the basics of life in the city—the public goods that make urban life dignified, humane, and sustainable. Inequalities in distribution are produced through what Max Weber once described as processes of "social closure," through which boundaries mark who is and who is not included in the distribution of resources. The state is a critical institutional sphere where such boundaries are drawn and redrawn. When Weber wrote about social closure in urban space, he recalled the history of medieval walled cities to illustrate in stark terms just how governing institutions mark who is on either side of the boundaries of social closure. Among more contemporary sociological treatments of the state, a closely related idea comes from Michael Mann's (1984) term *infrastructural power*. He defines this as "the capacity of the state to actually penetrate civil society, and to implement logistically political decisions throughout the realm" (1984, 189). My use of *urban power* refers to the distinct dimensions of such "infrastructural" statecraft at the urban scale, especially municipal government, which shapes such closure in the built environment.

Western sociology has traditionally understood the process of urbanization as a transition toward industrial, rational modernity.[3] Likewise, demographers have understood urbanization and the transition from slums to neighborhoods with access to basic services as critical factors in the "demographic transition" to higher life expectancy (Dyson 2011). These approaches assume a type of teleology about patterns of urbanization. But what urban planners call "the built environment" of cities is not a product of physical laws. The built environment is a product of social conflict.[4]

Today, the persistence of the urban informal settlement is a crucible of some of sociology's founding assumptions about modernity: the economics of urbanization without industrialization (Gollin, Jedwab, and Vollrath 2016), the politics of institutions that are unable to include all urban residents in the provision of adequate housing and basic services, and the largely informal social organization of collective action. By 2050, in large part due to climate change–induced migration in Latin America, sub-Saharan Africa, and South Asia, two of every three humans will live in a city. And 40 percent of those residents, an estimated two billion people, will live in slums (Rigaud et al. 2018). The exclusions of urban life are at both the practical core and the theoretical core of the contemporary nature of inequality. The relationship between these inequalities in the urban political economy is about the power to govern, which is ultimately defined by the strength and scope of democratic authority over private actors.

Why Is Urban Redistribution So Hard?

"Urban power"—the coordination of the formal and informal social relationships that produce the institutions that govern the distribution of public goods across urban space—can work either to enforce social closure or to build urban inclusion. Though cities today do not build walls like the medieval city, they can enforce closure through land use laws, prejudicial allocation of financial and institutional authority for building and maintaining infrastructure, and evictions. The extent to which cities mobilize law, finance, and policies toward creating a more inclusive distribution of public goods becomes the basis on which the bonds of social closure either harden or begin to break down. The question of why some cities are more effective than others in reducing urban inequalities is, in this sense, a question of under what conditions urban power gets mobilized toward breaking the boundaries of social closure. And this is no simple task.

We might reasonably wonder why local government matters at all. An interdisciplinary set of arguments about the political economy of cities emphasizes the structuring role of globalization. The past half century of transnationally integrated markets and political institutions has led many scholars of urban political economy to downplay the urban scale of politics. When the sociologist Saskia Sassen (1991) observed these changes in the early 1990s, she argued that the primary function of cities is to serve in a hierarchy of global relations of exchange, with a select few coordinating those relations as so-called global cities. This influential approach carries a couple of key implications for the questions that I pose in this book. This approach suggests that *all* cities have undergone—or are undergoing—significant restructuring due to their role in the global integration of markets. The global is the primary scale that counts. Further, the nature of this kind of restructuring is to increase inequality in cities. For "global cities," there is a clear spatial imaginary aligned to Sassen's vision of inequality. The cores of cities are where the wealthy work, particularly in the so-called FIRE industries of finance, insurance, and real estate. The peripheries are home to the vast populations of low-wage service workers who clean city center buildings and serve food and other amenities to these white-collar winners of the new global economy.

To be sure, the literature on urban neoliberalism has, at times, emphasized that local and municipal politics and institutions matter and can vary (Brenner and Theodor 2002). However, the emphasis on the structural shift toward neoliberalism, which focuses on global dynamics, constrains room for agency at the local level. This literature has highlighted the trend toward decentralization reforms for public administration down to the municipal scale. Such reforms assume a strong reliance on local generation of revenue. The trend of decentralization has accelerated what Harvey (1989) describes as the transition of urban administration from "managerialism" to "entrepreneurialism," as local governments compete for private development to secure local tax revenues. To the extent that local action matters, it only matters in one direction. Because so much of local administration is geared toward capturing footloose private capital, little effort and resources is expended on broadening inclusion in the public goods of the city. The privatization of public services, tax incentives, and public subsidies for profit-generating activities becomes the primary scope of local government action. The outcome has an inexorable tendency toward lifting up the drawbridge of social closure.

This structural logic is at work in more locally driven theories of urban politics as well. "Growth machine" theory (Logan and Molotch 1987), for example, has focused on local coalitions between business and political elites to maximize economic growth as the decisive relationship in urban political economy. Similarly, the collective capacities of a "regime" in "urban regime theory" are defined by the interaction between the configuration of the actors that make up the local regime with the capability to act and the policies that are the object of institutional action (Stone 1989). These approaches are commensurate with the more global view of neoliberal urban restructuring because of the propensity of local authorities to ally with business elites to respond to the competitive pressures of neoliberal decentralizing reforms. The "growth machine" approach highlights the structural forces that bring these groups together, in particular the precedence of the "exchange value" of urban land over its "use value." This approach suggests that established elite concerns are the relatively immovable force around which redistributive reforms must navigate.

The tools of "growth machine" and "regime" theorists are useful for identifying both the importance of local institutional configurations and the varieties of conflict between growth-oriented and redistributive policy goals. For example, Stone (1993) theorizes the possibility of two types of redistribution-oriented regimes, which he describes as "middle class progressive" and "lower class opportunity expansion." However, he sees these categories as largely "hypothetical" (1993, 18). Notably, work in the urban literature that looks beyond U.S. cases for comparative leverage has called into question the usefulness of the "regime" and "growth machine" frames, due to much greater variation in intercity competition across countries (Davies 2002; Stoker and Mossberger 1994). These critiques emphasize the possibility of social coordination between political and other social actors for realizing programmatic goals in cities. But the possibility for a more inclusive programmatic change—as opposed to a program of economic growth—is unlikely. Work on redistributive politics in cities in the United States, for example, has highlighted the constraints that federal government regulations pose for cities (Petersen 1981) as well as the possibility for redistribution through regulations such as minimum wage laws (Martin 2001).

I agree that the conceptual tools of "growth machine" and "regime" theorists are useful. But the assumption—sometimes explicit, sometimes implicit—of much of this work that assigns independent weight to local politics is that all cities are growth machines, which is not necessarily the case. Likewise, the "growth machine" and "regime" theoretical paradigms assume a relatively uniform regulatory and implementing capacity of the local state, which also does not hold, particularly in the Global South. Furthermore, there is a wide variety of interscalar governing relationships between national or federal, state or provincial, and local governments.

A different kind of interdisciplinary literature on the political economy of development, often called "power-resources" theory, emphasizes variation in governing regimes but does so only within a national political framework. The extent to which subnational institutions are subject to contingency and variation is relatively minimized in these accounts. The emphasis has been on variations of class coalitions aligned to programmatic political parties as enabling or disabling policies for economic development and/or redistribution (see Esping-Andersen 1990; Pzeworski 1985). In particular, the role of democracy has been seen as critical for redistributive outcomes (see Rueschemeyer, Stephens, and Stephens 1992). The role of left political parties in Latin America (Huber and Stephens 2012) and alliances between working-class organizations in civil society and a left political party in the Indian state of Kerala (Heller 1999), for example, have been found to drive gains in both human development and economic growth. In sum, under conditions of subaltern collective action in coalition with a programmatic political party, redistribution is possible, even given the structural constraints of global capitalism.

These "power-resources" approaches to theorizing the state and distributional outcomes are mirrored in the social movements literature. Instead of just a focus on class coalitions or political parties, the movements literature makes it possible to identify other kinds of collective actors that can matter for producing redistributive policy change. Recent work on a "political mediation" model of social movement action has highlighted the need for a responsive political elite to react to movement demands in order to make them successful (Amenta et al. 2010). This literature has readily acknowledged a focus on cases in the United States (Amenta 2014), however, and therefore assumes a degree of generalizable bureaucratic capacity to act that does not exist in other parts of the world. Even the more state-centric accounts of social movements seen in work on "political opportunities" take for granted the question of state capacity beyond the capacity to repress movements (McAdam, McCarthy, and Zald 1996; Tarrow 1994). The literature on social movements has emphasized that a range of collective actors can produce a bottom-up, demand-side dynamic for change. But it does not explore the mechanisms for generating state capacity to make it happen.

The most prominent way of theorizing how different sectors of society might generate internal state capacities is in Evans's (1995) concept of "embedded autonomy." Evans uses this concept to characterize how states achieve economic development. In his paradigmatic account of South Korea, autonomous bureaucrats work with organized groups of industrial elites to implement a national project of industrial upgrading and development of exports for economic growth. Heller (1999) has found a similar dynamic in Kerala, but with a different protagonist—the working class—driving gains in both social outcomes and economic growth. Both focus on the importance of the coherence of different social groups outside of the state as a support for state action.

These prior findings might lead us to expect that if we observe variation in distributional outcomes at the urban scale, the root of change must lie at the national level and not at the local level. The "power-resources" approach allows for the possibility of variation in distributive regimes in contexts in which the structural forces of global capitalism might otherwise be seen as overdetermining. In fact, the thrust of the work in this literature has increasingly focused on middle-income countries in the Global South (see Evans and Heller 2015) where state capacities are highly varied. Work in the "power-resources" tradition has generally focused on national-level issues such as wages and social welfare benefits. But once we begin to disaggregate the institutional sphere of the state, capacities of state institutions to regulate the wage relationship and to tax and redistribute may vary considerably from capacities to alter the distributional consequences of the built environment.

Projects of political change are always spatially uneven (Snyder 2001). It is one thing to pursue redistribution with the centralized authority and resources of a national state. It is quite another to do so at the local level, where government actors must coordinate delegated legal authority that is often unclear, may overlap with state or provincial government, and may lack requisite fiscal resources for implementation. This becomes even more complicated when political parties of a given ideological stripe control one scale of government but not another. And even if there is an alignment of political parties across different scales of government, this is no guarantee that they will all work together. As this study will show, the alignment of parties across scales can sometimes hinder, rather than enable, urban-scale projects of distributional change. At the same time, political party competition—and changes in power—may very well enable more responsive government. But there is no reason to expect that

TABLE 1.1. Existing Explanations and Predicted Outcomes

Theoretical School	Consequence for Inequality
"Power-resources"/movements	Variation
Neoliberalism/"growth machines" and "regimes"	Growing inequality

this is a sufficient condition for building the bureaucratic capacities that are required for projects of distributional inclusion. Table 1.1 illustrates how the urban literature has tended to focus on the sources of growing inequality in cities, while the nationally focused "power-resources" literature has analyzed the sources of variation in distributional outcomes.

We can bridge these literatures by asking: *Under what conditions does social mobilization translate into making the local state matter for redistribution?* Recent qualitative empirical work on urban governance in the Global South has explored this question through a focus on the role of neighborhood associations and movements themselves. For example, in Mumbai, India, neighborhood associations in informal settlements have organized to prevent likely eviction due to the redevelopment schemes of national and state government as well as multinational private firms (Weinstein 2014). In São Paulo, "insurgent citizenship" strategies of neighborhood associations have asserted land rights that had previously been denied or hidden in formal law (Holston 2008). Both of these examples, however, focus on the role of the courts to enforce (or deny) land occupancy rights, and they focus on social organization at the scale of the neighborhood. They do not directly implicate the role of bureaucratic action to deliver new infrastructure, such as housing, sanitation, or transportation, or the role of social movements that organize beyond the scale of the neighborhood. These findings underscore that democratic institutional arrangements are a necessary condition for residents to organize freely, assert rights to stay in the city, and demand public goods in their neighborhoods. Even across democratic and nondemocratic contexts, recent work has highlighted the importance of the relationship between local state organization and social mobilization. Ren's (2020) comparison of Indian and Chinese cities finds that the organization of local governance varies widely and shapes residents' struggles with significant consequences in the regulation of both land use and air pollution.

To summarize so far, the politics of distributing public goods in cities has largely been characterized by theories of "supply" of state capacity or "demand" from excluded social sectors. But this finding still does not address some larger questions about the processes involved in enacting change in cities around the globe. What are the characteristics of governing regimes that make such programmatic, city-wide outcomes in delivery possible? How do these demands translate beyond regulatory change or legal enforcement into concrete delivery at a city-wide scale by local governments?

Defining "Embeddedness" and "Cohesion"

I argue that the theoretical concepts of "embeddedness" and "cohesion" explain processes of change that bridge external social mobilization and the internal, organizational life of state institutions. This approach cuts across questions of "supply" of state capacity from above and "demand" from below. Social pressure and institutional capacity, I contend, are in dynamic interaction. And for the types of public goods I examine here, this interaction has concrete results—often, quite literally.

I define *embeddedness* as the connections of the local state to civil society, particularly a sphere of social movements, that produce the ideas and influence for policy change that realizes human development. And I define *cohesion* as the internal coordinating capacity of the local state to implement policy changes. The concepts of "embeddedness" and "cohesion" adapt prior explanations of social bases of state action like Evans's "embedded autonomy" to the unique dimensions of the urban administration of public goods. Furthermore, I argue that the analytical usefulness of these explanations depends on our ability to wield them to explain not only why an institutional configuration produces a given outcome in a particular moment but how those institutional changes occur over time.

Prior explanations of the role of embeddedness in generating state capacities do not fully account for the full range of influential social actors in the urban context (see Evans 1995; Heller 1999). The social sectors likely to induce changes in the distribution of public goods in cities are not likely to be either business elites or traditional trade unions. Due to their organizational focus on precisely these goods, social movements for goods of collective consumption, such as housing or transportation, are much more likely candidates for "embedded" connections to local state institutions to drive change in the distribution of public goods. In the literature on social democracy in both northern Europe (see Esping-Andersen 1990) and Latin America (see Huber and Stephens 2012), these movements are rarely as durable or as encompassing as traditional social actors, such as unions. The mobilization of such movements articulates and builds popular pressure for distributive goals. The connections that these movements have to both political parties and professional bureaucrats within the local state make it possible for these goals to enter the halls of formal power.

It is important to note that network ties between movements and the state are a necessary but not necessarily sufficient condition for "embeddedness" to exist, however. Social movements have a wide repertoire of strategies, which could be considered oppositional, on one end of the spectrum, or clientelistic, on the other. So how do we know when their relationship to the state is embedded? "Embeddedness" describes network ties that are oriented toward programmatic outcomes—that is, city-wide policies as opposed to discretionary or clientelistic ones. This criterion resembles Fung and Wright's (2001) model of "empowered deliberative democracy," which theorizes the relationship between participatory democratic reforms and institutional action. The kind of state-society embeddedness under examination in this study highlights the role of movements, as opposed to individuals, and emphasizes not just deliberation but changed modes in the state's delivery of physical goods.

My comparative analysis in the cases of São Paulo and Johannesburg in this book will show that the interplay between movements and political parties became vital for either mobilizing or demobilizing urban movements in each city. The role of political parties therefore had meaningful effects on processes leading toward configurations of higher or lower embeddedness and cohesion. Though bureaucrats and movements occupy the foreground of much of the empirical story I tell, the role of political parties in the background is never far from the field of action. Sociologists cannot theorize urban governance without paying attention to the strategies and tactics of political parties. A key takeaway for practice is that bureaucrats, planners, and movement activists alike cannot ignore the role of parties in shaping their strategies for generating policy change at the urban scale.

Embeddedness is critical for generating the disciplining impetus for institutional cohesion. Evans's theorization of embeddedness is largely a macro-level explanation of the relationship between state and society for economic development. His approach, along theoretical lines associated with Polanyi's (1944) description of market exchange being "embedded" in human social relation, focuses on the institutional sphere of the state and that of the market, primarily on channels of communicating information across the social spheres of market and state. My approach, however, considers embeddedness from a more meso-level understanding, which is commonly associated with Granovetter (1985). I focus not only on the abstract strength or weakness of network ties between actors in the civil society sphere—particularly social movements—and the local state but also on the temporal structure of those ties. In other words, sequencing matters for explaining the variation in configurations of embeddedness and cohesion. From this standpoint, the emphasis is not only on sharing information between different spheres of social action but on the formation of durable bonds over time between actors both within and outside the state that can produce the disciplining power of coordination that defines "cohesion." Sequencing matters because embeddedness and cohesion can be mutually reinforcing, but they may also undermine one another. For example, cohesion might undermine embeddedness. Likewise, embeddedness might overwhelm cohesion.

Institutional action at subnational scales is intrinsically about coordinating delegated authority from higher scales in order to deliver public goods. The concept of "cohesion" makes a parallel logical move to that in prior work that sought to bring the institutions of the state "back in" to sociological analysis (Evans, Rueschemeyer, and Skocpol 1985; Morgan and Orloff 2017). This work has regularly considered how national state institutions are in co-constitutive relationships with international, global, and transnational institutional configurations. The concept of cohesion that I advance here describes the distinct nature of subnational institutional capacity.

"Cohesion," therefore, comprises two axes of coordinating capacities that are relatively unique to urban—as opposed to national—government: "vertical cohesion," which is the capacity of municipal institutions to coordinate the delivery of public goods across institutions at state and federal levels; and "horizontal cohesion," which is the capacity of institutions to coordinate across multiple line agencies at the municipal level. We can compare the function of "cohesion" in urban public goods distribution with the role of the Weberian "autonomy" of state bureaucracies in driving economic development in East Asian developmental states (Amsden 1989; Evans 1995; Wade 1990), which focuses on single national agencies that manage economic policy. More recent work has found pockets of bureaucratic effectiveness within a single economic agency in Ghana (McDonnell 2017). Cities, however, tend to be nested in intermediate subnational (e.g., state) and national (e.g., federal) levels of authority, and the delivery of public goods tends to cut across multiple agencies. This makes it necessary to develop a concept that can address the interscalar (i.e., vertical) and transversal (i.e., horizontal) problems of bureaucratic effectiveness.

My focus on cohesion is not only concerned with Weberian autonomy or capacity in terms of characteristics such as rational procedures of appointment, clear rules and lines of accountability, and predictable careers of personnel. "Cohesion" is distinct from what is commonly referred to as "state capacity." The dominant, Weberian view of "state capacity" is that the rational, rule-following features of organization of personnel should produce effective bureaucratic action. The notion of discipline as a feature of bureaucratic coordination does not feature for Weber. This is, in large part, because his ideal type of bureaucracy describes a single agency aiming to act in a linear command structure. The Weberian view of state capacity therefore provides limited analytical purchase for describing bureaucratic action for delivering goods that require coordinating multiple agencies along with multiscalar regulations and funding flows. This notion of *disciplined* coordination builds on a critique by Chibber that rule-following is not a sufficient condition for state bureaucracies to realize developmental aims: "In order for it to be effective as a *developmental* state, bureaucratic rationality must also be structured in an appropriate apportionment of *power* among state policy agencies" (2002, 952).

Above I describe "urban power" as defined by the strength and scope of democratic authority over private actors. We can think of this "strength and scope of democratic authority" in terms proposed by the Brazilian political theorist Leonardo Avritzer (2002). He argues that democracy should not be "regarded simply as the institutionalization of political competition"—that is, formal characteristics such as elections and separation of powers—but, instead, as "a societal practice in need of institutionalization" (2002, 5). The link between social action and the institutionalization of that action is precisely what the concepts of "embeddedness" and "cohesion" allow us to recognize. They are concepts that allow us to specify when social action is institutionalized via the *configuration* of these two factors. And they allow us to specify the pathways through which different cases travel via alternating configurations of these two factors.

Such pathways also underscore the importance of *sequence* and *process* to understanding configuration. Social bases of state effectiveness cannot be theorized without an explanation of change over time. Configurations of embeddedness and cohesion exhibit aspects of both path dependence and institutional indeterminacy—structural weaknesses that allow for agentic change. Sewell describes the causal properties of historical events and sequences: "Although individual actions can be shown to have fateful social effects, it is also true that every act is part of a sequence of actions and that its effects are profoundly dependent upon its place in the sequence" (2010, 7). To illustrate, in order for movements to build lasting reform in state institutions, they need to navigate the institutional architecture that has been established through past struggles. In cities, this means reckoning with the deep and lasting influence of private-sector actors, particularly those invested in the value of urban land, who often act as central power brokers in urban politics.

In this study, I focus on the temporal dynamics of within-case variation. The precise sequence of change matters for assessing the causal pathways for the construction of institutional capacity to distribute public goods over time. I care not only about the configurations that exist in cities but also about the order in which those configurations change. Specifying the configuration and sequencing of these two factors—embeddedness and cohesion—makes it possible to categorize and compare how local political power is coordinated in cities, as illustrated in Table 1.2. For policymakers, planners, and other practitioners, the question of how to construct either or both "embeddedness" and "cohesion" is not a simple technical exercise of formal institutional design. Instead, my goal in introducing these concepts is, in part, to help practitioners see themselves as working both within formal institutional contexts and across a broader social terrain, shot through with private market interests and movements.

TABLE 1.2. Configurations of Embeddedness and Cohesion

		Embeddedness	
		Low	*High*
Cohesion	*Low*	*Rentier*	*Mobilizational*
		Narrow elite capture	Redistribution-oriented policies without financial and administrative capacity
	High	*Managerial*	*Integrationist*
		Programmatic top-down administration, often growth-oriented	Effective administration of redistribution-oriented policies

The Comparative Methodological Approach

This book argues that understanding the emergence of embeddedness and cohesion can explain why some cities are more effective than others in reducing inequalities. Studies of single cases can help us discover and theorize novel ways of thinking about urban change. But if we seek to understand variation across cities, a comparative method is necessary in order to develop explanatory concepts. The role of comparison in interdisciplinary urban studies has been subject to increasing methodological and conceptual debate, particularly as scholars have sought to include non-Western cases. Jennifer Robinson (2022) has underscored the importance of comparison for making cases from the Global South not merely objects of descriptive analysis but subjects for theoretical development. Sociology's methodological emphasis on structured comparison is particularly useful for variation-finding approaches to theoretical development. Within disciplinary sociology, Garrido, Ren, and Weinstein (2021) have taken as a starting point the many differences that Global South cities exhibit in relation to their Northern counterparts. In doing so, they have argued that Northern theory can be reconstructed through theorizing from Southern cases to develop a "truly global urban sociology" (2021, 4). This book shares with Garrido, Ren, and Weinstein the empirical attention to Southern cities and the analytical ambition to reconstruct urban theory.

The empirical heart of this book is a comparative investigation of São Paulo, Brazil, and Johannesburg, South Africa. Through this comparison, I test and develop the theoretical concepts of "embeddedness" and "cohesion" as configurational factors that enable distributional change in cities. I selected São Paulo and Johannesburg for this study based on a range of similarities that hold constant across the cases. These are cities in national contexts that had similar social movement bases for their transition to democracy, similar extensions of rights to urban public goods in new constitutions, and a similar decentralized implementation for those rights, including a primary role for municipal government. Furthermore, these cities are the largest in their respective national contexts and serve similar functions in terms of connecting to global networks of trade and finance. They are considered to be in the same "alpha level" category of global connectedness by the most common quantitative ranking of "global cities" (Globalization and World Cities Research Network 2020). Finally, they have had a similar proportion of residents living in informal settlements and started with similar deficits in access to the public goods under study here. Yet, as the next chapter will make clear, São Paulo has been more effective than Johannesburg in expanding inclusion through access to three kinds of public goods: housing, sanitation, and transportation. It is precisely the similarly high degree of movement mobilization in the period of democratization, along with the strong commitment to urban public goods distribution through local governments in both cities, that makes their subsequent divergence surprising. This is the empirical variation that makes it possible to evaluate the helpfulness of the concepts of "embeddedness" and "cohesion."

This comparative logic follows what Imre Lakatos, the theorist of social science, described as a "positive heuristic," drawing primarily on the "research programs" associated with the "power-resources" school of political sociology and the "institutionalist" school of sociology of development. The positive heuristic "is a research policy, made up of models and exemplars, for digesting anomalies by constructing theories consistent with the hard core [of a research program]" (Burawoy 1989, 761). Cases are selected largely because of similarities that these two related approaches emphasize regarding social mobilization for democracy and the extension of socioeconomic rights after democratization. The anomalies that I explain come into focus when we look more closely at specifically urban literature, which emphasizes different conflicts of distribution—namely, over urban land and public goods—that have not been featured in the literatures in political sociology and sociology of development. To extend their general research program to the scale of the city, therefore, requires the theoretical apparatus that I develop here.

Conceptualizing and Measuring Inequalities of Urban Public Goods

The variation in outcomes between São Paulo and Johannesburg that I describe in the next chapter makes comparison useful to find answers for why some cities are more effective than others in reducing inequalities. But how to measure the distribution of public goods is not an obvious task. While measuring inequalities of wealth and income is not without controversy, the purpose of such measurement is generally straightforward. Individuals are lined up in a distribution, and then their endowments of wealth and income are compared with one another.

It is rather simple to conceptualize a distribution of wealth or income, even though measurement can be quite difficult due to the fact that wealth and income are often hidden. Wealth and income can be represented by single monetary figures. Conceptualizing inequalities in the distribution of public goods is much more complex. In fact, the very concept of "public goods" itself can be slippery. Legal scholar Bob Hockett provides a particularly useful definition. He defines public goods as goods for "which private sector actors have neither the jurisdictional authority nor the coordinative or financial capacity to invest in socially optimal amounts" (2020; see Hockett 2017). This definition differs from the more constrained characteristics of a "public good" that any economist will learn in graduate school: "non-excludable"—it is impossible for one person to stop another from using the good—and "nonrivalrous"—using the good does not prevent another from using it.

This traditional approach from economics undergirds work by Elinor Ostrom (1990) on varieties of governance for natural resources, such as water basins. Ostrom emphasizes these natural resources as "commons," which are defined by the inherent costs of excluding any groups or individuals from their use. The central problem for her is that commons can therefore be overused or used in ways that generate undesirable outcomes across groups.

Ostrom's approach, while highly relevant to the profound questions of how we manage natural resources, is not particularly well suited to urban questions. The common public good in the urban context is the city itself. By this, I mean that one of the city's primary advantages is found in the goods it provides that enable public health and, increasingly, adaptability to the impacts of a warming planet. These goods are sometimes residential—such as housing— and sometimes networked—such as transportation. There are also goods, such as sanitation, that are both; a toilet is residential because it is inside the home, but it is networked because it is ultimately connected to a much larger sewage system. In practice, and in contrast to the more limited economic definition of a public good, these goods *are* excludable. In theory, they are the stuff of the common good that is intrinsic to the city itself.[5]

What determines whether these goods are or are not excludable is institutional power: the relationship between state, market, and society that regulates the realization of the theory of the city as a public good. Therefore, when we think about the notion of public goods within the urban context, there is good reason to opt for Hockett's definition. In particular, this definition's focus on "socially optimal amounts" emphasizes the question of distribution. In both Brazil and South Africa, the constitutions that were drafted after the transition to democracy define such a distribution quite clearly for the goods under examination here:

They are rights of all citizens. The theoretical goal of the city as a public good is indisputable.

Furthermore, Hockett's more expansive definition highlights the institutional characteristics of a "public good." The market, by itself, cannot provide such goods in the socially optimal amount. In contexts where rights to such goods are explicit in the constitution, which is itself a product of the struggles for enshrining those rights in the first place, it is therefore clear why they can be considered "public." Furthermore, the key characteristics of an institution that can provide such goods are legal authority, coordinating capacity, and financial capacity.

With these two concepts in mind, then, we can safely describe housing, sanitation, and transportation as public goods. This is very different from saying that there is something inherent about these goods that makes them subject to exclusive provision by public authorities. Rather, it is clear that the state is an indispensable sphere for ensuring that the provision of these goods gets closer to what is defined in a democratic constitution as "socially optimal"— that is, as a right.

This still does not resolve how we might empirically assess "success" or "failure" in producing a distribution of these goods that is closer to that "socially optimal amount." In order to think about access to these goods as a distributional question, it is helpful to begin with the concept of rationing. This goes all the way back to Weber's 1921 study of the medieval city as a place where those inside the walls had access to the city's benefits, while other villagers were literally walled away from those benefits. The de facto and de jure spatial inequalities of Brazilian and South African cities that this book analyzes carry obvious resonances with what Weber described. A key premise of this study is that it is best to think about the relative distribution of urban public goods as a matter of inclusion—who is included in the distribution and who is not.

This may not be as simple as it sounds, either. Inclusion in housing is not straightforward to measure, for example. The dominant mode of exclusion in these cities is not what we might think of as "true" homelessness—that is, sleeping on the street. This is not to say that such forms of homelessness are not a problem in either city, but the scale of this form of homelessness is dwarfed by the use of informal shelters, which are often built by residents themselves. These shelters are "informal" precisely because they lack the legal recognition of land rights conventionally associated with a shelter's location. This lack of land rights then generates vulnerability to the insecurity of eviction, by both the market and the state. When it comes to housing, therefore, the question becomes whether land policies enable the production of a more secure form of residence, in terms of urban residents' access to public goods as well as a reduction in the risk of eviction. This emphasizes the multisectoral nature of housing policy; it is not only about the physical production of housing but also about land use planning.

Among the three goods under examination in this book, sanitation is perhaps the easiest to measure. What share of residents of informal settlements has a flush toilet inside their home, and what share does not? While figuring out the answer to this question is relatively straightforward, I must emphasize that this is not to say that sanitation does not carry with it multisectoral coordination challenges as well. Provision of the infrastructure that enables a flush toilet to exist in a residential home, for example, requires sewer lines. To connect to water treatment facilities, these sewer lines have to be formalized. Of course, various forms of septic tanks (or pits) can exist quite easily with informal land tenure. But, generally speaking, some type of formal assessment of land tenure is de rigueur in almost all parts of the world for bulk sewer infrastructure to reach an urban residential home.

This is historically the case in both Brazil and South Africa. As a result, sanitation policy, like housing, also crosses over into land use planning. In contexts involving persistently high shares of informal dwellings, which certainly describes the conditions in both São Paulo and Johannesburg, one of the starkest ways to represent change in access to sanitation is by looking at how sanitation has changed *within* informal settlements in the city, that is, the share of residences within informal settlements that have a flush toilet inside the dwelling. Doing so also echoes recent calls in international urban planning scholarship to focus on "disaggregated, interurban performance metrics" in order to "give a clearer picture of the equity of water and sanitation services" (Carolini and Raman 2021, 101).

Transportation carries its own challenges. There is no widely recognized single quantitative metric for measuring equality or inequality in transportation. While there have been recent attempts to introduce quantitative measures of transportation inequality, these have generally focused on specifying what is meant conceptually by "distributive justice" in transportation (Pereira, Schwanen, and Banister 2017). Therefore, we should look at how a public transportation system does or does not include residents in the functioning of the city through at least three dimensions that are each largely about change over time. First, do reforms to the transportation system reduce the time required to get from residence to work? Second, do transportation system reforms make the cost of transportation cheaper for the city's poorest residents? And third, do reforms to the transportation system expand the geographic availability of the service? Compared with housing and sanitation, transportation has the least crossover with other policy sectors in terms of its provision. However, as we will see, it still carries with it great costs; financing these costs is a perennial concern for policymakers, and how they are financed has direct implications for assessing the degree of inequality in collective transportation.

Taken together, framing distributional questions of urban public goods as questions concerning rationing and inclusion underlines the political nature of these policy arenas. To distribute these goods more equally is a normative goal defined in both Brazil's and South Africa's constitutions. Questions about administrative capacity are therefore really about the distribution of power: What *share* (as opposed to the nominal number) of the city's residents will be included in the city's benefits?

Research Methods

In order to identify the institutional mechanisms that explain the divergence between São Paulo and Johannesburg, as well as the sequential pathways they have traveled to get there, I draw on fieldwork that I conducted in the two cities over sixteen months between 2015 and 2018. This includes 225 semi-structured interviews with current and former high- and mid-ranking officials in government departments, mayors, city councillors, housing activists in professional nongovernmental organizations and grassroots movements, private property developers, executives in sanitation companies and bus companies, consultants, and scholars. I conducted 110 interviews in São Paulo and 115 interviews in Johannesburg. A full list of these interviews is in appendix B. All interviews were recorded and transcribed. In Brazil, all interviews were conducted in Portuguese, and in South Africa, all interviews were conducted in English.

As a method of historical social scientific research, I conducted these interviews as an archivist of the recent past. For projects aiming to uncover processes of institutional change in earlier periods of time, a researcher would hope for a set of oral primary evidence along the lines of the interviews I conducted for this project. My goal was to reconstruct a series of events and relationships that are otherwise largely outside of the formal archive of press releases and media reports. Many of the conflicts that I documented escaped the gaze of the public record. They appear technical and forbidding, and their significance may have only been understood in retrospect. That being said, I collected hundreds of documents of additional primary written evidence, including legislation, newspapers, professional trade publications, and internal government and nongovernmental organization documents. For those conflicts that did appear in the public record, I cite contemporaneous documentation to contextualize claims made by my informants in interviews.

My aim in the interviews and archival work was to identify the relationships between key actors, institutional spaces, and events that explain how institutional arrangements for distributing public goods have changed over time in São Paulo and Johannesburg. I used snowball sampling until I reached a point of saturation for each type of actor. In practice, this meant that at the end of interviews, I would ask who else I should talk to, to understand the key events, policies, and institutions involved in a given interview. This particular question provided at least two kinds of useful information. It exposed broader social networks that were critical for piecing together a relational account of policy change, and it helped me understand when I was reaching meaningful degrees of informant saturation (Small and Calarco 2022) within my investigation of a given policy arena. I used archival documentation to corroborate or call into question accounts from interviews, as well as to assist in triangulating contradictory accounts from different informants. I collected legislative documents and urban plans in order to understand the formalization of political decisions.

I draw on these data to construct a historical account of change in local state institutions in São Paulo and Johannesburg. This account relies on specifying sequences of change, which roughly correspond to different mayoral administrations. Such a sequential method, or "process tracing," is useful "for establishing the features of the events that compose individual sequences (e.g., their duration, order, and pace) as well as the causal mechanisms that link them together" (Faletti and Mahoney 2015, 212).

Structure of the Study

The book documents the histories of institutional changes in the distribution of three public goods: housing, transportation, and sanitation. As we will see, the governance of each good is never entirely separate from that of another; just as city politics are nested in larger national contexts, these policy arenas have significant areas of overlap. However, each public good also thematizes a specific debate that emphasizes different dimensions of the concepts of "embeddedness" and "cohesion" as explanatory factors for the capacities of cities to reduce inequalities. These concepts are premised on some degree of social contestation. The policies of housing, transportation, and sanitation illustrate a spectrum of openness to social contestation. Housing is the policy area most obviously open to social contestation, transportation is an intermediate case, and sanitation is most clearly the preserve of insulated technocrats.

In the next chapter, I lay out a contextual history of each city, especially the social mobilizations that led to democratization in Brazil in the late 1980s and South Africa in the early 1990s, and illustrate how the distribution of these three public goods has changed in São Paulo and Johannesburg since democratization. This comparative history of the relationship between urban distribution and struggles for democracy sets the stage for identifying the sequence of change in both cities in the period of interest in this book—that is, after their transitions to democracy. I begin by focusing on how urban inequality was thematized as intrinsic to the struggle for democracy in each country. As a result, the new democratic dispensations made reducing urban inequality an explicit goal and empowered local government to be the governing scale to exercise the power to realize this goal. I then lay out in both quantitative and spatial detail what these inequalities in housing, sanitation, and transportation looked like in each city at the moment of transition to democracy and how they have changed over time. Before the second chapter concludes, I return to the substantive theories discussed in this introductory chapter to show how the variation between the two cases confounds expectations that emerge in the global literature on cities and inequality.

The third chapter concerns the distribution of housing in each city. Here I ask, Why did São Paulo manage to develop planning tools that generated power to relativize the rights of private property in order to deliver social housing in well-located areas, while Johannesburg did not? The politics of housing in both cities have been the most directly thematized by organized social movements. It is therefore unsurprising that this is a sector that has been shaped most clearly by the relationships between state and society. In São Paulo, I show that successive waves of movements developed durable relationships with politicians and bureaucratic officials, producing an incremental project of internal capacity within the state to conceptualize and deliver housing. In Johannesburg, I show that the municipal bureaucracy became progressively de-linked from its social movement base. In the wake of the transition from Apartheid, white real estate interests did not have the political legitimacy to openly challenge the largely black government, so they developed hidden strategies that disabled the capacity of the local government to implement reforms that were often aimed at redistribution. While strong embeddedness in São Paulo produced an increasingly cohesive governing capacity in the local state, the lack of embeddedness in Johannesburg made the local state vulnerable to relatively hidden challenges by traditional white elites that prevented the emergence of a similar capacity.

The fourth chapter focuses on the dominant mode of collective transportation in each city: in São Paulo, the bus; in Johannesburg, the minibus taxi. I ask, Why did São Paulo formalize its bus sector and reform it to be cheaper and to extend into the poorest neighborhoods of the city, while Johannesburg could not formalize or integrate its minibus taxi sector? In São Paulo, reforms in the sector focused on an institutional approach that allowed the municipality to develop relationships with key formal and informal actors in the privately owned bus sector, which built the requisite trust that the public sector would not exclude the interests of existing informal bus operators. In contrast, Johannesburg has placed a premium on the introduction of a new technology in collective transportation: bus rapid transit. By leading with technological reform, the city was unable to develop ties to minibus taxi operators that would enable a shared project of sectoral reform. The embeddedness of the local state in São Paulo pushed it to pursue the institutional path, while Johannesburg's lack of embeddedness pushed it into a confrontational relationship with the dominant informal operators. Furthermore, Johannesburg's cohesion was progressively undermined as it pursued a technological path driven by fleeting international events and alliances. This resulted in a new bus rapid transit system used by few residents, the vast majority of whom continue to opt for a minibus taxi system largely unchanged since the dawn of democracy.

The fifth chapter shifts its focus to sanitation, a policy arena in which São Paulo managed to generate downward, municipal accountability of a state-level sanitation company for slum upgrading, while Johannesburg struggled to generate higher-level support for municipal sanitation priorities. In both cases, the key delivery agent for water and sanitation is a semi-independent agency. In São Paulo, this agency is constituted at the state level, while in Johannesburg, it operates at the level of the city. São Paulo was able to build its own planning capacity and draw on new national mandates to create shared institutional spaces that made this independent agency accountable to the planning prerogatives of the city. In Johannesburg, the city was unable to establish clear planning priorities or create an institutional environment where the delivery agency would become accountable to those priorities. While São Paulo used its embedded ties with social movements to take advantage of new national policy to build up power at the municipal scale to direct the priorities of an independent water agency, Johannesburg's lack of embedded ties in the movement sphere left it vulnerable to increasingly particularistic and captured ties in its relationship with an independent water agency.

Taken together, these three chapters thematize debates over (a) expanding the rights of the poor versus creating openings for elite resistance, (b) organizing reform by prioritizing institutional change or technological change, and (c) the extension of public goods distribution through the establishment of accountability to municipal plans or faith in the independence of sectoral delivery agencies. In the concluding chapter, I return to the global picture of urbanization and efforts at redistribution with which this chapter began. I argue that the conceptual apparatus of "embeddedness" and "cohesion" can help us rethink questions of distribution in cities across the globe. And I argue that the concepts developed here are critical to a new global urban sociology that is centrally concerned with questions of distributional conflict in and about the slum, the quintessential territory of our rapidly urbanizing world.

The heart of this book is a paired comparison of two cities. But the arc of the book is an argument about the study of cities and urbanization globally. That is to say, this book is about the problems of social closure in cities through the distribution of public goods. If we see cities from the vantage point of the most excluded places in them, then we can begin to see what it means to break today's "walls" of social closure. The experience of place-based exclusion in the world's informal settlements, *favelas*, and *mjondolos* is the experience of a broad swath of humanity, one in seven people. Exclusion in these places carries profound implications for public health, economic opportunity, and adaptability to a warming world. By looking for variation in efforts to distribute urban public goods, we can begin to understand why some cities are more effective at breaking the bonds of urban exclusion than others. We now turn to the comparison that frames this study.

2

The Cases

COMPARING SÃO PAULO AND JOHANNESBURG

In order to explain why some cities are more effective than others in reducing inequality, I sought out a comparison that could at once leverage political, economic, and social dimensions to this question. This meant finding cases with significant similarities in their terrain of political struggle, their economic inequalities, and their social organization. The previous chapter analyzed a global debate on urbanization, development, and inequality that has been conducted through literatures focused on either the national or the local scale. The cases that I arrived at for this study—São Paulo and Johannesburg—require examining these two scales together, as well as understanding how they are interlinked.

In Brazil and South Africa, protests over inequality, and especially *urban* inequality, fueled struggles for political democracy. In both countries, an alliance of industrial trade unions with neighborhood-based organizations fighting for rights to urban public goods such as housing, public transport, and sanitation formed the social basis of the democratic transition in the 1980s and early 1990s (Baiocchi, Heller, and Silva 2011; Seidman 1994). As a result, Brazil and South Africa are rare among developing nations for their constitutional commitments and social spending to reduce poverty and inequality.

Even before the epidemiological and economic crisis of the COVID-19 pandemic, Brazil and South Africa were undergoing critical reevaluations of their young democracies. Dissatisfaction with the pace of economic change and political accountability is unmistakable. In Brazil, the rise of extreme right-wing politics and the election of Jair Bolsonaro in 2018 threatened a return to authoritarianism. South Africa, meanwhile, has become the "protest capital of the world" (Runciman 2015) due to frequent marches over municipal governments' delivery of basic services. COVID-19 further reinforced the desperate necessity of urban public goods provision. One key determinant for the initial spread of the virus and subsequent waves of variants lay in the built environment conditions of overcrowded housing and transportation in cities, as well as lack of access to basic services such as water and sanitation (Bhardwaj et al. 2020). In the absence of these urban public goods, "social distancing" became nothing more than an empty exhortation (Wahba et al. 2020).

It is no wonder that the very legitimacy of the democratic state persists on the basis of struggles for these goods. As it has for the past three decades, a significant preoccupation of modern social science echoes from the city streets to the halls of power: Is democracy able to realize its promise of equality?

The divergent trajectories of São Paulo and Johannesburg in the period since their respective countries' transitions to democracy transform this broad theoretical question as an empirical puzzle about "spatial inequality." The story of each of these cities is one of exclusion—"social closure"—that is manifest through the distribution of public goods across the space of the city.

Following Wacquant's (2008) comparison of urban marginality in France and the United States, we can understand exclusions across urban territory as "effects of the state projected on to the city." This is because the state "shapes not only the markets for housing, employment and educational credentials, but also the distribution of basic goods and services, and through this mediation governs the conversion of social space into appropriated physical space" (Wacquant 2008, 6). In other words, to observe an unequal distribution of public goods across the space of the city is to see how government action rations and encloses inclusion in the city.

My task in this book is to explain the processes of institutional change shaped by struggles that are both external and internal to government agencies. But first, we need to understand the origins of the deep inequalities that local governments in São Paulo and Johannesburg faced at the moment of democratization. These inequalities were characterized by exclusion and exception that were sometimes encoded in law and sometimes wholly outside of it. As we shall see, the observable material inequalities across the physical spaces of São Paulo and Johannesburg suggest a striking parallel between the de facto apartheid of São Paulo's urban exclusions and the de jure apartheid of Johannesburg's.

Brazil and South Africa are both newly democratic states with foundational commitments, explicit in their constitutions, to using the power of local government to undo this spatial exclusion. Though these commitments are clear on paper, they are extremely hard to accomplish in practice. It requires using housing and land use policy to produce more residential integration. It requires a mode of governing collective mobility so that all residents can move efficiently and cheaply through the city. And it requires extending water and sewer infrastructures to the excluded and informal peripheries of cities.

It is impossible to separate the stories of democratization in Brazil and South Africa from their stories of urban transformation. This is because each country's geography of economic development during its authoritarian period—and the policy apparatus that underpinned it—depended on urban exclusion. While the role of urban social and political change is critical to the institutional relationships that are the concern of this book, the reason democratization is an urban story goes much deeper. To understand how urban power—the social, bureaucratic, and political coordinating authority necessary to undo exclusion—has developed in São Paulo and Johannesburg after Brazil's and South Africa's national transitions to democracy, we need to understand why this power was necessary in the first place.

In Brazil, the authoritarian model of state-led development began after the 1964 military overthrow of Juscelino Kubitschek's government amid growing panic about communist political infiltration. Strong state investment and a form of import-substituting economic development policies were accompanied by a world-historic shift of Brazil's population from the country's rural hinterlands to its rapidly growing cities. This population growth was most pronounced in the São Paulo metropolitan area, which includes the municipality of São Paulo itself and thirty-six much smaller municipalities. Here, a growing labor force in factories, as well as in related service occupations, came to occupy the rapidly sprawling peripheries of the city.

With largely minimal public investment in services and a lack of private construction for rental accommodations, favelas (the Portuguese word for "slums") became the city's spatial signature. This amounted to a de facto policy of exclusion from the public goods that characterize opportunity in the city. A wide gap in wages meant that rent in both formal and informal markets was persistently out of reach for millions of new residents. This produced wave after wave of evictions, which pushed the poor further and further toward the favelas in the city's peripheries.

In South Africa, where an explicitly racial authoritarian model of state-led development underpinned the Apartheid policymaking regime, these dynamics of exclusion were explicitly de jure. The National Party, built on an ideology of white Afrikaner ethnonationalism, took power in a whites-only vote in 1948. The party's victory in this election marked a change in South Africa's governing ethos. The 1948 election suggested something of a sharp break within the relative continuity of racialized forms of government. Previously, small spaces of racial integration in neighborhoods like Sophiatown and relative tolerance for claims of black land ownership in neighborhoods like Alexandra existed even without a universal extension of the electoral franchise. After the 1948 election, the tide turned decisively against continued toleration of these ambiguous urban spaces. As Evans puts it, the National Party's initial victory that year marked a move from segregation "to its sterner and more notorious successor, *apartheid*" (1995, ix).

This shift was important because it signaled a mode of economic development rooted in a particular social hierarchy, what South African scholars of Apartheid political economy would refer to as "racial Fordism." This approach included job reservations for "poor whites," industrial training, Afrikaans language mandates, strong public investment to drive both private and para-statal corporate champions, and the growth of a white mass consumption base (Gelb 1987). Semiskilled work was initially reserved for white workers. But as they upgraded skills, they increasingly saw themselves less as in competition with black workers and more as complements. While white workers could do increasingly skilled activities, black workers could do menial tasks that whites did not want to do. As a result, the vast underclass of black workers became an essential excluded population to be "managed" by state institutions.

Such population "management" was largely regulated through space. In rural areas, the development of "tribal homelands" created a reserve of black labor. These strategies were coupled with a strong system of population control in the geography of cities that similarly relegated black populations of manual laborers to remote townships far from the economic life of the city. Taken together, this produced a highly regulated system of low- and semiskilled labor reserves.

In contrast to the case in Brazil, these reserves were produced through a formalized, legal apparatus of regulation that relied on a rigid racial hierarchy. However, residents of these reserves experienced a daily life that was more often one of neglect. As in Brazil's industrial heartland of São Paulo, the cities of the Witwatersrand gold reef—which includes Johannesburg and its eastern suburbs—were bounded by sprawling "townships" that veered wildly between states of exception and repression.

The link between authoritarian rule and urban social closure became effectively intrinsic. It is therefore not so surprising that urban rights were intimately tied to national struggles for democratization in both countries. In both São Paulo and Johannesburg, we see the emergence of urban movements rooted in the struggle for a more equal distribution of public goods. These local movements developed sophisticated practices of participatory governance and concrete demands that were linked together through broad emancipatory visions. These movements furthermore developed links to political actors involved in the shaping of democratic institutions that would reform the authoritarian state. As a result, intense social contestation shaped the design and scope of newly empowered local governments, which ensured the possibility of meaningfully embedded ties between the local state and social movements.

In this chapter, I first analyze how demands for urban rights became inter-twined with struggles for democratization in each country. For each city, I then proceed to enumerate the quantitative and spatial features of the inequalities that the newly democratic local governments faced upon taking office. Pro-found states of exception and exclusion characterized the urbanization process in both cities. While it is always difficult to control for all potential confounding variables in a cross-country, cross-city comparison, I establish two key points here. First, São Paulo and Johannesburg faced largely similar deficits in the distribution of urban public goods at the moment of democratization. Second, each city varies enough from its respective national context to make clear that relative "success" or "failure" at the city scale is not merely an artifact of forces playing out at the national level. The social pressure that emerged from this exclusion became the defining characteristic of attempts to deploy the levers of the local state to reduce inequality.

I specify the divergences between São Paulo and Johannesburg in distrib-uting housing, sanitation, and transportation after democratization. In the terminology of linear sociological interpretation, this chapter can therefore be understood as specifying the "dependent variable." The divergent trajectories of São Paulo—the "positive" case—and Johannesburg—the "negative" case— are worth comparing precisely because of the similarities of their origins at a moment of distinct contingency—democratization. The chapter concludes by considering why this empirical variation is also puzzling in the context of the global conversation on urban development, democratization, and redistribution that we encountered in the previous chapter.

São Paulo: The Struggle to Loosen the Bonds of Urban Social Closure

When Mariza Dutra Alves began occupying land as part of a strategy to access housing in the spring of October 1998, she was following in a long lineage of city-making in São Paulo. The link between authoritarian governance and residential exclusion by class and race has been the historic hallmark of life in the city.[1] As the city began growing in the middle of the twentieth century, so did informal settlements and active policies of eviction from the well-serviced core of the city. During the civilian dictatorship in the 1940s, an estimated 10–15 percent of the city's inhabitants were evicted from their homes, in direct contradiction of existing legal protections for tenants, who accounted for two-thirds of residents at that time (Bonduki 1994). Under Brazil's military dicta-torship, from the late 1960s to the mid-1980s, São Paulo underwent one of the largest explosions of urbanization anywhere in the world. The city's population grew exponentially, from 3.8 million people in 1960 to 9.6 million in 1990. This growth was marked by not just neglect but the expulsion of the city's working class from the city's center by ruling elites who were not bound by ties of local democratic accountability. These twin processes of urbanization and exclusion defined the city's harsh inequalities.[2]

Sparse public investment in housing had encouraged a market-led redevelopment of the city center—"urban renewal"—without any provision for those who would be displaced. While municipal rent control legislation cushioned the blow of rising inflation in the early 1940s, it also discouraged private investment in low-income housing—an estimated 70 percent of households were renting. The stark rationing of public goods between a wealthy core and sprawling peripheral neighborhoods became a defining feature of the spatial organization of life in the city. In 1968, 41.3 percent of *all households* in the city of São Paulo were without a sewage connection (Camargo et al. 1976). The proportion of residents living in informal settlements, or *favelas* in Portuguese, grew more than sevenfold, from 1.1 percent in 1973 toward the beginning of the dictatorship to 7.7 percent by the end in 1987 (Rolnik, Kowarick, and Somekh 1990). Generally lacking basic services such as electricity, water, and sanitation, these neighborhoods were marked by a form of development— often referred to as *auto-construção*, or "self-build"—operating entirely outside the ambit of any formal planning authority. Many other parts of the city housed the urban poor in areas with only limited services (Holston 2008).

The result was that private sector–led evictions became commonplace. Nabil Bonduki (1994), one of the city's most prolific researchers and practitioners, estimates that between 10 and 15 percent of city residents in the 1940s experienced an eviction. Many of the residents who experienced this wave of mid-century evictions ended up in the far peripheries of the city, especially in the eastern and southern zones (Zona Leste and Zona Sul). There, they built new cities within the city—wooden plank by wooden plank, brick by brick, and without access to the public goods that would make life reliable, let alone dignified.

In these peripheries, a new Apartheid-like São Paulo was being "autoconstructed." I refer to the "auto-construction" of São Paulo's peripheries as being "new" with an ironic view toward the city's history of urbanization. The mass migrations of poor rural residents of the country's northeast had led to the city's explosive growth in the latter part of the first half of the twentieth century. Now, these same migrants were the carriers of a new wave of urbanization—of the city's periphery instead of its core. Rolnik et al. (1990) report that in 1960, the city's density fell from 110 inhabitants per hectare in 1914 to twenty-five per hectare. In one of the largest areas of the Zona Leste, São Miguel Paulista–Ermelino Matarazzo, the residential population multiplied eighteen times between 1940 and 1960, from 7,634 to 137,908 (Holston 2008).

The laborers who occupied these peripheral settlements had long been granted only limited citizenship by the Brazilian state. The Vargas era, comprising two presidential periods in 1930–45 and 1951–54, saw the institution of labor passbooks, which meant that urban workers—agricultural laborers were exempted—could only work in occupational sectors in which employers explicitly agreed to recognize their right to work. As Holston puts it, "The Vargas state masterminded a social citizenship based on the universe of urban labor that modernized the paradigm of Brazilian national membership while adhering to its inclusive yet inegalitarian principles" (2008, 196).

The Brazilian military had taken power in 1964 by mobilizing sensationalized concerns of communist infiltration through the center-left government of João Goulart. The result was a suspension of institutional checks and balances, epitomized by the Fifth Institutional Act, or "AI-5," of 1968, which is most well known for its legalization of torture. This act also suspended the mandates of states and municipalities, which were superseded by national mandates. The military dictatorship therefore became a period of centralized state power nearly unheard of in postimperial Brazilian history.

The inegalitarian form of citizenship that characterized much of the twentieth century in Brazil was the result of both the nature and the geography of work; in other words, it was determined through labor *in the city*. Until the 1988 constitution, suffrage was restricted to literate Brazilians, which excluded the majority of voting-age citizens from actually participating in elections. And the differential between high land prices and low wages practically excluded most urban residents from owning property. This mix of de jure and de facto exclusions produced a social geography of cheap labor reserves that, as we will see, closely resembled those of legal Apartheid in South Africa.

In 1990, the first Workers' Party (PT) mayoral administration in São Paulo, led by Luiza Erundina, commissioned leading planning academics in the city to put together a report on the city's inequalities. The goal was to create a type of baseline study to inform an anticipated urban master plan. The report underscored the nature of segregation in the city:

> In truth, both the laws of the city and its effects attest to the institution of a land market and the built environment of the city to which the poorest residents will never have access. . . . It is possible to estimate that between 60% and 70% of residents of the municipality find themselves today in a situation that contradicts the models of land acquisition and organization of space provided by contemporary legal norms. (Rolnik et al. 1990, 90)

The residents of these exploding, excluded peripheries were imbricated in political winds blowing in from the city's "ABC" suburbs. This so-called ABC region is named after the saints who are eponymous to these peripheral municipalities: Santo André, São Bernardo do Campo, and São Caetano do Sul. In the prior decade, the growth of shop floor militancy in the auto factories had coalesced into the formation of a new trade union federation, the Unified

Workers' Central. The founding of Unified Workers' Central in 1983, with its focus on direct action and shop floor democracy, came close on the heels of the formation of the PT in 1980.

The social struggle that would eventually coalesce around the demand for direct elections in Brazil was born on the shop floors of the factories that ring São Paulo's southern and eastern peripheries. In the first months of 1979, metalworkers, most of whom worked in multinational automobile factories in this region, decided to strike. The previous year, autoworkers throughout the state of São Paulo had become concerned about the threat of future layoffs. The workers in the ABC region had bucked their counterparts in other parts of the state who had accepted employers' wage proposals.

Within a week of the strike, the Labor Ministry declared the action illegal. Strike leaders—including future president Luiz Inácio "Lula" da Silva—were briefly arrested and removed from their union offices, and military police patrolled the streets (Seidman 1994). Documentary filmmaker Leon Hirszman captured footage of some of the strike's important moments, including a May Day rally in 1979 that brought together an estimated 150,000 people. In the film, such scenes are coupled with key moments of internal negotiation within the metalworkers' union and popular media footage of automobile company executives. But only after the democratic transition in the late 1980s, and the emergence of Lula as the most important electoral figure on the political left, did Hirszman compile the footage into *The ABCs of a Strike* (*ABC da Greve*), a cinema verité chronicle of these epochal events.

Hirszman's footage provides a vivid window into Lula's vault toward national importance and the impact that events that originated on the shop floor would eventually have at the level of national politics. At the time of the strike, the PT was not a formal party. But the mobilization of workers, along with their families and their neighbors, was a key source of strength for the growth of the numbers and confidence of strikers. By the end of 1979, 13 percent of Brazil's industrial workers had gone on strike—more than three million people—and 40 percent of these striking workers were in the São Paulo metropolitan area (Seidman 1994). This marked the city as a unique hotbed of worker militancy. While the negotiations only led to a few wage gains, Lula assessed the year in terms of how organizing had generated power for broader fights ahead: "The struggle that occurred in ABC was for wages, but the working-class movement, while fighting for raises, had a political result" (Luiz Inácio "Lula" da Silva, interview in *História Imediata, A Greve*, quoted in Seidman 1994, 165). For him, the strike's primary contribution was in building a movement with enough breadth and depth to begin affecting political outcomes, including the end to authoritarian rule.

The 1979 wave of strikes also produced a turn to decentralized shop floor organizing methods, which stood in contrast to the country's traditional mode of top-down "corporatist" management of industrial worker organizations. This institutional legacy of state-led worker mediation had its roots in labor legislation and institutions introduced during Getúlio Vargas's presidency in the first half of the 1940s (Weinstein 1996). Workers and businesses were generally organized through sectoral associations, which had the effect of reduced militancy. The shift to the shop floor targeted individual enterprises, as opposed to sectoral action.

While this had the potential to limit the broad reach of worker demands, it also opened up worker organizing strategies to a much deeper form of labor democracy. This growth of shop floor–based cadres with leadership capacity would help enable stronger ties between worker organization and neighborhood-based organizing. The support of communities near factories and where workers lived made it possible to sustain more risky actions such as strikes. In building that support, broader demands progressively became part of the striking workers' political repertoire. These ties became the critical base for a more generalized political movement for democratization.

The PT joined other, largely middle-class, opposition forces—including intellectuals and moderate business leaders—in emphasizing the need for the end of authoritarian rule, thereby underscoring the priority of direct elections. But the PT insisted that it fulfilled the need for a separate working-class party to represent workers. From the outset, the PT articulated the working-class political identity in a way that extended far beyond traditional shop floor demands such as union recognition. During the election campaign for São Paulo's governor in 1982, part of a limited opening of electoral participation by the military government, the PT articulated a position that underscored the link between struggles in the workplace and struggles in the home:

> There is a division in society, and it was not we who created it. The *latifundiário*'s plantation house is not the field hand's shack. The industrialist's meal is not the laborer's porridge. The banker's profit is not the salary of the bank employee. The neighborhood where the businessman lives is not the part of the periphery where the laborer lives. If we are separated socially and economically, how can we be united politically? (Seidman 1994, 197)

For Seidman (1994), in light of theories of labor organization, the emergence of a broad community-based articulation of the working class as a political actor in the early 1980s was a surprising development. The relatively skilled nature of metalworkers, whose unionizing efforts were the lynchpin of the PT's organizational development, should have made them wary of broader alliances. But it was precisely the union's entrance into the political arena that changed the equation. By seeking to articulate a "social bloc" in the electoral sphere, these unionists quickly had to articulate a broader constituency. And they had to bring it into being.

The favelas of the urban peripheries were the natural place to turn. These informal neighborhoods of the city's growing majority had been hotbeds of local organization beginning in the 1970s, spurred by the "liberation theology" associated with the Catholic Church. The *comunidades eclesiais de base* (CEBs), or ecclesiastical base communities, became the street-level building block on which housing movements would emerge. These groups developed deliberative practices in communities on the urban periphery in order to decide on strategies to approach state institutions about day-to-day issues concerning access to public goods. Holston (2008) refers to the emergence of CEBs as the beginnings of an "insurgent public sphere."

Antonio Luiz Marchioni, better known as Padre Ticão, led the diocese based in the Ermelino Matarazzo neighborhood of the city's East Zone from 1970, when he arrived in São Paulo to support growing labor militancy in the area, until his death in 2021. For Padre Ticão, the early 1980s were a period in which CEBs became more explicitly politicized. I visited him twice in his church, where he had been lecturing to local senior citizens about homeopathic remedies. In our interview, he described to me his first encounters with activists in the legal profession and in the PT: "In that period of 1984, I came to know Miguel Reis [a leading housing rights lawyer in São Paulo], and this was combined with the liberation theology, the ecclesiastical communities, the movements, the unions, the Church, the parties—principally the PT."[3]

As he spoke, we were interrupted by visitors who wanted to talk to him about upcoming local election campaigns. After mulling over the jockeying for position of various candidates, Padre Ticão turned back to me and continued. "So all of this was channeled through the formation of the PT, okay? And we had just begun the housing movement. We would come to have an organization that scaled up to the national level. But it began here."[4] As he said this, he pointed to the grounds of his church.

The CEB organizational unit, at the street or neighborhood level, was soon networked into larger scales of activity. In large part, this was due to activist-theological leaders like Padre Ticão, who used their parishes to bring neighborhood activists together and connect what they were doing. On one of my visits to Ermelino Matarazzo in 2017, for example, Padre Ticão insisted on taking me with him to visit religious leaders of neighboring parishes. As buzz was building about the PT's electoral strategy in the next year's presidential election, he wanted to informally confer with his colleagues. In these conversations, he emphasized the historical role the church parish played in bringing neighborhood associations together.[5]

The oldest housing movement in São Paulo that would gain city-wide, and eventually national, scale was the União dos Movimentos de Moradia (UMM), or Federation of Housing Movements. Evaniza Rodrigues, who began organizing in the East Zone in the city with the UMM in the 1980s, is now a national leader of the UMM, which led her to occupy positions in the Federal Ministry of Cities and the municipality of São Paulo under PT-led administrations. She described her involvement in the housing movement as being thoroughly imbricated in religious organizations, worker struggle, and the fight for democracy:

> I was volunteering as a youth organizer in the church, and this time was very curious. You had various processes, from the formation of the PT in the 1980s, supporting worker strikes, later the discussion of a constituent assembly. So all of these processes and the role of the church were very mixed. You didn't have separate meeting places—"this one is for the PT, this place is for the housing movement, that place is for the things that the church does." No. It was all together. The youth group discussed the national political situation and the question of a constituent assembly. It discussed the movements that were emerging. So it was through the youth group that I came to these struggles. And what began to happen was the land occupations in our region. And it was through this that the youth groups in the church began to get involved and had to help these initiatives that were appearing at that moment.[6]

Rodrigues's experience was echoed to me by other long-standing leaders in the UMM, who, unprompted, would describe the intersection of these various organizations—church, the PT, unions, and housing movements—as typical of their formative activist experiences.

During the negotiations over a new constitution between 1985 and 1988, these activists joined with professional architects, urban planners, and other intellectuals to make up what was called the Movimento Nacional pela Reforma Urbana (National Movement for Urban Reform, or MNRU in its Portuguese initials). These reformers, inspired by the theoretical call of Henri Lefebvre's (1996) "right to the city" and the practical experiences of struggle in São Paulo's urban peripheries, aimed to take their demands into the constituent assemblies that would determine the shape of the country's constitution. At the time, the MNRU was exceptional in Brazilian civil society for its truly national scope (Avritzer 2007).

Key demands of the MNRU in these negotiations focused on empowering municipal governments to secure the rights to deliver basic services, especially housing and sanitation. Activists gathered twelve million signatures to endorse various draft provisions for the constitution to realize these demands (Friendly 2017). Many of these same activists would make up the core of bureaucratic leadership in PT-led mayoral administrations in São Paulo in the late 1980s and early 1990s.

Even critical reassessments of the MNRU have noted the surprising gains it made during this period. As two leading Brazilian planning academics have put it, "While the 1990s were, as in other emerging countries, marked by crises-driven macroeconomic adjustment and a neoliberal-inspired rollback of the state, the Brazilian national government nevertheless consolidated its recognition and some financial support (albeit from a shrinking national budget) for alternative praxis in informal settlements" (Klink and Denaldi 2016, 403). These gains were marshaled at the national level with the establishment of the Ministry of Cities, which was first founded under Lula's presidential administration in 2003. This cabinet-level ministry focused on housing, sanitation, and transportation had been a long-held dream of the MNRU, as it linked together the administration of policy for those three public goods. Now these crucial and intertwined elements of urban life could be overseen by a single ministerial body and guided by a spatial, urban perspective in policy and planning.

Clientelism as a mode of governance—characterized by a ruling cabal of political brokers and landed elites—has been the durable backdrop to widespread exclusion from the formal built environment of São Paulo. Brazil's transition to democracy in the mid-1980s culminated in a new federal constitution in 1988 and the country's first direct presidential elections the following year. This produced possibilities for urban governance with unheard-of degrees of local autonomy and accountability in the provision of basic services. Prior to the 1988 election, urban political rule and negotiation had largely mimicked the strategies of traditional rural clientelism (Holston 2008). But after the ratification of the constitution, a largely centralized mode of municipal governance, including mayors appointed by federal authorities, gave way to direct elections of municipal executives.

Since the ratification of the new federal constitution in 1988, the standard of living in São Paulo has improved substantially with respect to the distribution of core public goods. In the next section of this chapter, these improvements across housing, sanitation, and transportation are quantified and laid out in detail. While Brazil has generally improved along a wide range of social development indicators during this period, the process has been marked by significant subnational variation across cities. Recent work analyzing this subnational variation has found that these improvements are primarily a function of local provisioning (Gibson 2019). The constitution contained significant provisions for decentralizing the responsibility for distributing goods such as housing, sanitation, and transportation, as well as a transfer of financial resources to municipalities to fulfill these responsibilities (Arretche 1999).

Furthermore, recent analysis has suggested shifts in residential settlement patterns that do not comport with general expectations and the historic reality of core-peripheral spatial organization of wealthy and poor areas in the city. These studies highlight a decline in class-based residential segregation in São Paulo (Marques 2015). There is now a more even distribution of basic services across both poor and rich neighborhoods (Marques 2014). Drawing on both these academic studies and similar findings by a state-level public agency in São Paulo, Caldeira describes this shift as being from a "homogenous and vast periphery" to "a city that is a kind of patchwork" (2017, 10).

This history provides a sketch of the kinds of social movements and governing dynamics that would shape particular policy efforts in extending housing, transportation, and sanitation to the most excluded parts of São Paulo. These efforts are examined in the subsequent three chapters. Even before doing so, we can already see two key trends in Brazil's struggle for democratization, particularly in São Paulo. First, a political party of the Left rooted in a broader social base comprising both unions and housing movements emerged. This makes São Paulo a strong candidate for redistribution given the expectations of the "power-resources" literature. Second, at the same time, the growth of São Paulo under conditions of rapid urbanization throughout the authoritarian period produced extreme degrees of exclusion and inequality. As Brazil opened up to global markets after democratization, the pressures for an exclusionary orientation toward economic growth, as predicted by much of the urban literature, were likely to be extreme.

Inequality in São Paulo

During my fieldwork in Brazil, whether I was in a peripheral favela or an inner-city high-rise building occupation, I inevitably heard the same proximate cause from residents of how they came to live in their current home: Rent became unaffordable. There were many reasons for why this was the case: unemployment, underemployment, abusive partners, childcare, racial marginalization. But ultimately, the unaffordability of rent in the city was at the root of experiences of informal residence.

São Paulo has undergone a sea change in what living in an informal settlement means in terms of accessing the city's public goods. As we have already seen, it is hard to overstate the degree of state and market-driven exclusion from urban public goods that had built up over the half century preceding democratization. A de facto Apartheid made space a defining dimension of such urban inequalities in São Paulo; where one lived determined one's access to urban public goods. Often literally erased from the map, residents of São Paulo living in informal neighborhoods, largely arranged on the city's peripheries, had little to no recourse to claim or take advantage of urban public goods.

Since Brazil's transition to democracy, the country has undertaken three censuses—in 1991, 2000, and 2010—through its internationally renowned census agency, the Brazilian Institute of Geography and Statistics. Two leading urban social scientists in São Paulo, Eduardo Marques and Camila Saraiva, have conducted authoritative quantitative analysis of these census data crossed with municipal data on the location of informal settlements, which makes clear the ways that unequal access to São Paulo's public goods has and has not changed.

The municipality of São Paulo has also developed significant capacity for monitoring the extent and condition of its informal settlements. This is a stark reversal of the legacy of erasure and invisibility that marked the sprawl of informal residences that characterized the city's authoritarian period. Especially since the early 2000s, the municipality has developed multiple generations of digital monitoring tools. The first was developed in partnership with the World Bank and Cities Alliance (which was then itself a project housed within the World Bank). This produced a digital monitoring method to be used by the Municipal Housing Secretariat to guide the development of a Municipal Housing Policy. The resulting tool, called the Social Housing Information System of São Paulo, made it possible for the city's technical staff to use on-the-ground surveys to continuously update the database. In the early 2010s, the municipality also developed a new Municipal Housing Policy intended to coincide with a new master plan. It introduced a database called GeoSampa that included not only housing-related data contained in the Social Housing Information System of São Paulo but a much wider set of service indicators.

For our purposes here, the range of official administrative data on public goods in São Paulo represents a sea change in the legibility of informality in municipal decision-making. As a result, Brazilian scholars have produced important work documenting the distributional changes that can be measured through these data sources.

In terms of housing, studies show that the extent of legal informality has remained largely stagnant. In fact, the share of households living in informal settlements has grown slightly, from 9.2 percent in 1991 to 11.6 percent in 2010. The geography of informality has largely stayed constant, however, as we can see in Figure 2.1. This could mean that housing policy has failed, at least in relative terms over the period in question, and to a certain extent, this would be a fair interpretation; taken together, programs for public provision and the private market are not delivering enough housing to absorb demand. However, the extent of informality is not necessarily telling us what we actually care about in terms of the core questions of inclusion into the public goods of the city. In this sense, informality is not inherently "good" or "bad." Rather, it is what informality means *in practice* that matters.

When informality means that residents do not exist on maps and have no rights, as it did during the period of Brazil's military dictatorship, then it is a straightforward proposition to understand growth in informal residences as an unequivocal problem for inclusion. But living informally does *not* necessarily have to entail this type of subjugated rights-bearing citizenship. When these settlements become a policy priority for local government

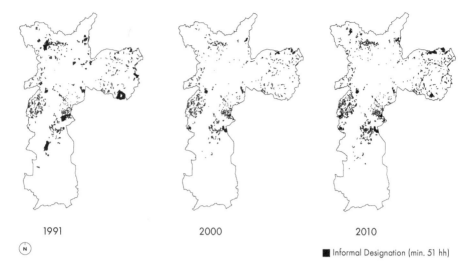

1991   2000   2010

Ⓝ

■ Informal Designation (min. 51 hh)

FIGURE 2.1. Informal settlements in São Paulo, by census sector. *Source:* Brazilian Institute of Geography and Statistics.

extension of a broader range of public goods, such as sanitation, then we need to more fully contextualize the informality of residential life with its material conditions.

So it is particularly notable how much sanitation provision has changed for people living in the city's informal settlements. This improvement can be hidden by more aggregated figures that show how overall sanitation provision is relatively high in São Paulo, especially compared with other municipalities across Brazil. In São Paulo, while only one in four (25.1 percent) residents of informal settlements had access to a flush toilet within their home in 1991, this share almost tripled to more than two of every three residents (67.9 percent) by 2010 (Marques and Saraiva 2017). This distribution in São Paulo is illustrated in Figures 2.2 and 2.3.

This is a remarkable gain, not only because of what it represents for the public health and basic dignity of residents of São Paulo's informal settlements. The extent of provision of a flush toilet is a useful indicator for the de facto inclusion of a dwelling in the infrastructural networks that make up the city. The extension of sewage systems to a home requires that the delivering agency accept a certain degree of tenure rights of the individual dwelling being serviced. Achieving this degree of accepted legitimacy is no small feat, and as we will see, São Paulo's main water and sanitation provisioning agency, the Basic Sanitation Company of the State of São Paulo, known by its Portuguese acronym of SABESP, had a long history of unwillingness to service homes and neighborhoods deemed to be informal.

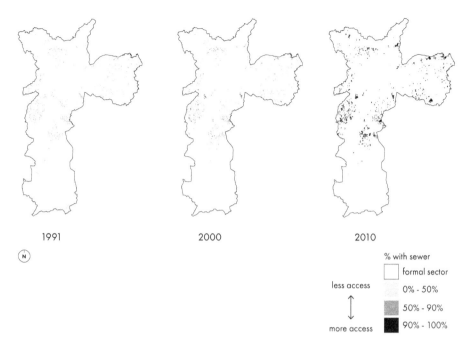

FIGURE 2.2. Access to sewer-connected toilets in informal settlement households in São Paulo. *Source:* Brazilian Institute of Geography and Statistics.

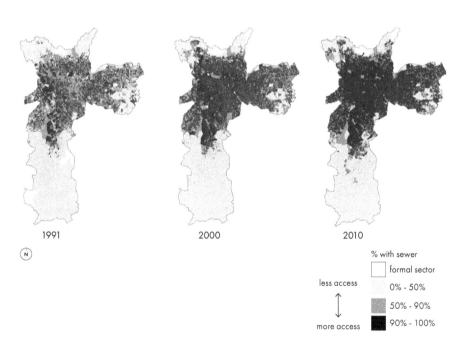

FIGURE 2.3. Access to sewer-connected toilets in all households in São Paulo. *Source:* Brazilian Institute of Geography and Statistics.

The gains in sanitation provision within informal settlements therefore represent a sea change in the lived experience of inclusion of informal residents within the city's infrastructure. And because of their implications for how informal residents are seen by the state, they represent not only an equitable improvement in sanitation policy. Instead, they need to be understood in a broader bundle of interventions in housing and land use policy that prioritizes what urban planners call the "upgrading" of informal settlements (Mitlin and Satterthwaite 2012), a process that accounts for the fundamental interconnection between housing, land use, and the provision of sanitation. In essence, while a shortage in formal housing persists and has even grown, the difference in quality of life between the city's various neighborhoods has narrowed significantly.

Distributional changes in collective transportation in São Paulo are nearly impossible to sum up in a single number. In part, this is due to the challenges of informality for formal recordkeeping in this policy arena. As I describe in chapter 5, the proliferation of clandestine buses and minibus taxis was hard to count in any reliable fashion. Even more to the point, calculating the overall number of vehicles in a city does not tell us anything substantial about individuals' ability to move around and get from home to work; the mere proliferation of vehicles is not a sure sign of increased connectivity. Instead, I describe changes in the unequal distribution of collective transportation as a public good by focusing on the inclusion of marginalized parts of the city through two mechanisms: (1) the connection of the formal network of collective transportation across the extent of the city and (2) the effective price implications of the network's ticketing system.

Changes in São Paulo over the past thirty years illustrate why each of these mechanisms is important and how they are interrelated to one another. The bus network is by far the city's most used form of transportation. A fragmented network of public, authorized private, and unauthorized private bus companies has been progressively integrated into a single network that is governed by the municipality of São Paulo. The city now puts out contracts to individual operators and collects all the fares into one system. This enables the municipality to establish a uniform policy of remuneration to bus companies on a subsidized basis. The administration of fare collection is also centralized, which has enabled the municipality to partially subsidize the cost to riders. This marks São Paulo as an outlier across Brazilian municipalities, where individual bus operators generally keep a tight hold on fare collection and administration (Cunha Linke and Andrés 2022).

It also has enabled a ticketing system whereby a user can buy a single ticket that gives the right to ride across a multileg journey. This is the most common kind of journey for residents of peripheral neighborhoods to the employment hubs in the city's center. The single ticket reduces the bus system's effective fare for poorer users. Where residents of the urban peripheries previously had to buy tickets for each leg of their journey to and from work, now they can buy a single ticket.

Taken together, these findings of change in inequality certainly do not suggest that São Paulo has become an egalitarian urban utopia. In fact, homelessness, informality, and inequality remain characteristic there. The purpose of describing São Paulo as a positive case is *not* to insist that it has become a paradise. Rather, it is to insist that large and meaningful reductions of inequality are possible even and especially in contexts where the pervasiveness of informality might generally lead us to expect their impossibility. In a case such as São Paulo, we can say that the boundaries of "social closure," instantiated through the built environment of the city, have loosened, and the city has become a more equitable space as a result. In the next three chapters, we will see how these gains are a consequence of the relationship between local government and the sphere of housing movements, as well as changes within local government itself.

Johannesburg: A Strong Basis for Redistribution

From the time Johannesburg was first settled in the late nineteenth century, it has been planned as two separate cities: wealthy, overwhelmingly white, and well-serviced neighborhoods in the northern and western areas of the city and poor, overwhelmingly black, and poorly serviced neighborhoods in the city's southern and eastern parts. This spatial separation was driven by successive waves of forced removals of nonwhite residents beginning in the early twentieth century (Van Onselen 1982) and codified into law under the Group Areas Act in 1950. The separate administrative apparatuses associated with this segregation were codified by the Bantu Authorities Act of 1951 and, later, the Black Local Authorities Act of 1982, which created a layer of Apartheid government, centrally appointed wardens of areas where black people were allowed to live. One consequence of these racially separated jurisdictions was that what would become the contemporary single administrative unit of Johannesburg was characterized by the fragmentation of, at varying times, eleven to fifteen separate municipal administrations.

In response to this fragmentation, the rallying cry of "one city, one tax base" united neighborhood associations, social movements, local branches of unions, and the African National Congress, as negotiations began at the local level in parallel to national negotiations for a democratic transition. These negotiations, which led to the elections of 1994 and the constitution of 1996, produced an extensive enumeration of socioeconomic rights that define the country's democratic dispensation. While Apartheid was a political economic program rooted in racial ideology, the spatial logic embedded in the name of this policy defined its institutional trajectory. "Apartheid" characterized a specific political economy that rested on the creation of reserves of cheap black labor for extractive mining and industrial production under the aegis of strong state-backed corporate monopolies (Fine and Rustomjee 1996; Wolpe 1972). The geographic divides within and between cities and towns constituted the social groups that continue to make and remake the institutions that govern fiscal distribution, land use planning, access to basic services, and, ultimately, access to economic freedom and social recognition.

Some of the most intense battles of the internal struggle against Apartheid in the late 1980s coalesced around protests against urban containment. Rent boycotts, rising militant protest, and calls to render cities "ungovernable" contributed to an increasingly unstable political environment ripe for change (Turok 2014). When the ANC was unbanned in 1990, the party doubled down on its decade-long call for South Africans to disobey Apartheid movement controls and "occupy the cities" (Pithouse 2008), moving into areas that had previously been prohibited. The demand that the black majority should reap the benefits of urban life and economic opportunity was a political priority in the struggle against a system designed to ration access to the city.

South Africa's democratic state is rooted in a social movement history that precedes its current formal structure: the United Democratic Front (UDF). Formed in 1983, this broad-based organization was made up of civic organizations, trade unions, and other citizen associations as a wide-ranging front against the Apartheid regime. In his landmark history of the UDF, South African social scientist Jeremy Seekings emphasizes that between its formation and 1986, the actions of the UDF were very much like those of a social movement:

> The UDF was not a party, did not have branches, and never allowed for individual or personal membership. . . . Having the form of a front facilitated effective activity over agreed, specific and discrete issues, whilst preserving the formal autonomy of affiliates. Organisations could affiliate even though they disagreed with other affiliates over broad ideals or even over the strategies they used in their individual activities. This loose form represented a choice on the part of the UDF's founders, an acknowledgment of the fragmentation, vulnerability and diversity of South Africa's extra-state opposition. (2000, 15–16)

Because the African National Congress was banned, its leaders either in exile or in prison, it could not maintain any formal links with the UDF. But clandestine links were established between party and movement throughout the 1980s. The strength of the UDF was tied to the emergence of militant industrial unionism, reminiscent of that in Brazil at the same time, through the Federation of South African Trade Unions. In 1973, strikes in the eastern port city of Durban were joined by nearly a hundred thousand workers across the country. Three years later, student protests, which first emerged in Johannesburg's Soweto township, took on a national character. This provided a strategic basis for linking student movements, community associations, and trade unions.

The Federation of South African Trade Unions was initially skeptical of joining forces with community organizations, arguing that they would distract or potentially subsume its emphasis on workplace demands. Seidman, for example, situates the 1970s in South Africa as a "kind of prehistory in which activists gradually created a basis for organization but made few concrete gains" (1994, 176). Increasing strikes around the country eventually coalesced in response to the National Party–led government's proposal in 1983 to institute a tricameral parliament, which would be divided along racial lines. The move was seen by organizers as a Trojan horse to defeat efforts at true universalization of the franchise and democracy. The number of UDF affiliates nearly doubled in the immediate aftermath of this proposal. Community organizations in townships grew more plentiful and were tightly organized around street-level committees. Unionists increasingly allied with these groups, linking economic concerns in the workplace *and* the home with broader demands for racial recognition and a universal electoral franchise.

By 1987, the trade union federation, now renamed the Congress of South African Trade Unions (COSATU), which united autoworkers, miners, teachers, nurses, and textile workers, among others, had a list of national demands that included a living wage for all, housing for all, political rights, land redistribution, and adequate education. This alliance saw broad-based terrain for struggle that extended far beyond the shop floor, as articulated in one of the aims in the UDF-COSATU National United Action campaign of 1987: "build organs of people's power in the townships, factories, schools, universities, etc." (Seekings 2000, 203).

Even as COSATU looked to unite the shop floor with the neighborhood and the university, it faced tension with connecting the class dimension of labor struggle to other struggles in the country, namely, that for racial equality. This was most evident in the arguments that raged over the relationship between COSATU and the broad community-based umbrella alliance of organizations known as the United Democratic Front. Seidman (1994) notes the strong alliances that COSATU was able to build with broader community groups to link labor struggles to the struggle for racial equality. By broadening beyond just shop floor demands, claims for universal dignity and racial equality appealed to a much wider base, linking identities of race and class.

But it was an uneasy alliance, and as it became clear that a democratic transition was approaching, tensions flared again. For example, at a COSATU congress in 1989, shortly before the unbanning of all political parties, while "COSATU reaffirmed the federation's 'strategic alliance' with the UDF (and, implicitly, the UDF's illegal ally, the ANC), it acknowledged that workers and community groups had separate identities and interests" (Seidman 1994, 251). In essence, it was not clear that worker demands would necessarily always be aligned with those of movements oriented toward housing and basic services. For example, the membership of the latter group might include many who were outside of the formal workforce.

In 1990, when the National Party–led government unbanned the ANC and began negotiations to end Apartheid, the UDF was increasingly subordinated to the political organizing imperatives of the ANC. The "civics" movements that composed the heart of the UDF had prepared to play a significant role in local government. A summary report from a meeting of the UDF on March 1–3, 1991, described the agenda that the movement foresaw:

> It is no longer enough to destroy apartheid. We now have to begin rebuilding what apartheid has destroyed. This means the civic movement has to formulate alternative forms of local government, propose more equatable [sic] health systems, study alternative transport systems, propose formulae for determining "affordability," put forward viable solutions to the housing crisis and begin to address the crisis in education.

Documentation prepared for this meeting noted that "there has been a resurgence of civic activity since February 1990. The main issues have been land, housing, electricity, taxis/transport and local government" (Ebrahim 1991).

Even at this early point, four years before democratic elections, the UDF was debating how it could restructure local government to address these issues. Cas Coovadia, then a leading activist in the UDF, prepared an internal report in 1990 that highlighted the basic thrust of these proposals, which had a clear orientation toward redistribution from local government in white urban areas:

> Civics are examining methods of subsidization of services. In the interim period, some civics are demanding that neighbouring white municipalities, because of their access to expertise, capital equipment and resources, take over the provision of certain services, i.e. rubbish removal and the maintenance of roads and stormwater drains. Where white municipalities are involved in the provision of water and electricity to black townships, they are being challenged to provide these services at a rate equal to, or below, the rate that applies in the white areas, thus effectively subsidizing costs. In the longer term, civics are looking to the introduction of a single administration, based on an integrated local metropolitan or regional tax base, as the way in which the provision and supply of services to low-income areas can be cross-subsidized. (Ebrahim 1991)

These debates over cross-subsidization across formerly separate municipalities in Johannesburg would reverberate with critical consequences.

The ANC's slogan of "one city, one tax base" encapsulated the drive to ensure a strong redistributional model; the wealthy and overwhelmingly white areas of the city's northern suburbs would subsidize the development of the poor and overwhelmingly black areas of the city's southern and northeastern peripheries. There could be little doubt that the long-standing economically dominant sector stood to lose its political supremacy.

As negotiations toward democratic elections progressed, most structures of the UDF quickly fell apart, despite the argument from some quarters in the leadership that "whilst the ANC would assume 'national political leadership,' especially in negotiations with the government, the UDF should continue to coordinate socio-economic struggles, help to build the ANC, and pull the political 'middle ground' into support for the ANC" (Seekings 2000, 21). In effect, the ANC took a strong ideological position that while social movement allies were essential for the struggle for democracy, they were likely to be obstacles to a "vanguardist" orientation of an ANC-led post-Apartheid state that could drive redistribution and development. As Madlingozi has argued, "The hegemony of the ANC and its allies over the national liberation struggle had devastating consequences for ideological and organizational diversity represented by grassroots organizations affiliated to the UDF" (2007, 85). This would be compounded by the fact that the ANC has maintained electoral dominance. Since the first democratic election in 1994, it has never come close to losing a national election.[7] In Johannesburg, it maintained the mayoral seat for the entire period of this study, finally handing over power to the center-right Democratic Alliance in 2016.

Significant features of this dominant relationship of the ruling party to social movements and organizations have carried through to the democratic era. And key features of this dominance were established through policy struggles over the provisioning of public goods. In 1994, riding high on its leading role in the UDF and in subsequent negotiations to end Apartheid after the unbanning of the ANC, COSATU played a big role in policymaking. The Reconstruction and Development Program (RDP), for example, which instituted a range of social welfare initiatives, including the administration of a new housing subsidy, was, in large part, crafted by people in COSATU's policy research wing. The trade union federation's secretary general, Jay Naidoo, was also appointed by President Nelson Mandela with the portfolio of minister in the presidency, widely understood to oversee the RDP. But just two years later, in 1996, the ANC had solidified its hold on the national government, and COSATU's waning influence was in plain sight. The ANC government's new Growth, Employment, and Redistribution program moved away from the more radical redistributive and labor-friendly policies of the RDP in the name of "global competitiveness."

The housing subsidy program that was initiated as part of the RDP would come to forever be associated with it. To this day, any government-built house is commonly referred to as an "RDP house," decades after the formal demise of the program. This approach to subsidizing private contractors to build houses for low-income residents was crafted through a tense series of negotiations as preparations for a democratic government were well underway in 1993 at what was called the National Housing Forum. This meeting was convened by a group of business leaders who had pushed the Apartheid government to prioritize investment in housing in informal settlements as a necessity for economic growth and stability. But it was joined by ANC activists and COSATU leaders, as well as members of the township-based "civics" that had been at the heart of the UDF. The National Housing Forum culminated in a series of working papers, consecrated in what is known as the Botshabelo Accord (Rust and Rubinstein 1996). This formed the basis of the national government's Housing White Paper in 1994 (Mackay 2007).

The country's newly democratic constitution of 1996 included commitments to socioeconomic rights, as well as the empowerment of municipal authorities to enable participatory deliberative politics and inclusive local economic development. This was affirmed by further legislation such as the Local Government White Paper, the provision for participatory planning through what is known as the Integrated Development Plan, and the creation of national grants for municipal infrastructure and local economic development. The rationale of housing and land use policies in the country, though rarely structured around a distinctly *urban* policy, has always been aimed at spatial integration to overcome Apartheid divides. For example, the Housing White Paper of 1994, the primary document that guided housing policy during the first ten years of democracy (Adebayo 2011), stated that the first goal of public regulation of land use, especially at the provincial and local levels of government, should be "to redress the spatial inequities and distortions that have resulted from planning according to apartheid and segregation policies of the past" (Department of Housing 1994, 50).

In a recent consideration of the compromises that defined the post-1994 settlement, Alan Hirsch, who between 1995 and 2013 held senior posts in the Department of Trade and Industry and the presidency, argues that a number of redistributive issues were ignored or downplayed during the early years of democratically elected government. "Assets such as wealth and land could have been more radically redistributed," he writes. After enumerating key issues in macro-economic policymaking, Hirsch concludes with one final concern that animated the anti-Apartheid struggle: "The Apartheid structure of cities could have been more urgently addressed" (2015).

Though much of the literature on institutions and the role of the state has tended to focus on the national or global scale, the regulation of markets for urban land and housing is often mediated through subnational institutions. And in the case of South Africa, land use has been regulated through a combination of provincial and municipal institutions. The conflicts between these different levels of institutional regulation of land have structured the persistence of ambiguous institutional legacies at the municipal level in Johannesburg that were intended to transform the city's spatial configuration. The city's traditionally white central and northern areas have enjoyed Western standards of near-universal basic services and infrastructure, while the traditionally black south and far northeast of the city have been vastly underresourced.

The Johannesburg case suggests the consequences of the emergence in South Africa of a "commandist logic of local governmental reform" (Heller 2001, 134). Local state-led attempts at reform have been increasingly insulated from the demands of both civil society activists and business elites and have therefore not been able to mobilize either popular or fiscal support to see them through. The ideological decision by the ANC to demobilize the UDF produced a fractured sphere of movement activity. South Africa has had some of the highest rates of protest anywhere in the world over the past fifteen years, with Johannesburg as a persistent epicenter of such activity. But organizing in poor communities rarely reaches beyond the scale of individual neighborhoods. The ANC either has been able to keep such organizing out of formal politics altogether or can easily co-opt such small-scale activity (Paret 2022). While grassroots activists have been unable to make their voices heard, business elites have been able to organize along geographic area–based lines to repurpose moments of reform to reinforce prior distributional trajectories that have defined the spatial logic of the city.

Inequality in Johannesburg

In Johannesburg, life in the *mjondolo*, the isiZulu word for "shack," is a life of physical distance. The "shacklands" of informal settlements are often side by side with older formal townships and newer publicly subsidized, detached, single-story housing developments. Getting to and from workplaces is a perennial challenge for residents, who wake as early as 3 a.m. to catch minibus taxis to take them from their extreme southern and northwestern homes to their places of work in the city's leafy northern residential suburbs and the shiny business nodes of Sandton, Melrose, and Fourways.

Especially given that Johannesburg is cast in this book's comparative design as a negative case, we should be clear about what has changed. Racial segregation at the city-wide scale has *decreased*. Dynamics of this form of desegregation are most prevalent in middle-/upper-middle-class neighborhoods, as black people have increasingly moved into white-collar professional occupations (Crankshaw 2008, 2022). That being said, the racial makeup of poorer neighborhoods—where we see gaping deficits in access to public goods—remains persistently black. In this sense, the reproduction of Apartheid in

housing informality
■ informality ≥ 10%

1996	2001	2011
84/504 Subplaces	171/674 Subplaces	179/782 Subplaces
146,187 informal hh	169,260 informal hh	196,339 informal hh
535,827 formal hh	624,740 formal hh	984,833 formal hh

FIGURE 2.4. Informal settlements in Johannesburg, by census subplace. *Source:* Statistics South Africa.

Johannesburg after democratization cannot only be understood in purely racial terms. Instead, the way race articulates with class and space defines Johannesburg as what can be described as a "neo-Apartheid" city. Most notably, even as the most positive assessments of residential change in Johannesburg readily note, the townships and informal settlements are just as racialized as they were before democracy.

Since South Africa's transition to democracy, the national statistics agency, Statistics South Africa (StatsSA), has undertaken three censuses: in 1996, 2001, 2011. Reliable data collected by municipal government in Johannesburg are in shorter supply than in São Paulo, and I am unable to rely on any analyses of a similar sort as I was able to accomplish in São Paulo. That being said, we can make some direct comparisons with the available national census data.

The share of the informal settlement population in Johannesburg actually dropped slightly from 18.8 percent in 1996 to 14.1 percent in 2011. The spatial dimensions of this quantitative change are represented in Figure 2.4. With this decrease, we might therefore consider Johannesburg to have more successfully increased housing equality compared with São Paulo. But recall, the reason I analyze housing and land use together is that land use policy enables the regularization of land for slum upgrading. What we care about is not only the regulated status of land on which people reside but what this status means functionally in terms of both security of tenure and the capacity for other city services to be brought to the home.

Access to sanitation in informal settlements in Johannesburg, in notable contrast to São Paulo, barely grew from 36.0 percent in 1996 to 47.4 percent in

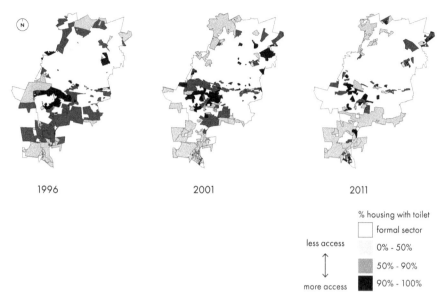

1996   2001   2011

% housing with toilet

☐ formal sector

less access   0% - 50%

↑   50% - 90%

↓

more access   ■ 90% - 100%

FIGURE 2.5. Access to sewer-connected toilets in informal settlement households in Johannesburg. *Source:* Statistics South Africa.

2011. Recall that São Paulo nearly tripled the share of households with access to sanitation in informal settlements in the same period. Figure 2.5 illustrates just how minimal this change appears in spatial terms only in areas with at least 10 percent of households living in an informal shack. And Figure 2.6 illustrates how little changed in terms of access to sanitation across the entire city. These data lead to a clear conclusion that the provision of sanitation in informal settlements in Johannesburg has been markedly worse than that in São Paulo. Furthermore, they make clear that the regulatory status of informal settlements in Johannesburg does not afford the same kind of tenure security as in São Paulo. In São Paulo, informal settlements continue to experience eviction by private landowners and the state government, but the municipal government has functionally ended all evictions on land that it owns. In Johannesburg, by contrast, informal settlement residents continue to face eviction from all three types of landowners. Prior spatial analysis of residential patterns in Johannesburg suggests persistent reproduction of class-based segregation despite a slight reduction in racial segregation (Kracker Selzer and Heller 2010). The effect has been a compounding of "neo-Apartheid" spatial inequalities (Harrison et al. 2014; Murray 2011).

Finally, we consider the difference in collective transportation. While São Paulo has seen significant changes in terms of regulation, ride integration, and functional user costs in its bus system, Johannesburg's minibus taxi system,

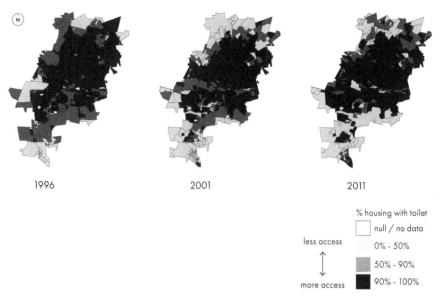

FIGURE 2.6. Access to sewer-connected toilets in all households in Johannesburg. *Source:* Statistics South Africa.

which remains the city's dominant form of collective transportation, is largely the same as at the end of Apartheid. It remains a fragmented, informal system, with users paying for each leg of a journey. While fine-grained municipal-level statistics are hard to come by for the system of minibus taxis, at the national level, StatsSA estimates that two-thirds of households in the bottom quintile of earnings spend more than 20 percent of their income on transportation. In the top quintile, only 3 percent of households spend a similar share of their income on transportation (StatsSA, 2015).

What These Cases Can Tell Us about Theorizing "Urban Power"

To state the empirical variation that motivates this study: In each of these three policy arenas, housing and land use, sanitation, and transportation, São Paulo has reduced inequalities in access to these urban public goods, while Johannesburg has reproduced these same types of inequalities. Table 2.1 summarizes these findings.

It is helpful to think about this variation in outcomes in light of the theoretical models discussed in the previous chapter. The urban literature focused on the effects of the global integration of markets hardly allows for redistributive outcomes in globally connected megacities, such as São Paulo and Johannesburg. The "urban regime" approach is focused on the historical construction

TABLE 2.1. Key Measures of Public Goods Inequality in São Paulo and Johannesburg

Measure	São Paulo		Johannesburg	
	1991	*2011*	*1996*	*2011*
Households in informal settlements	9.2%	11.6%	18.8%	14.1%
Households in informal settlements with a toilet	25.1%	67.9%	36.0%	47.4%
Dominant mode of collective transportation	Privately operated buses, no multileg fare integration, no subsidy	Public network of privately operated buses, single fare for multiple legs, partial subsidy	Privately operated minibus, no multileg fare integration, no subsidy	Privately operated minibus, no multileg fare integration, no subsidy

of coordination between public and private actors in cities, generally in order to realize goals of urban growth. The case of Atlanta, which Stone (1989) uses to develop his theory of "urban regimes," shows how white business elites were willing to cede political power to new black political elites in the second half of the twentieth century and strategically coordinated with black politicians to redevelop the downtown of the city. This often came at the expense of investments in black working-class neighborhoods.

Whereas a coalition of political and business elites worked together toward explicit policy and project outcomes in Atlanta, Johannesburg's policy goals and the development goals of business elites have largely remained at odds in the city. In São Paulo, business elites have actually had much closer relationships with political elites than in Johannesburg. But as I show in the next chapter, in São Paulo, and unlike in Johannesburg, these relationships have developed around the persistent countervailing power of social movements and their own ties with city officials and politicians.

The role of the color line in Johannesburg's politics is worth further examination in comparison to Stone's theorization of the Atlanta case. In Atlanta, black political power emerged through previously white-dominated structures of the Democratic Party and was constantly subject to pressures for compromise from within the party even before black politicians took power. In Johannesburg, by contrast, black political power emerged through the African National Congress. The shift in national politics was therefore much clearer on the race question in the South African case, while the articulation of race in party politics was much more ambiguous in the United States. The upshot here is that groups of white property owners and developers in Johannesburg faced an uphill battle to realize coordinated "regimes" oriented toward their goals of economic growth. They were therefore more likely to pursue strategies that disabled unfavorable government policies instead of more programmatic approaches.

Those who have examined post-Apartheid South African national political economy have highlighted similar strategies of traditional white elites in the country's democratic settlement (Bassett 2008; Bond 2005; Hart 2014; Marais 2011). On the one hand, this approach at the national level suggests an affinity to the "growth machine" approach: returns to capital arguably win the day. On the other hand, there is an explicit trade not anticipated in the "regimes" approach. Political power would surely be easier to coordinate with natural allies of business. Instead, we see a trade-off. In exchange for ceding the formal political terrain, largely white business elites win a degree of autonomy that allows them to later disable the implementation of policies.

Many post-settler-colonial societies are characterized by stark divisions of race and caste. But there are few with a clear articulation of both race and class in the party-political arena. There is no African country with as large a proportion of a white settler population. In Latin America, the one case of explicit race-class articulation in the party-political sphere is Bolivia's Movement towards Socialism (MAS), which governed between 2006 and 2019. Similar to South Africa, the MAS instituted policies geared toward transforming the racial composition of the bureaucracy to incorporate indigenous groups in the service of what the country's new constitution called a "plurinational state" (Anria 2018). However, the particular question of urban transformation has never been as central to the MAS political program as it has been for the ANC in South Africa and for the Workers' Party in Brazil.

Each of these countries has features of a social welfare state that the "power-resources" approach would predict, as it emphasizes the importance of parties and social movement allies in driving redistributive policies. In fact, when discussing comparative implications of his work on redistribution in the Indian state of Kerala, Heller (1999, 248) argues that South Africa was *more likely* to achieve redistributive outcomes because the working class was more "cohesive" than that in Brazil. It is not surprising, then, that Evans, Huber, and Stephens (2017) cite the varying trajectories of Brazil and South Africa, despite similar social and political transitions in the late 1980s and early 1990s, as an emblematic divergence that requires further investigation in order to elaborate a theory of state effectiveness in the twenty-first century.

The role of political parties, their relationship to social movements, and electoral competition are particularly hard to parse in these two cases with the tools of the "power-resources" model. The PT is a left political party aligned to an alliance of unions, social movements, and intellectuals. It is credited with programmatic redistributive policies in sectors such as labor, social security, education, and health (Gibson 2018). However, there were good reasons to expect that São Paulo's experience after democratization would not be a good candidate for the expectations of "power-resources" theory. Given the durable oligarchic tendencies of local rule prior to this historical inflection point, we would not necessarily anticipate even strong national policy reforms to deliver change at the municipal scale. In contrast to Johannesburg, where the ANC ruled continuously for the period under examination here, the PT has never had successive terms in office in the city. And, especially in São Paulo, trade unions have not been the unique or even primary civil society actor associated with the programmatic delivery of public goods in the city. This suggests that the role of a political party is insufficient, on its own, for explaining inclusionary changes in São Paulo's distribution of public goods. My own findings about the role of overlapping, and sometimes fractious, housing movements are surprising, given expectations that movements require formal cohesiveness for achieving programmatic welfare outcomes (Lee 2012).

Even if we expect that greater degrees of electoral competition in São Paulo might produce more political accountability that in Johannesburg, we still would lack a clear mechanism for building internal bureaucratic capacity to actually deliver the physical infrastructures that are the concern of this study. And, unlike in Johannesburg, the ruling party in local government in São Paulo has rarely been aligned to the party in power at the national level. This may very well lead us to predict counterproductive friction in interscalar coordination; state or federal government might very well try to undercut efforts by local government (or vice versa).

Though both countries remain highly unequal, significant parts of both the Brazilian and South African states retain and have developed strong institutional capacities for redistribution-oriented policies. Brazil's ratio of tax to gross domestic product (GDP) has been slightly lower than the average of the thirty-eight members of the Organisation for Economic Co-operation and Development (OECD) but well above the Latin American average. And by 2010, its tax-to-GDP ratio was still below the average but outpaced seventeen of the OECD member countries. South Africa has routinely collected taxes at a tax-to-GDP ratio equal to or above that of the United States, with a higher share of tax revenues coming from both income and corporate taxes than the respective averages of the member nations of the Organisation for Economic Co-operation and Development (OECD, African Tax Administration Forum, and African Union Commission 2018). Brazil's social welfare state includes a national public health care system and one of the world's largest conditional cash transfer systems, Bolsa Familia (Kerstenetzky 2014). South Africa's post-Apartheid system of social welfare grants manages to deliver cash transfers

TABLE 2.2. How Existing Theory Would Predict Outcomes in the Cases

Theories	São Paulo	Johannesburg	Predicted Outcome
Neoliberalism/ "global cities"	Deindustrialization, growing knowledge/ service sector	Deindustrialization, growing knowledge/ service sector	Should be the same
"Growth machines"/ "regimes"	Close ties between developers and city government	Arm's-length ties between developers and city government	Johannesburg should be more redistributive
"Power-resources"/ class coalitions	Working-class movement + programmatic party of the Left	Working-class movement + programmatic party of the Left	Should be the same
Organization of coalition	Less cohesive class-based movement	More cohesive class-based movement	Johannesburg should be more redistributive

to one in every three citizens (Rossouw 2017).[8] While national institutions have proved themselves capable of managing complex tasks of taxation and redistribution, well-capacitated municipal institutions in Johannesburg have been unable to achieve similar gains in their management of a property regime that defines the distribution of public goods in the city. All of this suggests that the national conditions for redistributive politics share a number of critical characteristics, which makes the variation in urban outcomes a puzzle with useful leverage for theorizing why some cities are more effective than others in reducing inequalities.

My presentation of the quantitative outcomes in distribution across these two cities in Table 2.2 should not be misconstrued as saying that São Paulo is a paradise without any inequality whatsoever. It is also not to say that Johannesburg is an ungoverned disaster. Rather, it is to say that each of these cities has struggled to deal with the truly wicked problems of urban growth amid persistent informality—typical challenges of urban management in most of the world—and that we see meaningful outcomes associated with the institutional changes that are the heart of the analysis in this book. What this chapter has done is establish precisely why the outcomes in São Paulo and Johannesburg should be understood as divergent and why their divergences are helpful for developing theory about the institutional conditions of distributional change at the scale of the city.

3

Housing

SUBALTERN RIGHTS AND ELITE RESISTANCE

The struggle for housing has long animated cultural and political life in São Paulo and Johannesburg. Of the many activists I interviewed across these two cities, almost all identified first and foremost as housing activists. Their movements were always articulated around housing concerns, and the bureaucratic agencies they targeted were almost always first responsible for delivering housing. Of the three public goods analyzed in this and the chapters that immediately follow, housing has been subject to the most sustained open political contestation as a both cause and consequence of struggles for democracy in both Brazil and South Africa. Much of this can be attributed to the intrinsic intersection of the politics of housing and rights to urban land. The nexus of housing and land continuously exposes the core interests in city-making and urban conflict: real estate finance, state authority, and the social need for collective meaning in everyday life.

In both São Paulo and Johannesburg, the politicization of housing and residential quality of life was intrinsic to broader struggles for electoral democracy. Rent strikes, land occupations, and contestation over local political power and neighborhood organization were central aspects of nationalized social struggles demanding a universal electoral franchise and new civic constitutions with socioeconomic rights. The role of movements that organized around the explicit theme of housing rights was critical to the inclusion of these rights in constitutional documents in both countries. And local government was empowered to realize these rights in both countries.

Both cities began their democratic eras governed by mayors with explicit commitments to redistributing wealth in the city to support the extension of adequate housing to the most excluded neighborhoods. These commitments were initially backed by strong capital investments. But the delivery outcomes and land use policies for sustaining these kinds of investments sharply diverged. This chapter asks why São Paulo managed to develop planning tools for housing that generated power within the local state to relativize the rights of private property to deliver social housing in well-located areas, while Johannesburg did not. What accounts for the divergent paths these cities took when it comes to the construction of municipal institutions to deliver housing and reform land policies to enable slum upgrading?

This chapter shows how one of the core challenges in coordinating governing power over housing and land use policy is the sanctity of private property rights. Cities can prioritize the market "exchange" value of housing and land over their social "use" value. When cities make choices to prioritize the social value of property, and are effective enough to implement those choices, they can be said to pursue a path that "relativizes" the rights of private property. In other words, they refuse the inviolable sanctity of private property rights.

I argue that an explanation for the contrasting municipal institutions in each city lies in the way that São Paulo's municipal bureaucracy relied on its ties to housing movements—*embeddedness*—thereby generating the capacity to coordinate within the bureaucracy—*cohesion*—to use new national mandates to challenge the power of private real estate interests. Conversely, Johannesburg's municipal bureaucracy was progressively de-linked from its social movement base, thereby weakening its internal capacity to challenge the relatively hidden strategies of largely white private real estate interests.

São Paulo: Erundina's "Inversion of Priorities"

Neighborhood associations and housing movements formed a critical bloc in the social alliance that propelled Brazil toward democratization in the 1980s. While the Workers' Party's Lula made it to the second round of the country's first direct presidential elections in 1988, he was soundly defeated, notwithstanding strong support in the industrial cities of the country's southeast, including São Paulo and its neighboring municipalities. The municipal elections in 1988, however, produced historic breakthroughs for the left-wing party. Even the party itself was surprised by its mayoral win in São Paulo, alongside victories in the adjacent municipalities of Diadema, Santo André, and São Bernardo do Campo (Rocha de Barros 2022). It was in these municipalities that the party could begin building its grassroots-oriented governing credentials at the local level, through a focus on the distribution of urban public goods. This, party leaders made clear, would establish a "PT way of governing" (*o modo petista de governor*) (Palocci et al. 1997). The party aimed to do so without first winning a national governing position.

The social movement sphere that brought Luiza Erundina to power as the first PT mayor of São Paulo in the 1988 municipal election provided a strong basis for embedding the local state in a new set of distributive demands. But her mayoral administration struggled to build the cohesion necessary to institutionalize them, particularly in the face of constrained fiscal resources at the municipal level. The first generation of grassroots housing movements in the city emerged in the 1970s and 1980s, as rapid urban industrialization and growth put significant pressure on housing availability. In particular, the extreme eastern and southern parts of São Paulo were home to new land occupations and the growth of informal settlements (Holston 2008). By the early 1980s, many of the neighborhood associations that had led these occupations were uniting under the common banner of the Federation of Housing Movements, or the *União de Movimentos da Moradia* in Portuguese (Earle 2012). All three of the veteran leaders of the UMM in the city with whom I conducted in-depth interviews reported to me that they first got involved in organizing around the issue of housing through the Catholic Church. Catholic priests who preached the Marxist-inflected "liberation theology" were growing their parishes in the city's peripheries (Burdick 1996). These were the areas of the city with the most rapid growth of in-migration and the neighborhoods most excluded from the city's distribution of public goods.

The city-wide ecosystem of housing movements, anchored in the UMM, was instrumental in shaping the electoral base of the Erundina administration from 1989 to 1992. Governing programs for all PT electoral campaigns in the city have been debated with housing movements, and professionals affiliated with such movements occupied prominent positions in all three elected administrations. UMM leaders and city councillors frequently mentioned this relationship in my interviews. This link would turn out to be decisive in embedding the municipal state in civil society under the Erundina administration, and this generation of movements was involved in many of the self-build (*mutirão*) housing projects that would be the prime target of support by her government.

Erundina's PT administration was therefore well placed to construct embedded ties between the municipal state and the sphere of the city's housing movements. Erundina herself had previously been a social worker in the city's eastern zone and had long-standing connections with many in the neighborhood movements of the city's periphery. One longtime UMM leader argued that this background was critical for getting her community's mutirão project in the city's southern periphery approved: "[Erundina] practically knew all of the favelas in the city. I would mention the name of a neighborhood, and she would say that she already knew it."[1]

Erundina, who speaks with a thick rural accent that betrays her roots in Brazil's impoverished northeast region, was known across the eastern zone of São Paulo as a "woman of the people." In 1988, she won her mayoral seat in a first-past-the-post election, taking 29.8 percent of the vote. Despite her narrow electoral mandate, she promised to run the city with an "inversion of priorities" in the city's budget (Singer 1995) in order to establish the "PT way of governing."

This "inversion" was to signal a break with what the PT saw as the way the municipal budget and administrative operations had previously served to perpetuate a divided city, whose inequality was marked across urban space. This division was most obvious in the distribution of public goods in which municipal administration had a direct role. Housing policy was therefore at the center of such an "inversion of priorities."

Even with a constrained municipal budget in a time of high inflation, Erundina focused on redistributive programs for public goods. Her administration used national social welfare funds to seed housing and slum-upgrading programs in peripheral areas of the city. This included funding for the self-build programs demanded by housing movements. Both Erundina and her right-wing successor, Paulo Maluf, spent 3 percent of the total municipal budget on housing. In the same time period, the Erundina administration funded the construction of ten thousand more houses than the thirty thousand built or started under Maluf (*Folha de São Paulo* 1996), affecting an estimated two hundred thousand individual residents. The two administrations preceding Erundina's had provided homes for a total estimated three thousand families. Furthermore, the Erundina administration was responsible for slum-upgrading projects that brought services to an additional twenty-five thousand families in favelas. In doing so, these projects regularized the residence of previously illegal squatters on municipal-owned land (Macaulay 1996).

The Catholic Church and housing movements were the primary backers of Erundina's candidacy within the PT (Couto 1995). In part, this was because of the intellectual and political leadership of both the liberation theology priests and a generation of architects and urban planners who began working with communities in the favelas of São Paulo's periphery. These professionals formed groups offering technical assistance (*asistências técnicas*) to neighborhood associations looking to improve their built environment.

Many of these architects were also part of intellectual circles that were uniting around the banner of "urban reform" as their main political input to the evolving PT agenda. These progressive architects and planners first began working in asistências técnicas before Erundina's administration. During the beginnings of democratic opening in Brazil from 1982 to 1985, Mario Covas, an appointed mayor of the Brazilian Democratic Movement, then the only legal opposition political party, began funding slum-upgrading projects in the city's periphery. These few projects produced key modalities for slum upgrading and self-build housing that were scaled up under the Erundina administration (Abiko and Oliveira Coelho 2004).

One of the key researcher-practitioners of this era was Nabil Bonduki, who would become the second-highest official in Erundina's housing department under the leadership of Erminia Maricato. His experience as a practitioner and documenter of self-build, mutirão projects was instrumental in making them part of the administration's official housing policy. The mutirão projects were designed by neighborhood associations, through his work in asistências técnicas. Building was often undertaken directly by these associations. Subsequent iterations of mutirão-style projects were increasingly built by contractors appointed by neighborhood associations, while the process for design remained more or less the same.

After Erundina's election, funding for *mutirões* became a priority demand of housing movements. In his position, Bonduki was able to take this demand to the city bureaucracy and spearheaded the creation of a new municipal fund for slum upgrading, known by its Portuguese initials of FUNAPS (*Fundo de Atendimento à População Moradora em Habitação Subnormal*, or Fund for People Living in Substandard Housing). This fund was designated for self-build projects managed by the housing associations linked to these movements. Its main revenue source lay in the *outorga onerosa*, or "onerous grant," a municipal tax levied on private building construction rights in the city. During the Erundina administration, these self-build, mutirão projects accounted for one-quarter of the homes built (Macaulay 1996).

According to both housing movement leaders and officials in the Department of Housing, Erminia Maricato, the department's top official, was initially opposed to self-build projects due to concerns about quality control. When I spoke with her, however, she said that she learned to take pride in these self-build projects. She came to view such projects as being of much higher quality and much cheaper than the few large-scale projects undertaken by later administrations, particularly those in the federal housing program launched in 2009. In large part, this was due to an obsession over quality control through the direct oversight of the communities that would go on to live in these new developments.

It took bureaucrats like Bonduki, who had extensive links to housing movements, to bring movement demands into the formal policymaking process. Bonduki had worked with housing movements as a leading architect in the network of nongovernmental architectural practices (*asistências técnicas*) focused on community-driven slum upgrading that grew in the city throughout the 1980s.

When Maricato began in her role as secretary of housing, such an active, receptive orientation to housing movements had not been her initial inclination.

Erundina insisted that municipal staff open their doors to these movements. "In that period, social movements would occupy our offices, one week on, one week off. They always wanted to speak with us," Maricato told me. "My life wasn't easy, because they were placing constant demands on our office."[2] When I interviewed Maricato in a café in the upscale bohemian neighborhood of Vila Madalena, she remembered this dynamic with a wink and an exasperated roll of her eyes.

Maricato was at the upper echelons of São Paulo's municipal bureaucracy. But the bureaucracy's street level is where we really see the development of deeply embedded ties between movements and the local state in this period. At this entry-level rung of the bureaucratic ladder, many young planners and architects who had been working with housing movements got their first taste of working inside the local state. Geraldo Juncal, who had just qualified as an architect, described the "capillary" work of city government architects at this time who were based in peripheral neighborhoods of the city.[3] "The difference, I think, was the capillary nature of policy," he said, emphasizing the Portuguese *capilaridade*. "You had technical officials in different parts of the city who worked directly with the people, the people were their primary reference point, and they were always near a housing project. This was the embryo of what we called 'local government.'"[4]

Juncal's contemporaries in this group, many of whom would end up in senior posts in housing and planning under subsequent mayoral administrations, recounted similar experiences. These developments created a corps of professionals focused on redistributive policy implementation who would go on to work in later municipal administrations. The social housing division of the housing department under Bonduki doubled its staff complement during this period, from 350 to 700, constituting 58 percent of total staff in the department (Cities Alliance 2004). The purpose was to bring a significant group of activist planning professionals from asistências técnicas into the "street level" of the housing bureaucracy.

The Erundina administration's focus was to reorient services toward the urban periphery, which had been woefully underserved by prior administrative logics that saw the peripheries of São Paulo exclusively as a cheap labor reserve for centrally located business activity. During the Erundina administration, bureaucrats worked to produce a vision of redistribution in the city that was tied to the civil sphere of housing movements.

But this was by no means a mayoral regime with durable coordinating capacity. Political attacks in the courts and in the press made implementation difficult. Erundina faced a constrained municipal budget and a minority on the city council, and she only ever had minority support in the city's legislature and had to continuously struggle to get her budgets approved. Likewise, despite the creation of new municipal funding arrangements for movement-led slum upgrading, few funds were available from state and national governments to support these efforts. Most dramatically, a court-imposed reduction in the increasingly progressive property tax made it difficult to continue to cross-subsidize spending on public goods across the geography of the city, from the wealthy core to the poor periphery. One case in the Court of Municipal Accounts was brought by opposition representatives in the municipal legislature. A former president of the São Paulo state chamber of real estate developers, the *Sindicato das Empresas de Compra, Venda e Administração de Imóveis* (SECOVI, or Syndicate of Purchases, Sales, and Administration of Property of São Paulo), was blunt in his description of Erundina's administration, describing the mayor as an undeserving interloper, "a northeasterner elected here in our city who was a total disaster."[5] The Erundina administration's combative relationship with right-wing-controlled state and federal governments sealed this lack of cohesion.

But even with these obstacles, the PT's first mayoral administration in São Paulo was embedded in a civil sphere of housing movements. This made it possible to establish new guiding priorities for the distribution of public goods. The Erundina administration reforms would continue to serve as a benchmark for subsequent mayoral administrations. However, the administration's lack of institutional cohesion made it difficult to achieve programmatic outcomes in practice and made any progress particularly vulnerable to reaction.

São Paulo: The Rentier Reaction of Maluf and Pitta

The PT's chosen successor to Erundina was defeated by over 17 percent in the second round of the 1992 mayoral election (Patarra 1996). If the Erundina administration lanced the boil of traditional urban political economy in São Paulo, the right-wing mayoral administrations of Paulo Maluf (1993–96, of the Popular Party) and his successor, Celso Pitta (1997–2000, of the Brazilian Progressive Party), were the virulent effect. This electoral switch set in motion a distinct ideological indeterminacy in São Paulo's mayoral elections moving forward. Erundina was the first of three mayors from the Left (always running with the PT), none of whom won reelection.

During Erundina's administration, a local state open to the sphere of housing movements was hamstrung by battles over financing and constrained legal authority without allies in state and federal government. This enabled a backlash that brought to power representatives of a particularistic traditional elite. Across the tenures of Maluf and his handpicked successor, Pitta, the oppositional relationship between local government and housing movements combined with disjointed, fragmented, and often obstructed modes of bureaucratic action. But housing movements' fleeting experience of programmatic, policy-oriented ties with the local state encouraged them to maintain mobilization that could serve as a counterpower to the reactionary logic of the Maluf and Pitta administrations.

Paulo Maluf was known for large public works projects that mostly benefited well-established neighborhoods in the city and for using these large projects to fund narrow patronage networks. This was the basis for his enduring nickname, *rouba mas faz* (he steals, but he gets things done). As an electoral figure, Maluf, whose formal political career was forged during the military dictatorship, was a strong representative of the middle class and the business establishment (Puls 2000). Pitta was much weaker. The first Afro-Brazilian mayor of the city, he was not as personally connected to traditional brokers of power. His rise was prefigured by Maluf's strong endorsement as he left office, but Pitta himself was never able to establish an independent political base (*Estado de São Paulo* 2009).

To the extent that Maluf was concerned with the distribution of public goods, he focused on using the municipal housing company, officially known as the Metropolitan Housing Company of São Paulo, or COHAB, to build high-rise buildings that often hid much larger favelas. These projects were called "Cingapuras," named after state-led housing projects in Singapore under Lee Kuan Yew. Under both Maluf and Pitta, there was no public housing outside of the "Cingapura" developments. These did little to actually provide security of tenure or housing to the still largely informal populations of the city's periphery. They eliminated the role of housing movements and neighborhood associations in project design and policymaking. Private construction companies took the place of housing movements and neighborhood associations in the little low-income housing that was produced. And the Maluf and Pitta administrations did away with the in situ logic of slum upgrading and mutirão and focused on moving favela residents into high-rise towers in new locations, often dispersing communities.

While this period witnessed the emergence of new business nodes in the western part of the city, they were not pursued on a programmatic basis. Beginning in the mid-1990s, new development zones in the city's western sections were dedicated to the particular interests of a few local developers. Favelas were evicted to make way for high-rise buildings that would become home to the Latin American headquarters of multinational firms (Fix 2007).

What was seen as an attack on housing movements became a source of profound renewal for a movement sphere that was licking its wounds from the lost policy momentum after the PT's ejection from municipal office. Leaders from UMM argued that fights against these evictions as well as against the paralysis of Erundina-era housing programs made the Maluf-Pitta era one of the most mobilized periods in the movements' history. Evaniza Rodrigues, a longtime leader in UMM from the East Zone of the city, recalled that movement organizing during this period was something akin to a warlike footing.

"From the beginning of 1993 until the last mobilization [before the municipal elections in 2000], the response from the government was against us," she told me. "They began an attack on the housing movements."[6]

The movements were able to respond. They had not been demobilized in their relationship with their allies in the PT. And they used the antagonism of local government to reinvigorate their own organizing. This meant both mobilizing against the growing frequency of evictions and fighting for the reinstatement of the self-build, mutirão housing programs that had been the hallmark of their relationship with local government under the PT's Erundina.

In the private real estate sector, this period was seen through a strikingly different lens than in the sphere of housing movements. Claudio Bernardes, a recent president of SECOVI, described Maluf as a "fantastic" mayor.[7] At the same time, Bernardes and other leading developers with whom I spoke viewed the broader period of right-wing rule by Maluf and Pitta as one of weak governance. In making this assessment, Bernardes emphasized the long-standing personal relationships that leading developers had with this mainstay of right-wing politics in Brazil. All of this suggests a personalistic mode of private sector–friendly intermediation by the successive administrations of Maluf and Pitta. This was not a programmatic, policy-driven orientation toward economic growth.

Housing movement protests against favela removals and the poor quality of housing units increasingly discredited the "Cingapuras." These projects were described by the city's leading daily newspaper as "one of the principal electoral banners" of Maluf and Pitta (*Folha de São Paulo* 1999). Though Pitta won his election as Maluf's handpicked successor, he ended his term claiming to want to return to the "Erundina line" through a focus on self-build low-income housing programs (Gentile and Navarrete 1999). This led Maluf to brand Pitta a "traitor," going so far as to suggest that Pitta be impeached (Gentile 1999).

The Maluf and Pitta administrations courted confrontation with housing movements while delivering narrowly distributed profits through a series of poorly coordinated private real estate and public infrastructure projects. The prior experience of programmatic ties to local government under Erundina had given housing movements the capacity to demand not only an end to evictions but a return to the self-build housing programs that had been such movements' policy banner: a positive and programmatic set of policies. As Maluf's chosen political inheritor faced political instability in the late 1990s, he even attempted to bring back the housing policies of the Erundina administration. These were precisely the policies that Maluf had so firmly rejected upon taking office at the beginning of 1993. Such a reactive sequence in the movement sphere held the promise of renewing programmatic, policy-oriented ties to local government bureaucracy.

São Paulo: The PT's Return under Suplicy and Durable Change across Party Lines

When Marta Suplicy took office on the first day of 2000, she cut a decidedly different profile than Erundina, who had been, up to that point, the only other PT mayor of the city. Suplicy came from a wealthy family and spoke with the accent of an elite *paulistana*, in contrast to Erundina's rural northeastern twang. Suplicy's arrival in office was made possible by a perception of growing disorder and narrowly corrupt rule after the years of Maluf and Pitta, along with a mobilized coalition centered on the same housing movements that had put Erundina in office a decade before. The key contrast lay in the durability and increased coordinating capacity of the Suplicy administration's efforts to build a more programmatic set of municipal housing policies.

Compared with Erundina's, Suplicy's political strategy was much more reconciled to the traditional mode of favor-trading with other political parties ahead of the election in order to secure a workable majority for passing legislation in the city council (*Folha de São Paulo* 2000). This presaged the institutionalization of the Suplicy administration's priorities beyond the working-class base of the PT and, ultimately, across party lines. Such an alignment of strong social mobilization and increased coordinating capacity was so strong that it would endure across Suplicy's administration as well as the subsequent center-right governments of José Serra and Gilberto Kassab.

Just as Suplicy's mayoral administration had some strategic contrasts with Erundina's, the grassroots movement sphere was undergoing its own changes. A second generation of housing movements had emerged in the late 1990s, with an initial affiliation with the UMM in São Paulo. Disinvestment of the city center in the 1990s under Maluf and Pitta had led to a loss of population in central areas. Younger activists occupied abandoned buildings in the city center and refurbished them. Leaders of this new generation reported to me that their aggressive style grated on older movement activists, who had become accustomed to the boardroom jujitsu of negotiations with local authorities for accessing land and housing.[8] The new groups were eventually ejected and formed the umbrella Frente da Luta por Moradia (FLM, or Front for the Housing Struggle). FLM-affiliated groups built their own links to PT politicians in the Suplicy administration, and the city's housing department began a new program designed to attend to the concerns raised by the front's affiliated groups in the city center. This was sea change for a city that had previously considered only the peripheries for public housing intervention. FLM-affiliated groups later united with UMM groups under the umbrella of the Central dos Movimentos Populares (Popular Movements Front) (Earle 2012). Both UMM and FLM leaders were quick to emphasize to me that despite previous differences, they now work together closely.

The watershed national elections in 2002 created new structures of opportunity for municipal administration in São Paulo. In 2002, the PT won its first national election, and Luiz Inácio "Lula" da Silva assumed the presidency. A new Ministry of Cities was initially staffed by figures from São Paulo housing activist circles, including officials from the Erundina administration. The creation of this national ministry made it possible to reinforce the Suplicy administration's local priorities through federal injection of funds for housing, sanitation, and transportation, the ministry's three focus areas.

Beyond the creation of a new federal ministry, a new federal law—the City Statute of 2001—enabled a planning framework that was critical for producing cohesion across the federal, state, and municipal governments. Previous efforts to build support for a master plan during the Erundina administration did not gain much traction with housing movements (Macaulay 1996). But now, the broader institutional support for master planning made this a more attractive arena for these movements, enabling a self-reinforcing interaction between their ties to local government bureaucracy and the internal coordinating capacity of the bureaucracy itself.

The passage of a master plan in 2002 and the passage of a master plan in 2014 in São Paulo have become key moments for two reasons: First, these were moments that made it possible to reconnect housing movements to their political allies within the PT. Second, these were moments when housing movements and the private real estate sector, while at odds, generated a common language of policy debate. These master plans used concepts in the federal constitution of 1988 and the City Statute, especially concerning the "social function" of property, to designate areas as Zonas Especiais de Interesse Social (ZEIS, or Special Zones of Social Interest) and to regularize areas without individual title.[9] This made it possible to use the zoning code to take well-located land off of the market for social housing provision and to enable slum upgrading in areas where, absent this special designation, it had been legally impossible (Fernandes 2007). As we will see in chapter 5, the Companhia de Saneamento Básico do Estado de São Paulo (SABESP, or Basic Sanitation Company of the State of São Paulo), the state sanitation company, was historically wary of providing a water or sewer connection as part of a slum-upgrading project anywhere without clearly established property rights. The master plans strengthened the municipality's hand to designate land for upgrading that would be acceptable to SABESP.

São Paulo's master plan of 2002 was the first of any major Brazilian city to come after the previous year's passage of the federal City Statute. The statute was the product of two decades of activism by the Urban Reform Movement, which drew mainly from urban professionals and activists from sectors such as architecture, engineering, and planning (Saule 2001). The plan was first drafted through Suplicy's planning department, led by renowned architect and planner Jorge Wilheim. Bonduki, who had been the housing secretary under Erundina, was now an elected city councillor. He took primary responsibility for shepherding through the plan, managing legislative and public debates around its provisions (see Caldeira and Holston 2015).

Many of the master plan's innovations were debated by PT-aligned professionals and housing movements. The municipal housing council and public meetings about the master plan convened with representatives from both housing movements and the real estate sector. Concepts such as ZEIS were a response to housing movement occupations. The master plan drew on constitutional provisions that allowed for the municipality to pursue nonmarket expropriation of vacant buildings, as well as for the state water company, SABESP, to install water and sewer connections on land without formal title.

A senior leader of the UMM said that the emphasis on master planning under Suplicy "introduced the concept of ZEIS, and housing movements made this a major part of our agenda." He argued that the willingness of the Suplicy administration to use new national legal tools to make São Paulo one of the first major cities in the country to pursue a master plan created new opportunities for a programmatic redistributive agenda for housing movements.[10]

In particular, it meant that housing movements could exploit land use policy as a tool to achieve their aims. This connection between housing and land use policy is generally a hard nut to crack for housing movements because they are otherwise left demanding housing policy that is made within the strictures of an existing property regime. By moving into the land use policy-making space, housing movements took up a voice in actively pushing the city to continue to relativize its private property regime, even if on a limited scale.

A key mechanism for doing so was making use of formal participatory dimensions of the city's governance, which were increasingly given attention under Suplicy. Participatory councils in Brazil—especially for budgeting—have mostly been evaluated on two metrics: their direct effect on distributive outcomes and their effect on the strength of associational life in civil society (Baiocchi et al. 2011). In São Paulo, participatory councils do not have direct power over distributive outcomes, but they have made it possible for otherwise opposed interests to mediate conflicts in a formal arena that is empowered to translate such mediation into policy change (Tatagiba, Paterniani, and Trindade 2012).

Whereas informants in housing movements emphasized their interest in upholding the "social function of property" on participatory councils, private-sector informants consistently emphasized the sanctity of rights to private property. SECOVI has had the same point person representing the chamber on public councils and in master planning processes since the Erundina administration. He described the deliberative dynamic he encountered in these participatory forums:

When you enter into the game of the master plan, you have to enter—and I'm speaking as a representative of a stakeholder or as a leader of a housing movement—we can't enter this game thinking that we're going to get everything that we want. The master plan, for it to be good for our city, it should mediate and perceive what is relevant from society's point of view, what is the public interest.[11]

This perspective underscores how institutional processes, especially under the Suplicy administration, began to create a mechanism for ensuring that the real estate sector would shape its strategies to account for the distributional demands of housing movements. For example, leaders of the FLM described the master planning deliberations in 2002 as a moment when the movement learned to negotiate demands for the expropriation of vacant private buildings. As one leader told me,

It [the master plan] is something that belongs to the people. So for us from the FLM, we know that to be approved by the government, there has to be popular participation. It is not enough simply for the government to just go and say: "Look, I have this law to approve," and not have popular participation. Participation is essential not only in the master plan but also in all of the plans of the government. So the FLM has this understanding of political participation, right? It's not party politics, but the politics of discussing a set of laws that is for the good of the citizen.[12]

From the perspective of both the SECOVI representative and the FLM leader, the participatory master planning process produced a sense that deliberation could produce acceptable results. I do not want to be mistaken as interpreting these quotes as a Pollyanna. If we take the example of the SECOVI representative, this was a globally connected professional who wanted to give an agreeable spin to a foreign researcher. But in the context of how his putative antagonists in housing movements also interpreted these spaces, there is good reason to take seriously this view of countervailing power. Both the SECOVI representative and the FLM leader pointed to legislative outcomes like the ZEIS as critical examples. Similarly positioned figures in Johannesburg were much more dismissive of the roles of both housing movements and local government and further tended to present their interests as equivalent to "the public interest."

Formal participatory institutions became a setting in which the local state intervenes directly in the process of mediating a core conflict of the urban political economy. This resembles a form of what labor scholars would see as neo-corporatism (Offe and Wiesenthal 1980). This is not to dismiss the very real pitfalls of co-optation associated with these kinds of spaces, as has been documented across a number of Brazilian cases (Wampler 2008). Rather, these experiences underscore the role that deliberative spaces have played in mainstreaming the distributional demands of housing movements in a context where this would otherwise be unlikely.

Suplicy's failed reelection campaign at the end of 2003 had the paradoxical effect of ushering in a moment in which São Paulo's integration of ties to housing movements and internal coordinating capacity crossed party lines. The growing role of the Lula administration's federal investment in urban public goods created a national fiscal and political context for this. Redistributionist claims in the realm of public goods governance in São Paulo moved from a single party affiliation to a capable trans-partisan administration. Moreover, before leaving office, Suplicy's administration created a Municipal Fund for Urban Development (FUNDURB) that drew from the sale of private construction rights to finance public investments. Successive administrations increasingly relied on this new source of funds, and their role in financing public investment by local government increased from 4 percent in 2005 to 11.4 percent in 2013 (Whitaker et al. 2020).

This was a period of significant continuity of staff across PT and center-right administrations, according to recent network analysis of bureaucratic appointments (Marques 2017). So though there was changeover in mid- and high-level staff in the housing department, the redistributive emphasis of the department remained entrenched. I spoke with three senior bureaucrats who had continuous tenures dating back to the Erundina administration. For example, Ricardo Pereira, who served as housing secretary under Gilberto Kassab, was previously in the leadership of SECOVI. He argued that he was quickly acculturated to the policy orientation of career bureaucrats when he entered municipal government: "Look, in the private sector you are a capitalist. But when you enter the public sector you become a communist."[13]

Senior officials in the housing department under Serra and Kassab compared their work in slum upgrading favorably with that of their predecessors in the administration of the PT's Suplicy, citing work in favelas of the Guarapiranga Reservoir in the far south of the city.[14] From a technical perspective, the upgrades in this section of São Paulo were some of the most complicated anywhere in the city, due to the proximity of the informal settlements to one of the largest bodies of water adjacent to the city's landmass.

These officials credited the combination of social movement pressure and increased alignment between sanitation investments by SABESP and municipal plans for making these projects possible. Elisabete França, who directed many of the slum-upgrading efforts in the southern parts of the city, described the critical role played by housing movements: "In São Paulo, we have serious movements. They have histories and representativity. And they should exist, no? They are always there fighting. And public authorities are sometimes struggling to keep up with them."[15] This was a surprisingly forthright statement.

Many of the housing movement leaders I interviewed referred specifically to França as an official with whom they saw themselves in contentious battle. But taking these divergent accounts together suggests that the pressure of movements on França's office was conducive to producing institutionalized delivery outcomes.

The federal government created necessary, but not sufficient, conditions for the interscalar dimension of cohesion through law (e.g., the City Statute of 2001) and budget (new funds for slum upgrading and a low-income housing subsidy). In this period, we see increased cohesion in both "horizontal" and "vertical" dimensions. Horizontal cohesion is illustrated by the continuity of bureaucrats across mayoral administrations and integrated master plans that focused line agencies on common goals and accounted for the full geography of the city. Vertical cohesion is illustrated by the increased accountability of the federal government and the state-level SABESP to support the distributional goals of municipal authorities. But the increased coordinating capacity of the local state in housing and land use introduced new forms of instability to the durability of ties between the local state and housing movements.

São Paulo: Haddad and the Temptations of National Policy Dominance

While housing movements continued to engage and make demands on the local state, their attention increasingly moved to national programs. This was especially so after the introduction of new urban infrastructure grants in 2007 as part of the federal Growth and Acceleration Program and a federal housing subsidy (Minha Casa, Minha Vida) in 2009. From 2013 through 2016, the mayoral term of Fernando Haddad, an academic who had served as a minister in Lula's governments, was a period when we began to see the sources of fragility in the sequential dynamics in "embedded cohesion." The mayoral terms of the center-left Marta Suplicy and center José Serra and Gilberto Kassab saw a configuration of strong ties between housing movements and the local state along with growing coordinating capacity to deliver public goods. When the PT took over once again under Haddad, it inaugurated a more top-down "managerial" style for a center-left administration.

The campaign was marked by the São Paulo PT's increasing distance from housing movements. Haddad chose to include as a coalition partner Maluf's Popular Party, with an agreement to grant the party the housing portfolio. This deviated from expectations that were set during Suplicy's administration, the only other municipal coalition government led by the PT in São Paulo. Her housing secretary had been Paulo Teixeira, a PT student activist and human rights lawyer with links to housing movements in the eastern periphery of the city, where he grew up. Haddad's approach to coalition-building even led

Erundina to end her support for the ticket. One senior leader of UMM told me that housing movements viewed the inclusion of the Popular Party as "absolutely horrible,"[16] and they appealed to their allies in the PT to intervene on their behalf. Haddad promised that housing movements would still have a direct line of communication with him, a claim that he repeated to me. However, leaders from multiple movements to whom I spoke did not perceive this to have been realized. Having the PT in office had clearly been critical for housing movements to gain access to the bureaucracy under Erundina and Suplicy. This time around, under Haddad, the administrative apparatus was a much more forbidding space.

The Haddad administration's absence of ties to housing movements can be explained in two ways, which need not be seen as exclusive. First, housing movements—the PT's partner for realizing an embedded regime—were increasingly focused on securing subsidies from the federal housing program and did not mobilize the mass support for city-wide policies that they had commanded in earlier years. A new, third generation of movements united under the banner of the Movimento dos Trabalhadores Sem Teto (MTST, or Homeless Workers Movement) in the mid-2000s. The MTST shunned engagements with formal participatory institutional structures, such as the municipal housing council, instead favoring strategies of direct action. MTST occupations in the São Paulo metropolitan region began in the mid-2000s, though rarely within the municipality's official boundaries. Occupations have tended to be quite large, often topping one thousand families.[17]

The federal subsidy offered through the Minha Casa, Minha Vida (MCMV, or My House, My Life) program produced new connections between movements and the private sector that did not require the local government's mediation. Due to its scale compared with municipal programs, leaders of all three generations of housing movements—the UMM in the municipal peripheries, then the FLM in the city center, and the new MTST in the metropolitan region—increasingly considered the federal subsidy the only game in town for building new social housing. The MTST's notoriety among elite *paulistanos* is such that it was the only movement described as a true antagonist by the private property developers I interviewed. Even so, developers who worked with the federal housing subsidy maintained open lines of communication with this movement. Ricardo Yazbek, the chief executive of one of the most established property companies in São Paulo, described the relationship as follows:

> They invade the city, and we are against invasions. And they are in favor. But we talk to them. And there are other housing movements, various movements, that act in favor of popular housing and social interest housing. They talk a lot with us, and we support that because we need to focus on housing, social interest housing, and the low-income market. What we don't always

have is resources. So we are always fighting at the federal level. We have participated actively in Minha Casa, Minha Vida.[18]

In fact, the Minha Casa, Minha Vida program became a lifeline of sorts for a substantial segment of the private property development sector. The program itself was negotiated at the federal level between major property developers and the Lula administration as a fiscal stimulus measure in response to the global financial crisis of 2008. The model of a per-unit construction subsidy to private developers was based on similar programs that emerged in the 1990s in Chile and South Africa (Rolnik 2015). This model created incentives for developers to seek out the cheapest, largest plots of land in order to maximize their profit margins. Every developer I interviewed who had taken part in the program repeated the same line about their business model: "There was life before Minha Casa, Minha Vida, and there was life after Minha Casa, Minha Vida." For these developers, MCMV had opened up gushers of new public projects and money.

Second, despite some interpersonal political conflict with the federal government, the Haddad administration was characterized by institutional cohesion across scales. In a reflection on his time in office, published in a popular monthly magazine in May 2017, Haddad criticized Lula's successor, Dilma Rousseff, for not prioritizing federal investment in São Paulo (Haddad 2017). Interviewed shortly after this article's publication, Haddad also told me that all of his regular contact with the national PT was with Lula and that he almost never spoke with Rousseff.[19] Without a strong connection to local social mobilization, Haddad was reduced to weak personal appeals to continue to build interscalar "vertical" cohesion.

Despite these weaknesses, the Haddad administration was still able to draw on the gains of the prior embedded ties to housing movements and cohesive local administration. After the 2002 master plan passed under Suplicy, the subsequent center-right administrations of Serra and Kassab (2006–12) had pursued a planning vision that was often aligned to the interests of developers, especially through the new zoning tool of "urban operations" (Alvim, Abascal, and Moraes 2011). Even so, the Serra and Kassab administrations faced binding constraints for land use enumerated in the 2002 master plan.

Haddad would extend these restraints for market-driven development in a new master plan passed in 2014. The key instrument here was the demarcation of additional ZEIS in order to continue to relativize private property rights, especially in centrally located areas, which theoretically expanded the scope of well-located low-income housing. This new master plan required that 30 percent of funds from the FUNDURB established at the end of the Suplicy administration should be dedicated to the acquisition of land for social housing (Whitaker et al. 2020).

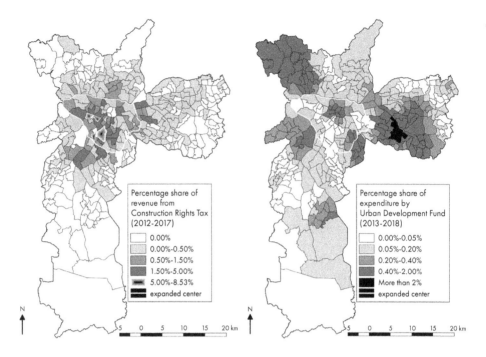

FIGURE 3.1. Share of construction rights tax collection and share of investments by the Municipal Fund for Urban Development, by enumerator area. *Source:* Reproduced from Leite et al. 2019.

A recent analysis of the sources and expenditures of the FUNDURB of the period directly before and after passage of the 2002 master plan highlights its redistributive dynamics. In Figure 3.1, the darker areas of the map on the left are the enumerator areas of the city that generate greater revenues from the city's tax on construction; the darker areas of the map on the right depict the share of investment from the FUNDURB (Leite et al. 2019).

Taken together, these maps show that construction in the wealthiest central areas is generating funding for projects in the poorest peripheral areas of the city. The darkest areas correspond to the largest slums in the city, in areas such as Sapopemba in the eastern zone, with an estimated population of three hundred thousand, and Paraísopolis in the southern zone, with an estimated population of one hundred thousand.

Ronaldo Cury, a scion of the Cury Development Company, described the logic of how ZEIS combined with the federal subsidy for low-income housing to incentivize private development of social housing:

If you have the zoning available through demarcation of an area as a ZEIS, I am coming to search for ZEIS areas to develop. This is because I can go to the landowner and say, "Look, friend. You don't have anyone to sell this land to. You can only sell this land to me because you can only build [low-income housing] on your land. You can't do anything else on your land." In municipalities where this hasn't been done, we can't act with the same leverage in planning. But once this federal subsidy was available, we worked wherever we could.[20]

While ZEIS unlocked land in theory for private developers targeting the low-income market, the federal subsidy was understood to unlock it in practice for actual development. This is because the subsidy greatly reduced the perceived risk associated with such developments in a city in which the cost of land is at an absolute premium. This also produced a perverse outcome in the geography of low-income housing, because private developers secured subsidies on a per-house basis irrespective of land value. This pushed developers to design projects for the city's farthest, undeveloped reaches, where land was cheapest. This geographic outcome undermined the gains of key initiatives under prior local administrations, such as those of the self-build *mutirões* under Erundina and Suplicy, which focused on in situ slum upgrading.

The Cury company is considered one of the three major developers of low-income housing through the MCMV program and in 2017 claimed to have developed more than two thousand units of low-income housing in the municipality of São Paulo. While the SECOVI leadership expressed a great deal of skepticism about Haddad, executives in the three companies that focused on delivering MCMV projects were much more positive, always citing the expansion of ZEIS as a mechanism for expanding their work in the lowest reaches of the housing market.

The advent of the federal subsidy through MCMV increased the perception of administrative competence on the part of the private real estate development sector. But it also took local housing movements out of the project *and* policy development pipeline. Mutirão, self-build projects were largely sidelined except for a small carve out in the subsidy program called MCMV *entitades*, literally "entities" but understood to mean housing movements (Marques 2021). Furthermore, MCMV made local government less important to housing movements for securing support for such projects, as contracts were signed with the federal government's Caixa bank. This was a critical ingredient in undermining the embeddedness of the local state under Haddad.

In the 2014 master plan, Haddad tried to present himself as an urbanist modernizer who could demonstrate a new twenty-first-century "PT way of governing," similar to Erundina's ambitions twenty-five years earlier. He told me that at the time, he aimed to establish a new "socio-environmental" political coalition, exemplified by a program to build a network of bike lanes throughout the city. He also aimed to burnish a reputation for fiscal rectitude.

In June 2013, six months after Haddad took office, he attempted to push through a proposed hike in public transport fares. Protests erupted. The challenges morphed into more generalized protests against corruption and took on an increasingly middle-class tinge that criticized the entire political class (Alonso and Mische 2016; Purdy 2017). This groundswell produced energy on the Right to call for the impeachment of Lula's successor, Dilma Rousseff, which occurred shortly before Haddad's failed reelection campaign in 2016.

As the anti-PT groundswell grew in the lead-up to the 2016 municipal elections, Haddad's campaign ended in an unprecedented failure for the PT in São Paulo. There was not even a second-round runoff, something that had occurred in every election since 1992. João Doria, an uncharacteristically reactionary candidate for the historically center-right Social Democratic Party of Brazil, was a business impresario and TV host of the Brazilian version of Donald Trump's *The Apprentice*. He was elected with 53 percent of the vote.

The experience of the Haddad administration suggests that institutional cohesion can breed a top-down managerial governing style that makes it less likely for formal political leaders to tend to the "embedded" side of the equation. Upon leaving office at the end of 2016, Haddad did not point to a redistributive outcome as the major achievement of his tenure, instead highlighting improved finances, a new public works plan, and a new master plan (Scruggs 2016). This weakness of the relationship between party, local state institutions, and the social movement sphere echoes Robert Michels's theory of the "iron law of oligarchy" in political party organizations, as well as arguments in the social movement literature that highlight the tension between mobilization and institutionalization (Armstrong and Bernstein 2008; Baiocchi, Braathen, and Teixeira 2012; Seippel 2001). The ties to housing movements that had helped produce an increasingly coordinated and redistribution-oriented local government under prior PT mayors such as Erundina and Suplicy had now fallen apart. Cohesion overtook embeddedness under Haddad, leaving the local state without a social base through which it could pursue its distributive goals.

The emerging weaknesses in the configuration of embeddedness and cohesion that characterized São Paulo's governing regime for housing and land use under Haddad highlight just how far the city had come since its first direct mayoral elections. Erundina's administration in 1989–92 enabled a durable set of ties between housing movements and bureaucrats that established the basis for programmatic, policy-based engagements over the next three decades. A period of right-wing reaction ensured that the movement sphere, which had found strong footing within the local state under Erundina, could now develop its capacity to renew mobilization outside of the local state. Once the PT was back in power, local government could draw on this renewed mobilizational strength to produce high embeddedness combined with high cohesion—a much stronger coordinating capacity both horizontally (across line departments) and vertically (across scales of government). As we will see in Johannesburg, a very different trajectory of housing movement mobilization was similarly critical for dynamics of embeddedness and cohesion.

Johannesburg: Demobilization and Fragmentation

In São Paulo, the progressive construction of local government capacity to change patterns of production of low-income housing was driven by the increasing embeddedness of local government institutions in a sphere of housing movements and the cohesion of the bureaucratic sphere of local government. In Johannesburg, beginning in 1994, relatively well-capacitated local government institutions introduced a range of policy reforms designed to produce similar outcomes. But as local government institutions became increasingly distant from the movement sphere, the internal cohesion of municipal government was increasingly vulnerable to strategies of hidden resistance by largely white property owners and developers. In the following sections, I document two types of strategies—ring-fencing of tax contributions and "venue-shopping" between scales of government for development permits—that disabled the capacity of local government to alter patterns of production of low-income housing, thereby reproducing a spatial structure of the city that largely resembled Apartheid inequalities in the distribution of public goods.

Critical to this story is the relationship between the ruling African National Congress and the movements and neighborhood associations—collectively known as "civics"—that had served as a critical base to "render the cities ungovernable" during Apartheid and bring the ANC to power in the first democratic elections. These civics were progressively demobilized by explicit decisions made by the ANC, largely on an ideological basis. The party saw itself as the primary governing authority to drive redistribution-oriented policies at all levels of government, and this had particularly stark consequences at the urban scale in Johannesburg (Mayekiso 1996).

In South Africa, because the democracy movement was also specifically an anti-Apartheid movement, the urban housing question was arguably even more central to the country's process of democratization than in Brazil. However, unlike in São Paulo, the movements that had led rent strikes, service rate boycotts, and endless marches in the 1980s and early 1990s faded away soon after democratization. This left local government in Johannesburg unable to counterbalance the traditional elite interest in maintaining the value of their properties and restricting efforts at redirecting public expenditure to excluded parts of the city. In turn, this created openings for traditional elites, who were largely white, to organize strategies of hidden resistance to a local government policy regime that was otherwise geared toward using land and housing policy as the lynchpin of "deracializing" the city. The result was that, unlike São Paulo, Johannesburg did not produce a similar suite of policies able to relativize rights to private property in land use planning, create municipal institutions for financing, deliver affordable housing at meaningful scale, and support community-led slum upgrading.

Johannesburg: Ring-Fencing

The animating idea for municipal government in Johannesburg in the democratic transition of the early 1990s was to address the fundamental fragmentation of Apartheid subnational administration by bringing a patchwork of eleven white and black local authorities together into a single municipality. The basic thrust was to cross-subsidize the extension of adequate housing and services to poor, black areas through a centralized municipal collection of local tax revenue. The strategies deployed by wealthy, white neighborhood associations and property developers responded to the swift efforts of the first post-Apartheid government in the city to prioritize spending on public goods in peripheral black townships. I define the first strategy—"ring-fencing"—as area-based hoarding of taxes for local infrastructure improvement.

The irony of this strategy is that it had previously been deployed by some of the most marginalized parts of the city as a method of protesting Apartheid. In 1986, residents of Soweto, the sprawling dormitory township for black residents in the southwestern part of the city, refused to pay rent and utility bills to protest the legitimacy of the Black Local Authority (BLA) that administered the region. The mayor of the Soweto local authority, Nelson Botile, was elected on the basis of an estimated 6 percent turnout, emblematic of the hollow legitimacy of BLA leaders. These boycotts were part of a broader campaign by the growing anti-Apartheid movement to "render the country ungovernable" (Bonner and Segal 1998, 121). For the Soweto protesters, the BLA would never be capable of delivering adequate services if it relied only on funding for those services from the overwhelmingly poor residents under the BLA administration. In order to avoid the perception of intimidation by rent boycott leaders, the National Party–led government set up offices in the center of Johannesburg in 1987 for Soweto residents to pay their rent (Chaskalson, Jochelson, and Seekings 1987), but the response underscored the administrative fiction of the BLAs as separate from the urban functions of Johannesburg.

By 1991, negotiations were underway between the National Party local government and the Soweto People's Delegation, represented by African National Congress Secretary-General Cyril Ramaphosa, the former secretary general of the National Union of Mineworkers and currently president of the country. Two years prior, the Soweto People's Delegation had released a paper arguing that Soweto residents were subsidizing the rest of the city because they conducted most of the work in industrial and commercial activity, which made up 70 percent of the city's economy, yet were not receiving any services from the Johannesburg city council. Their demands included a write-off of arrears owed by rent boycotters, the transfer of home ownership from local authorities to current renters, upgraded services, affordable service charges, and the fiscal and political unification of Johannesburg and Soweto (Tomlinson et al. 2003).

These negotiations eventually led to the creation of the Central Witwatersrand Metropolitan Chamber (CWMC). This body had broad legitimacy and included fifty-three organizations, including the Transvaal provincial administration,[21] local governments in the Johannesburg metropolitan region, rent boycotters, white ratepayers and resident associations, organized business, labor, church groups, schools, and political parties, including the recently unbanned ANC. A group of urban planning professionals in an organization called PlanAct, which had been a key hub of technical support for United Democratic Front–linked organizations in Johannesburg, served as a form of technical consultancy for the grassroots movements participating in the CWMC. Over two decades after the fact, participants still described the CWMC as an exhilarating period of rethinking the city. The negotiations were punctuated by heated arguments with old bureaucrats about loosening the reins of power to young activists from townships and progressive planning and architectural professionals. Erky Wood was a leading architect hired by a group of civic associations from Soweto and associated nongovernmental organizations. In an interview, he recalled the role of these organizations from the black townships in the CWMC negotiation sessions:

> They literally beat down the doors of all these local authorities and, and regional authorities and things like that. Literally would storm into meetings and take seats, and the people running these meetings had no ability to, to throw them out. They just hadn't been invited before and now they were there, and I can remember, and they're very polite people of course, those Afrikaans people. They'd say, you know, And so we'd like to welcome our guests from the Jabulani [a neighborhood in Soweto] Civic Association," and, you know, the guy from Jabulani would say, "Point of order, we're not your friends, you didn't invite us and you can't welcome us," you know, because we beat the door down.[22]

The CWMC negotiations became a national model for local government transitions throughout the country. This influence was institutionalized in the 1993 Local Government Transition Act. This piece of legislation governing negotiations over local government institutional designs across the country emphasized fundamental principles first established through the CWMC, including the goal of deracializing cities and unifying fragmented tax bases

(Tomlinson 1999). But in Johannesburg, the empowerment of the previously excluded majority was short-lived.

As negotiations for democratic elections neared their conclusion in 1994, the ANC began to demand greater control of city councils. The pluralistic planning mechanisms still in development as part of the CWMC were pushed aside. The entrance of national ANC cadres into the negotiation of a set of post-Apartheid local government structures proved to be a countervailing mechanism against the strong demands of black township resident groups and civic associations in the CWMC. Actors with links to the South African Communist Party, an ally of the ANC, but with relatively autonomous local structures, did not accept the ultimate compromise to resolve the end of rent boycotts.

Trevor Ngwane was a civic movement leader from the Jabavu and Pimville neighborhoods of Soweto and a onetime Johannesburg city councillor. He insisted in an interview that the uneven acceptance of what many grassroots civics saw as an ANC-imposed compromise in the outcomes of the CWMC explained why agreements to begin paying rents and rates for basic services in many townships were not implemented effectively. Current and former ANC officials I interviewed echoed this assessment.

Negotiators at the national level wanted to move quickly to elections in April 1994, amid threats of coups and insurrections (Harris 2010). One consequence of this rush was that the municipal negotiations in cities such as Johannesburg were essentially short-circuited. There, a compromise of four submunicipal structures was agreed to on a transitional basis, in the north, south, east, and west. Each of the four zones was granted proportional representation on the central city council, as opposed to making representation subject to city-wide apportionment. This arrangement paralleled efforts to dilute the authority of national government through strong provincial powers being negotiated by white elites in the National Party. As Ngwane put it regarding the distribution of power in the city council, "They gave more power to the white section by making it proportional rather than based on an open vote, where it is obvious we would have swamped them."[23]

A key consequence of this arrangement was that the project to build "one city, one taxpayer" was structurally undermined from the start. The arrangements for revenue collection and land management were delegated to the submunicipal scale. These institutional relationships were central to the prospects for realizing the metropolitan spatial plan that had been backed by the more progressive elements of the CWMC. The scale of Johannesburg was where the project of "deracializing the city" and undertaking a project of deep spatial transformation was to be undertaken. But without strong powers to build up the centralized city government's fiscal capacity to cross-subsidize investments in poorer areas with contributions from wealthier ones, such a project faced stark vulnerabilities.

The starkest vulnerability concerned the ways wealthier areas of Johannesburg were able to dictate the use of their local tax revenues. The effect of ring-fencing by wealthy neighborhoods was to compound a quickly deteriorating fiscal situation. The central city administration had moved quickly to expand spending in the most excluded areas of the city—essentially, those areas previously governed by BLAs. But submunicipalities could not keep up in bringing in necessary revenue. In fact, some of them were negotiating away revenue from the central coffers. In the mid-1990s, for example, Anne Stephny, known in developer circles as the pioneer of city improvement districts (CIDs) in Johannesburg, began organizing property owners in the Illovo neighborhood, which was part of the northern municipal substructure. CIDs were bodies composed of property owners in given areas who took joint responsibility for urban management functions for shared infrastructure and also lobbied municipal authorities. By 1996, Stephny had begun establishing CIDs in key northern business nodes such as Rosebank, Melrose, and Illovo and farther north in Sandton and Bryanston. These neighborhoods, home to the leafy, jacaranda tree–lined residential avenues of the city's largely white professional classes, became the lynchpin for fiscal hoarding that helped undermine any attempts to close the distance between the black townships and these wealthy suburbs.

Stephny described a well-developed set of relationships between business owners and Eastern Municipal Sub-structure officials: "We spoke to the head of our substructure. He sat on our management forum. We had a very tight relationship, a very good understanding. And also with the property owners. We had a northern corridors working group, thirty-five different groups."[24]

The key issue for CID participants was to ring-fence their required "development contributions" so as not to lose them to the newly centralized fiscal management of the city. As multiple property owners and developers active at this time reported to me, there were deep fears that a redistributive orientation of local government would lead to the neglect of maintaining standards of infrastructure in their neighborhoods. For example, Stephny emphasized these concerns in describing the rationale driving participants in CIDs that she helped organize to coordinate:

> It was a group of people who understood they were not working in isolation. You couldn't get any of these projects to work if you didn't have access and egress, if you didn't have bulk services. Sewerage, water, stormwater, all those things. Who was going to pay for that? And we definitely weren't going to give our contributions to the city, because there would be no guarantee that it would be spent in the area. So we did a deal.[25]

Local government had undergone a massive reorganization premised on fiscal consolidation in order to enable investments in public goods in previously excluded spaces in the city: housing, sanitation, and other basic infrastructure. Area-based property owners in wealthy parts of the city were seizing on a temporary compromise of institutional design—the municipal substructures—to ensure precisely the opposite of this redistributive fiscal consolidation. The particular arrangement of the CID by property owners instead ensured their fiscal independence. The municipal substructure would not demand that their property taxes go to the centralized municipal coffers.

While the upper echelons of city government had changed hands—with an expected shift in the racial makeup of the bureaucracy—the submunicipalities were still handled by career, mostly white bureaucrats familiar to business elites. As Stephny put it, "Luckily, we had very good city officials at that time. . . . The city wasn't a metro at that stage."[26] The substructures provided an opportunity for business elites to draw on preexisting connections to these veteran officials to secure bespoke deals on property taxes within a system whose policy goals were no longer aligned.

This accelerated the rapid deterioration of extensive infrastructure in the traditional central business district (CBD) of Johannesburg, while the city was forced to continue to spend on expensive bulk infrastructure to reach new business nodes in northern areas such as Sandton (formerly a separate municipality) and Fourways. In fact, Sandton had already begun attracting new business development away from the CBD through competitive tax rates and less strict planning regulations, especially around parking limits (Todes 2014). By 2000, the Johannesburg Stock Exchange moved from its long-standing location in the CBD to Sandton, underscoring the geographic shift in business activity and investment in the city. Meanwhile, a project aimed at the historic poor, black area adjacent to Sandton in the north, the Alexandra Renewal Project, was given presidential-level priority. However, it was riven with local political battles, and its levels of service delivery are similar to those in most poor, black areas of the south and northwest of the city (Clarno 2017). After 1994, the largely black informal settlement of Diepsloot mushroomed in the northwest of the city, and service backlogs increased (Harber 2011).

The growth of informal settlements in new areas in the northwest such as Diepsloot, as well as in the far southern and eastern reaches of the city, produced increasing demand for public housing through national housing programs. The lack of programs and policies specifically targeted at these informal settlements until the mid-2000s represents a clear dearth of ties between organizations in informal settlements and the local state. The formal city—where every parcel of land has an individual title and a housing structure based on formal standards— was where institutions of the state, from the local to the national, had trained their sights. This stood in sharp contrast to the growing recognition of informal settlements in São Paulo's housing policies beginning in the Erundina administration in 1989.

The first low-income housing program to impact Johannesburg in the post-Apartheid era was part of the national government's Reconstruction and Development Program. It provided a per-unit subsidy to private developers, which structured similar incentives to those that would later play out in Brazil's Minha Casa, Minha Vida program. A successor program to RDP aimed to undo these incentives by providing regulatory mechanisms for "in situ" slum upgrading in the locations of existing informal settlements (Bradlow, Bolnick, and Shearing 2011), which had long been part of the approach to housing in Brazil. This program, Breaking New Ground, continues to disburse housing subsidies along the same lines as RDP, while there have been very few in situ slum-upgrading projects in the largest cities in the country. National government provision of housing created many of the same incentives for housing movements to focus on national as opposed to city government as we saw in São Paulo under Fernando Haddad's administration (2013–16). But unlike in Brazil, in South Africa the emergence of a national housing subsidy came much earlier on in the phase of consolidating democratic local government. This meant that housing movements had much less incentive to coalesce around city-oriented strategies.

In Johannesburg, the national approach to subsidized housing largely outpaced more local efforts to produce well-located low-income housing. City agencies such as the Johannesburg Social Housing Company produced some of the few formal low-income rental units available in the inner city, while a small group of for-profit and nonprofit developers produced additional low-income units for rent as well (Mosselson 2017). In my interviews across this range of developers, executives frequently invoked difficulties in securing dedicated funding streams and policies in city government that hindered efforts to institutionalize and grow their approaches. And grassroots housing movements were absent from such efforts altogether.

Eventually, the distancing of predominantly white property owners and developers from predominantly black local politicians and bureaucrats was realized in spatial terms. Gerald Olitzky focused on developing the Gandhi Square neighborhood of the CBD since 1994. In many ways, he was an exception to the pattern of white-led real estate investment and is part of a small but growing class of investors focused on the inner city (see Mosselson 2017). "[White people] said, 'Here come the blacks, there goes the city.' They created the problem by fleeing to the north," he told me, describing the flight to Sandton from Johannesburg's inner city and its subsequent decline.

> This, for me, was a bloody annoying thing because they caused the problem right? . . . All the major guys, all the heavyweights, the public companies, the big financial corporations. Cleared them out of the city. Any developments that happened by these chaps were done in the north. They were done in Sandton.[27]

Olitzky used the widespread disinvestment in the inner city (Crankshaw and White 1995) as the basis for insisting on two provisions in order to begin his own investments: a declaration in the city's bylaws to ban street trading and a private lease over the large public transportation terminal in the Gandhi Square neighborhood. This private lease would allow him to hire his own security and refuse removal services—in essence, a one-person CID.

"You guys know how to fight a struggle. You know a freedom struggle," Olitzky recalled telling municipal officials. "But you don't know—you don't have—let's level with each other. You don't have the acumen to bring back the city, and you certainly don't have the budget for it. Nobody's giving you the money for it."[28] He proposed an arm's-length division of labor. In São Paulo, local government officials were critical to the development of housing projects in partnership with housing movements; in Johannesburg, the developer vision was to have a much more hands-off local state, tinged with a barely veiled disdain for the perceived competence of local government officials.

To summarize, two key facts enabled the strategy of ring-fencing. First, the strong powers of submunicipal authorities in the years immediately following the transition to democracy ensured the fragmented nature of city administration across the geographic extent of the city. This incentivized new organized forms of local associations of wealthy property owners and developers. These associations made use of relationships with submunicipal government representatives through which advantageous deals could be struck. The production of institutional fragmentation was a body blow to efforts to unify such a highly unequal city in order to cross-subsidize the universal distribution of urban public goods.

The alliance of property owners and property developers was not a fait accompli. But the combination of common "skin-in-the-game" of property ownership and associational ties with submunicipal bureaucrats allowed these actors to overcome potential collective action problems and work the front lines of the state. This allowed both actors to realize gains while remaining out of the limelight of a straightforward attack on the redistributive policies that the local state was introducing.

Furthermore, the compromise of administrative fragmentation in the democratic transition was coupled with the steady deprioritization of movement-oriented activists from poorer neighborhoods in both making and implementing policy. Activists struggled to be heard in proposing an alternative, more centralized institutional vision. While the city was investing in poorer areas, there was little prospect of building a sustainable bureaucratic environment for managing these investments. Its capital expenditures required consistent operational investment. While the former was splashy and attractive to political principals, the latter required a longer-term investment strategy, which was difficult with increasing attacks on the central city's finances. As a result, the balance between revenue and expenditure in the municipal fiscus was increasingly unstable.

By 1997, the city's finances were under increasing strain. The fiscal imbalances that began in 1994 were due to the interaction of increased capital investments by the centralized municipal authorities in black township areas and the submunicipal ring-fencing of taxes. The city required the budgets of the substructures to balance in the aggregate, which theoretically enabled some form of cross-subsidization across the geography of the city. But each substructure could budget independently. David Savage, a national Treasury official responsible for local government finances in the late 1990s and early 2000s, described Johannesburg's fragmented governing arrangements as an "outlier" among large cities in South Africa:

> There was a fair degree of variation in exactly how specific powers and functions were assigned between the substructures and the metros. So in Joburg's case, what kind of really hit them was very—a fairly weak center at the metro level, I think, compared to elsewhere, which translated into things like—for example—their substructures used to hold their own cash reserves at a net significant cost to the metro. So you would have the Sandton substructure sitting on a big cash surplus in its bank account, while the other substructures were completely broke.[29]

The divergent priorities for capital expenditure for new infrastructure in poorer parts of the city and for maintenance of existing infrastructure in wealthier parts of the city like Sandton drove this kind of imbalance.

The issue of centralizing municipal powers had become increasingly fraught as a matter of both racial politics and institutional capacity in the city. Former ANC Mayor Parks Tau, who previously served on the Southern Metropolitan Local Council's Urban Development Committee, described the link between the racial and institutional dynamics of municipal budgeting under the "two-tiered" arrangement of municipal subcouncils and the metropolitan authority:

> Suddenly you had complex negotiations happening from within the subcouncils and the metro council. And even people of the same party were representing different interests of their subcouncil. So, the people from what would have been the white subcouncil area, which would have been in the east—that was Rosebank—would have said, "Look, we don't understand why we should cross-subsidize the program of the southern subcouncil." This would have been the poorer subcouncil that inherited the bulk of the staff, the bulk of the poor people in Johannesburg, and therefore the bulk of the challenges that we're dealing with. So, those disparities almost became stuck as we were trying to implement the two-tier system.[30]

Ultimately, this intersection of race, geography, and bureaucracy made the "transitional" institutional arrangements of local government in Johannesburg both politically and economically unstable. These transitional measures, especially the division of subcouncils, had provided mechanisms for wealthy, white areas to preserve effective economic control. And all of this was despite an overall mission in the democratic transition to develop fiscal arrangements that could spread investment across the geography of the city.

In São Paulo, dynamics of sequencing attached to shifts in political regimes were punctuated by changes in the party in control. But in Johannesburg, during the period under examination in this study, the same party remained in control throughout. Consequently, the dynamics of sequencing are more closely tied to shifts in the fiscal basis—as opposed to the political basis—of the local state. This emphasis on the fiscal basis of the local state underscores just how marginal housing policy was to housing politics. That is, activism around housing development for the poor quickly disappeared. Instead, these more invisible contests over financing the city enabled a de facto set of housing and land use outcomes that were largely outside of official policy.

Though political power seemed to become more consolidated during this time, effective economic power lay elsewhere, and the emergence of an explicit capital strike compounded this gap. The Sandton Federation of Ratepayers, which encompassed a geographic area inclusive of multiple CIDs, initiated a widespread boycott of property taxes. This was followed by appeals by ten thousand out of a total of 180,000 property owners in the subregion in order to contest property valuations. The move was designed to minimize the tax liabilities of property owners in the area. Kenny Fihla, an ANC city councillor from 1995 to 2002, described the crisis as a "double whammy." "You are growing your staff complement to try and address, as a matter of urgency, your service delivery needs. You are ramping up your capital expenditure to address backlogs and all of that. You are experiencing a revenue squeeze because the property owners are effectively withholding their rates."[31] By 1998, the Eastern Municipal Sub-structure was owed R220 million, which was equal to over two-thirds of the R314 million debt that the city was unable to pay its creditors after exhausting its reserves.[32] Rates boycotts in Soweto and the CBD paled in comparison to this loss: R7 million and R15 million, respectively (Beall, Crankshaw, and Parnell 2002).

The growing fiscal emergency would eventually lead to a reorganization of the city under a unified local authority in 2000. This was coupled with the creation of municipal-owned entities (MOEs) for key services such as trash, electricity, water, and roads and a new development agency, known as the Johannesburg Development Agency. For the first time, the city conducted a review of the finances of all substructures, but with specific guidelines from national and provincial authorities to do so in order to find where to cut capital expenditures. The newly unified metropolitan municipal government dissolved the municipal substructures. Governance of the city relied on the mandate of a clearer one-person, one-vote system that was headed by an executive mayor (Todes 2014). The ANC was able to consolidate its political power in the city. Amos Masondo, a veteran activist who cut his teeth in politics during anti-Apartheid protests in Soweto, was elected mayor.

The concurrent consolidation of the city's finances, introduction of a municipal corporate structure based around the operation of MOEs, and a more austere budgetary regime was opposed by the South African Municipal Workers' Union. These changes, which were part of the city's "iGoli 2002" plan, resulted in large protests (*The Star* 1999). The South African Municipal Workers' Union cast its resistance as part of a broader opposition by the Congress of South African Trade Unions and the South African Communist Party to the Growth, Employment, and Redistribution macro-economic policy led by then–Deputy President Thabo Mbeki, which had attacked labor regulations and limited growth in social spending (Marais 2011). This also spawned one of the more significant, non-ANC-aligned social movements of the anti-Apartheid era, the Anti-Privatization Forum (Runciman 2015).

The view in the city council was that fiscal consolidation would be impossible without first resolving the antagonism of wealthy property owners and developers. "We engaged very well with labor, with community organizations, and so on, but we were very bad in engaging with business because it was not our traditional constituency so to speak," Fihla said, describing it as a new type of engagement for the ANC-led city council. "But because there was a boycott, there was a need for us to start engaging because that was the only way we could solve it. So we engaged with the South African Property Owners Association [SAPOA], and, through SAPOA, we agreed on a mediation process."[33] This process of mediation with SAPOA did not produce any kind of new formalized relationship, but it did catalyze a period of regular engagement between property owners and the city council.

The eventual agreement included limits on future increases on rates and negotiated settlements on payment of arrears. Fihla said,

> Gradually property owners started to come on board and started paying, especially the big boys, because the big boys are not interested in a stand-off with government. It is not in their interest. I mean, they participated because this was a big issue for them to have given in to strengthen the viability of their entities.

He saw this as an emerging meeting of the minds between council and large property owners, despite their deep-seated wariness.

As soon as a practical and a logical solution was put on the table, the big boys were the first to accept it, and once many of the big boys, the large property owners, were accepting an agreement and starting to pay, it was easy then for the rest of their constituency to follow suit.[34]

Multiple representatives of SAPOA, as well as individual private developers who are part of its membership, all reported that their subsequent engagements with the city were infrequent and that they did not plan major investments together. Parks Tau had succeeded Masondo as Johannesburg's mayor in 2011, and in 2015, the last full year of his administration, top planning officials told me that it was the first year in which they were beginning to hold regular meetings with SAPOA.

Ring-fencing, however, still made operative the distance between the economic power of the overwhelmingly white class of property developers and owners and the political power of the overwhelmingly black city government. "Effectively, developers are paying for the upgrading of the cities because the municipalities are bankrupt, they don't seem to have the skill on a financial basis to control the fiscus, that's sitting within them," one private architect who worked with the largest developers in Sandton's business district put it to me. "They're putting the onus of development onto the developers for general infrastructure—build this road, pay for this intersection, put in these robots, and we'll give you more bulk [infrastructure]. . . . The city [of Johannesburg] is trying, but it is getting eaten up by developers."[35]

He suggested that the operational costs of maintaining new infrastructure were rarely being factored into the city's fiscal planning. As a result, what seemed like advantageous development contributions by private developers ended up adding to the fiscal strain, foreclosing capacity to plan for more redistributive investments in poorer parts of the city.

It would be hard to characterize a coordinated project of business and political elites in the sense of a "managerial" regime in which the now-well-established low embeddedness of the local state is coupled with high cohesion. The gains to land development are captured on ad hoc, nonprogrammatic terms. Private returns are realized not by coordination with the public sector but by forcing the public sector to capitulate. In a "growth regime," local political and business elites coordinate to maximize rents. But in the Johannesburg case, we see a state capacitated to plan, without the fiscal powers to implement its plan. And fiscal capacity becomes a pivot for advantaging economic over political power. Post-Apartheid Johannesburg had begun its democratic era animated by the roots of democratization in popular mobilization on the basis of a "mobilizational regime." But the politics of housing, and especially land use, in the early years of democratic local government were hampered by property-owning elites' subterranean attacks on the city's fiscal capacity by ring-fencing their tax contributions.

Johannesburg: Venue-Shopping

The newly consolidated city authorities overcame the fiscal standoff through a reorganization of the city that produced significant fragmentation of key service providers as part of the iGoli 2002 plan (Beall et al. 2002). Water, electricity, and trash collection, among others, were all now separate "municipal-owned entities" that were not directly accountable to the executive mayor and, instead, were supposed to answer to an independent board of directors. Even so, the city also tried to assert a land use planning vision of its own. By 2001, the city approved, for the first time, a spatial development framework, which included the formal establishment of an urban development boundary; the active creation of development nodes, including in the inner city; the promotion of mixed use and densification along transport corridors; and attempts to "avoid patterns of decline coupled with new growth elsewhere" (Todes 2014, 88). Though this period has been cast by some as a move toward neoliberal "world-class city" development, significant redistributive outlays persisted, especially in terms of continued physical infrastructural investments in Soweto (Harrison et al. 2014).

Over the course of the 2000s, and especially under Tau, area-based development became more central to the city's planning approach. The idea was to focus on "transit-oriented development" under the slogan of "corridors of freedom."[36] This strategy anticipated that public investments in a new bus rapid transit system would incentivize private investments in both commercial buildings and residential housing near bus stops. However, city officials from the Tau administration—and Tau himself—readily acknowledged to me that this had not had the desired impact.

Herman Pienaar, the city's head of planning until 2017, described the role of spatial planning in the city at the beginning of his tenure in blunt terms. "The department had no credibility. No political credibility. No institutional credibility. It was really the weakest link in the city."[37] The urban boundary was intended to ensure that private development did not force the city to build and maintain new bulk infrastructure such as roads and sewers that would undermine the fiscal capacity of the city to invest in its planned infrastructural goals. The introduction of tools such as an urban boundary could, in theory, put some clear limits on the spatial trajectory of private developer plans. But the relatively austere capital expenditures of the city throughout the 2000s and the lack of institutional capacity to enforce either land use regulations or interagency coordination meant that private developers were still able to shape the spatial trajectory of the city.

While planned corridors did see some significant increases in development, the sprawl of business nodes to northern suburbs continued to stretch public infrastructure, including "congestion in Fourways, a lack of sewer capacity in Bryanston, underprovision of schools and electricity blackouts due to lack of network capacity" (Todes 2014, 89). The major growth in privately financed middle-class residential housing was entirely separate from publicly financed housing for the poor. This was especially the case when seen in the context of what has become known as the Gauteng City-Region, which includes Johannesburg's neighboring municipalities. A recent spatial analysis by Götz, Wray, and Mubiwa concludes that public housing developments are

> all in the poorer areas of the city-region, usually on the edges of municipalities and with a preponderance in southern and western Johannesburg. . . . By contrast, the growth of [townhouse clusters and estates] is almost exclusively located in the wealthy core of the province, most on the edge of the existing built-up area, on sweeping diagonal from the north-west of Johannesburg to the south-east of Tshwane. (2014, 54)

In the years after the reorganization of the city in 2000, planning officials slowly began to generate bureaucratic tools and political momentum to unite land use management and agencies responsible for infrastructure. But in the meantime, developers had begun to exploit contradictions in the planning apparatus both within local government and between different scales of government. This occurred in two ways: first, by undermining the approvals process within the local bureaucracy and, second, by exploiting contradictions in planning priorities between the local and provincial governments.

Beginning in the early 2000s, with Pienaar as the leading bureaucratic official and Tau as the political principal on the city council, the city introduced a centralized system for budget priorities. This system, known as the Capital Investment Management System (CIMS), required every department to justify its annual budget requests on the basis of the city's spatial plan. CIMS was a system designed to "institutionalize macro processes of investment prioritization that seeks to actively mediate the tension between short-term delivery imperatives and long-term developmental objectives to alter the space economy of the city and address the imperative of spatial transformation in the interest of the urban working classes" (Pieterse 2019, 21).

In order to illustrate the critical role that CIMS served for budget planning and to mediate short-term delivery imperatives, Tau described to me the extent to which department heads felt bound by its strictures. Political principals of line departments often complained that the process undermined their autonomy to set priorities. As Tau recounted in an interview, members of the Mayoral Committee would say to him, "When did this Councillor CIMS contest elections? We don't know when he contested elections to represent a constituency."[38] The algorithmic approach to investment prioritization often felt alien to the normative goals of political department heads.

And absent effective political legitimacy—members of the Mayoral Committee had an electoral mandate—CIMS could not coordinate the patterns of private investment. With developers able to get approvals through agreements to pay up-front capital costs for new bulk infrastructure, the city was in a particularly weak position. "[Developers] had almost free rein, the only thing that could hamper them was the lack of capacity infrastructure," Pienaar told me. "[The year] 2008 is a blessing in disguise for us because the [global] financial crisis slowed everything down, and it gave us time to catch up and a bit of breathing time."[39]

The city's bureaucratic consolidation promised to introduce an era of city planning instruments that could now coordinate the spatial trajectory of land development. A veteran leader in the South African Association of Consulting Planners described a situation where the transition to a single authority created new choke points to gain approvals for private developments.

> There used to be towns called Sandton and Randburg and Roodepoort and a whole lot of towns. And they merged into one big metro council, which sounds efficient if you have everything in one building. But it's not efficient. Because you might be dealing with an application on the northern part of the area or in the southern part of the area, which is about fifty kilometers apart, and the guys who are dealing with the one area don't know the other area. And in the past you could have sent them down to that branch or that town and dealt with the town planner, dealt with the city engineer. Now you deal with this one massive big monster.[40]

As a result, developers began building first and getting approvals only after they had established facts on the ground.[41]

This did not impede private investment in land and real estate, as long as developers felt that they could extract zoning and building approvals when required. Private planners and developers both reported that rezoning approvals, while still required, were easily obtained even when projects did not fit key goals of the city's planners such as densification, mixed use, and corridor development. City officials in planning and land use management likewise acknowledged this. While there was a general sense that there were cases of bribery on occasion, the overwhelming view of my informants was that the bigger issue was simply a lack of capacity to keep ahead of the approval process. When I visited the offices where land use approvals are made on two different occasions in 2015 and 2017, I saw piles of approval applications covering approval officers' desks.

The urban boundary, first introduced in 2000, became the basis of competition between the municipal and the provincial scales. According to many current and former officials I interviewed, the goal of the urban boundary was to drive private development toward existing transportation corridors within the city, so as to encourage density and transit-oriented development. A further goal was to minimize the extension of infrastructure networks to new peripheral neighborhoods of development that would then require recurring municipal operational maintenance.

Municipal authorities insisted that the boundary was theirs to enforce on the basis of the Development Facilitation Act. However, in the decade after the introduction of the boundary, it had become an open secret among developers that if a given development fell outside the municipal boundary, an appeal could be made to Gauteng provincial authorities, who enforced a more permissive development boundary.

This form of real estate "venue-shopping" undercut the authority of municipal bureaucrats responsible for managing development approvals. "The main objective [of the Development Facilitation Act] was to facilitate reconstruction and development. Those type of developments—the backlog of housing," Gina Zanti, a veteran mid-rank staffer of the city's Department of Land Use Management told me.

> The idea was to allow the process to be faster. Not to go through all the stringent processes. So that was supposed to fast-track. But the way it was written it did not prevent any other developer from using this system. So these guys, they saw a loophole, and then most applications were processed by province. Now they had powers to disregard any of our policies.[42]

This bureaucratic sensibility was shaped by a distinct sense of powerlessness on the part of municipal officials. Tools aimed at increasing coordinating authority within the municipality disregarded the vertical dimension of bureaucratic cohesion. Gauteng provincial officials were able to use the more permissive boundary to implicitly incentivize development in neighboring municipalities; they also continued to stretch the bulk infrastructure requirements of the Johannesburg municipality. Beyond previous northern business nodes such as Sandton and Bryanston, new nodes were consolidated on the edge of the city and beyond, in places such as Weltevreden Park, Randpark Ridge, Lanseria, Midrand, and Kempton Park (Murray 2015). In Honeydew, another node on the city's northwest edge, Genesis Holdings has built more than ten thousand "greenfields" housing units in addition to multiple shopping centers.

Charl Fitzgerald, Genesis CEO, expressed typical complaints about the ways that developers maneuver around city officials to get new developments off the ground in these peripheral areas:

> The problem was created by the local authority. I mean, my personal opinion is that there was not proper planning from their side to coincide with the growth of a particular town and their excuses are normally budget.

But if you budget correctly years in advance, that should also be fine, and if you allocate your money correctly as a [city] council, I think it can also, if you don't waste your money on unnecessary stuff. So it is quite a process to get all the services negotiated, and then we install those services. We sit with engineers who design the services. We submit it to the council, it gets approved, and then we install those services. We build the roads and everything ourselves. Put all the stormwater, electricity, water, sewer lines.[43]

Although Fitzgerald acknowledged that installing these services removed significant tax burdens for the development, he insisted that this was counterbalanced by requirements for higher up-front capital investments. From the perspective of the city, the operational maintenance of the infrastructure always remains its responsibility. And while Fitzgerald criticized city budgeting practices, the fact is that the extent of development in Honeydew was not part of the city's original spatial plans. Throughout the 2000s, new spatial plans were introduced in attempts to address a growing realization that private development patterns—and the budgetary strains they placed on the maintenance of new infrastructure—continued to reproduce existing spatial divisions (Todes 2014).

The area of the city where Fitzgerald and others were developing would become a major source of conflict between the city and province and an opportunity for institutional arbitrage. Developers sought to continue to grow private property holdings in Honeydew and adjacent Ruimsig, which was over the city's official development boundary but not beyond the province's. In 2003, while the city of Johannesburg had not agreed to rezone land that would establish a township to enable new development, the province did, and development began.

In 2007, the conflict came to a head when the metropolitan municipality of Johannesburg took Gauteng province to court; the case eventually reached the Constitutional Court in 2010. The Development Facilitation Act of 1995 had given the authority for development approvals to provincial authorities. The city argued that the constitution granted this power to municipalities. The Constitutional Court ruled in favor of the city but also supported the recommendation of an amicus curiae brief by the South African Property Owners Association that the act could not be scrapped entirely without a provision for a new law specifying how zoning rights could be established in areas without municipal control, primarily rural areas administered through provinces.

In essence, just as the city seemed to have found a way to get control over its own planning tools, its momentum was foiled by SAPOA's appeal for new legislation. The court's decision included a clause that delayed the scuttling of the Development Facilitation Act until new legislation could be passed in parliament within twenty-four months. After a series of delays, this new legislation was finally gazetted in July 2015, under the Spatial Planning and

Land Use Management Act. The city's director of land use management, Gina Zanti, reported that the Constitutional Court case that ruled in favor of the city did not actually stop further instances of developers achieving development rights in areas beyond the city boundary by getting approvals from the Gauteng province.[44] The way that a moment of reform was repurposed to reproduce the existing spatial trajectory of the city was slightly different in this case. New institutional scales—the national Constitutional Court and the Gauteng province—were mobilized by developers to prevent the assertion of city authority.

By the time the Spatial Planning and Land Use Management Act was passed, developers and city officials were beginning to pursue something that increasingly resembled a rentier form of governing regime. David Savage, of the national Department of Treasury, described it as follows:

> I think in private-sector development, there has also been—there is a coalition, it is there, it is not a declared coalition—but certainly operated. It works between provinces, municipalities, officials, politicians, private developers, contractors, and the financial sector—that isn't necessarily always delivering a strong public benefit. In fact maybe capturing public benefit.[45]

Critically, this kind of growth coalition was not oriented toward a programmatic form of economic growth. Instead, it was a coalition of rentier-like capture.

The Tau administration began touting its spatial development framework known as "the corridors of freedom," which was supposed to target new market and subsidized development around the nodes of a planned bus rapid transit network. This mirrored popular approaches to "transit-oriented development" across the globe. In 2015, city officials were keen to talk about "corridors of freedom,"[46] aiming to show visible progress before the next year's elections. In this same year, city officials began holding regular engagements with SAPOA leadership and key members. A senior official in the development planning office in the city reported that this was the first period in which such regular engagements had ever taken place.[47]

Conclusion

This chapter has argued that the connections between housing movements and local government bureaucracy became a critical factor in determining the capacity to either weaken or succumb to the power of private real estate interests in shaping the politics of housing and land use. In São Paulo, the proliferation of these connections—embeddedness—made it possible to build internal bureaucratic capacity—cohesion—to meaningfully relativize rights to private property to deliver housing for the poor in decent locations in the city. As a result, we see a sustained "integrationist" governing regime of high embeddedness and high cohesion across much of the 2000s and early 2010s in housing and land use policy. In Johannesburg, the absence of these connections meant that private property rights were exclusively sacrosanct. The city began its democratic period with a strong base in housing movements that could have enabled a comparable path to coordinating power in housing and land use policy. But this was pushed aside: The ANC made an ideologically motivated decision that movements should demobilize, and the lack of party competition meant that this decision became reality. As a consequence, largely white property owners and developers could protect their property in ways that undermined the capacity of the local state to deliver on policies aimed at altering housing inequalities in the city. Where São Paulo moved from a "mobilizational" to an "integrationist" configuration of embeddedness and cohesion, Johannesburg moved from a similar starting point to something approximating a narrow "rentier" regime.

Electoral politics were a critical background condition. At the local level, São Paulo's elections were much more competitive than Johannesburg's. In fact, the PT—the party with organic links to housing movements in the city—never won reelection. For all three PT administrations (Erundina, Suplicy, and Haddad), these connections were critical for mobilizing electoral support. In Johannesburg, the ANC won elections throughout the period under examination here. Independent housing movements were not understood by the ANC as critical for electoral success, an accurate assessment. While these dynamics of electoral politics make up a critical difference between the two cities, they cannot explain why the construction of policy and delivery outcomes ultimately transpired so differently. This chapter has shown precisely how movements mattered for what happened after elections. It is in the process of governing, and not just campaigning, that policies emerge, face resistance, and either become more durable, in the case of São Paulo, or get deconstructed, in the case of Johannesburg.

The politics of land rights in both cities impeded the construction of classic urban growth regimes, which I theorize as "managerial" configurations of low embeddedness and high cohesion. In São Paulo, the ingredients for a growth machine were abundant. We see a well-organized set of real estate interests with long-established connections to government institutions at all levels. And yet, it was difficult for joint governing projects to emerge between these interests without the countervailing role of housing movements. Local government cohesion was buttressed through the emergence of interscalar supporting policies, especially federal mandates that helped the city loosen the primacy of private property rights through tools such as ZEIS, as well as increased funding for local government provision. In later years, the increased role of the federal government in providing direct funding for housing meant that the provision of low-income housing ended up reinforcing the incentive structures associated with private land markets. And furthermore, housing movements began focusing on the federal government as their primary target of contestation, leaving the city more isolated.

In Johannesburg, the ingredients for preventing the emergence of a growth machine were clear. The shift in the racial basis of political power meant that there was a much less established set of relationships between the real estate sector and local political elites. As this chapter documents, largely white economic elites deployed relatively hidden strategies to undermine local government capacity to implement policies pitched at reducing housing inequalities and pursue narrow rentier-like gains. A joint project of urban growth was just as elusive as a joint redistribution-oriented project.

As the next chapter shows, the challenge of not only accessing a home but traveling to and from home relies on different kinds of institutional coordinating capacities, much more internal to local government bureaucracies. How these transportation bureaucracies managed the comparatively more subtle dimensions of social embeddedness would have significant effects on the extent to which local government could produce effective governing arrangements for collective transportation.

4

Transportation

INSTITUTIONS VERSUS TECHNOLOGY

From every point of view—philosophical, moral, economic—a bus has to have its own lane.
—FERNANDO HADDAD, FORMER MAYOR OF SÃO PAULO

You guys fought for freedom just so that you plan your city for transit?
—PARKS TAU, FORMER MAYOR OF JOHANNESBURG

By the late 1980s in South Africa, sixteen-seater minibus taxis were easily the dominant mode of collective transportation across the country's cities. The sector was largely unregulated and was increasingly championed as a growth sector for black entrepreneurialism. The question of its legal formalization was central to what black participation in the economy might look like as the country entered the final decade of the twentieth century, with the future of Apartheid's grip increasingly unclear. In 1989, Knox Matjila, a spokesman for the leading association of minibus taxis in South Africa, reflected on the future of the industry: "The taxi industry has reached the limit of its development as part of the informal sector. The 1980s have been the decade of the informal sector; the 1990s must be the decade of transition to the semi-formal sector" (McCaull 1990, 113).

In São Paulo, more than a decade later, in 2001, the city was faced with a similar growth in informal collective transportation. In both cases, this was, in part, a consequence of rapid urbanization and a need for transportation to new informal settlements unmet by the formal transport sector. That year, three former officials in the Erundina administration in São Paulo wrote an article in *Folha de São Paulo* about the growing role of informal *peruas* and *vans*, the common terms for minibus taxis in Brazil: "It makes sense to develop this service, which today operates as a 'barbaric solution' to the problem, because it attends to a need that is at the same time both real and ignored by the state" (Gregori, Zilbovicius, and Varoli 2001).

In both cities, the question of how to grow and govern notoriously patchwork, unregulated, road-based collective transport to improve possibilities for residents traversing each city has bedeviled generations of politicians, bureaucrats, and ordinary riders. It is a question that has been subject to both loud political contention and entrenched, often illicit business interests. Collective transportation is not only a public good that changes how users can or cannot access the benefits of city life. Participants in the industry—such as drivers and vehicle owners—have frequently taken their lives into their hands to do so. Likely more so than housing or sanitation, transportation is the public good under examination in this book that has been most prone to violence, including severe assaults and murder. Across the Global South, the cash basis of informal transportation has long made it attractive for illicit organization (Agbiboa 2022). Though much remains to be documented in this regard in either city, the role of organized crime in the transportation sector in both cities is an open secret. Building a regulated, integrated, extensive, and affordable system out of such an institutional chimera is a common dilemma of city management across the rapidly urbanizing Global South (see Agbiboa 2022; Mutongi 2017). And like housing, in São Paulo and Johannesburg, it proved to be a critical crucible for revealing the nature of each city's coordinating power to govern.

Both cities began with highly fragmented bus services, dominated by a diversity of operators, many of which operated outside of any government regulation. This meant that residents not only had to use an inefficient and slow service. It was expensive. Routes changed without notice or were subject to unplanned deviations. Users had to pay for each leg of a trip, and it was impossible to contemplate the provision of any subsidy due to the lack of formal recognition and regulation of many operators in the sector.

This chapter contrasts two approaches to improving transport policy after democratization and decentralization. In São Paulo, I chronicle the city's "institutions-first" attempts to integrate and extend a reliable network of municipal buses. In Johannesburg, I find a "technology-first" attempt to do the same. São Paulo's decision to lead with reforms that changed the institutional governance of an existing network of both formal and informal service providers to improve bus service produced a heretofore unheralded, yet instructive set of successes. In Johannesburg, the decision to introduce a brand-new bus rapid transit (BRT) service has captured little market share and done little to change the costs—in terms of both time and money—to the majority of collective transport users in the city.

These comparative findings stand in contrast to the dominant approach in literature on transportation planning, which has focused on top-down, design-led innovations, either through the introduction of new modes of collective transport or through data-led operational improvements. In this chapter, I trace the history of transportation reforms in both cities. São Paulo's approach focused on the social basis of an infrastructure sector generally thought of as highly technical. The goal was to improve, extend, and reduce the effective price of existing municipal bus services. In turn, this enabled the staying power of subsequent technological reforms to bus operations. This "institutions-first" approach is explained by a history of political action by social movements that brought up demands for low fares and better services to reach the most marginalized parts of the city.

In Johannesburg, by contrast, the local government focused on establishing a brand-new BRT system and treated institutional integration of the informal taxi sector as a secondary concern. This was influenced by a narrow class of international consultants focused on policy transfer from, ironically, cities in Brazil and Colombia. The result was that the city's already dominant mode of transportation—semiformal minibus taxis—was largely excluded from the reform. The social distance of the African National Congress–led government from the taxi sector made it nearly impossible to import brand-new transport system technologies like BRT.

The resulting divergence is illustrated in Table 4.1. São Paulo's reforms produced an integrated bus system that enabled the introduction of a single ticket across multiple legs of a journey. This cut the effective price that users paid, and a system of centralized fare collection enabled the municipality to provide subsidies to disadvantaged groups such as the elderly and students. Johannesburg's reforms failed to realize similar goals, due to its struggle to become relevant to the majority of city residents who rely on collective transportation. This failure left in place the dominant system of informal minibus taxis inherited from the Apartheid era. In sprawling and fragmented megacities such as São Paulo and Johannesburg, where the poor live on the peripheries and end up spending hours in a daily commute in multileg journeys, these divergent pathways to reforming collective transportation have had far-reaching consequences.

The variation between these two cases can be explained by virtue of processual path dependencies in the development of the bus sector in each city. I argue that São Paulo's transportation reforms were explicitly part of a broader political project that helped build bureaucratic cohesion that was able to respond to the demands of movements in the city's extreme peripheral zones. In contrast, Johannesburg's transportation reforms were driven by a technocratic image of international "best practice" that was disconnected from a meaningful political dialogue with either operators or users. The

TABLE 4.1. Bus Sector Reforms in São Paulo and Johannesburg

Temporal Marker	São Paulo		Johannesburg	
	Industrial Organization	*Ticketing/Pricing*	*Industrial Organization*	*Ticketing/ Pricing*
Before reform	Fragmented service between municipal provider (Companhia Metropolitana de Transportes Coletivos) + private companies (formalized) + *peruas* (informal)	Ticket for each leg of a journey	Fragmented service across all informal minibus taxis	Ticket for each leg of a journey
After reform	All service providers in a consortium-based contract with the municipality: (1) prior private operators—central and trunk segments of network; (2) former *perua* operators— "local"/peripheral neighborhoods in the network	Centralized fare collection, integrated single ticket across all legs of a journey; range of municipal subsidies for students and the elderly	Fragmented service across all informal minibus taxis	Ticket for each leg of a journey

"institutions-first" approach in São Paulo was well suited to developing the interplay of social mobilization and increased institutional cohesion necessary to sustain reforms over long periods of time. In contrast, the "technology-first" approach in Johannesburg offered a tantalizing but elusive goal: to overlay a new transportation technology that would largely bypass a system of collective transportation that was deeply rooted in how riders were already moving through the city. Once the new BRT system did not capture market share and scale up quickly, it struggled to develop social support and quickly diminished institutional capacities for effective municipal administration.

São Paulo: Leading with Institutions

Brazil's contemporary crisis of governability reached its first major popular expression in what are known as the "June Days" of 2013. This cycle of street protest and police repression quickly coalesced into a more general protest against corruption, eventually metamorphosing into a wave that crushed the

popularity of President Dilma Rousseff and fueled the rise of politicians calling for her impeachment. These protests began with the apparently quotidian
outrage of a municipal bus fare hike proposed by São Paulo's Fernando Haddad, who had taken over as mayor at the beginning of 2013 and quickly found
himself barely on speaking terms with Rousseff.

The June Days arrived on the back of not just the immediate political conjuncture of snowballing corruption investigations known as Lava Jato (Car
Wash) and a stagnating economy. They were filled with echoes of earlier
moments in São Paulo's history as well. The wave of worker strikes in the
city in 1979, the first major labor actions since the beginning of the military
dictatorship in 1964, included strong participation by municipal bus drivers.
As far back as 1958, a protest by transport users in the city against fare hikes
had also led to standoffs with police in which four protestors were killed by
the authorities.

As the city's population grew in the 1970s and 1980s, along with its vast
and largely informal peripheral residential areas, a patchwork of public and
private bus operators provided disjointed services with significant resource
implications—of both time and money—for public transport users to access
employment and the rest of the city. The Free Tariff Movement that started
the protests in 2013—known by its Portuguese initials of MPL (Movimento
Passe Livre)—had its roots in the interplay between Workers' Party municipal bureaucrats and grassroots activists during the Erundina administration
(1989–92). During this period, the municipal authorities lent lasting credence
to the redistributive dimension of policy in collective transportation and established the institutional focus of intervention in order to achieve redistribution.
In the city's newly democratic era, this mix of formal and informal institutional
settings, as well as the mix of public and private provision of services, framed
political choices for ordinary residents, social movements, political parties,
and urban administrators alike.

When Erundina took office, she encountered an institutionally heteroge-
neous system of buses. The Companhia Metropolitana de Transportes Coletivos
(CMTC, or Municipal Company for Collective Transport) ran approximately
30 percent of the overall bus lines in the municipality. The rest were operated
by a range of private operators, with a varied patchwork of regulatory oversight.
Some were officially sanctioned, while others operated fully in the shadow of
municipal regulation. In the city's extreme peripheries, where the growing favelas were often located, informal minibuses and vans called peruas transported
residents to access more formal bus routes.

São Paulo's municipal government has a long history of a well-trained,
Weberian-style bureaucratic corps in the transportation sector. The Com-
panhia de Engenharia de Trafego (Traffic Engineering Company) and the
CMTC each cultivated career professionals with reputations as highly skilled

employees who were loyal to their agency. The Traffic Engineering Company has generally focused on managing the roadways for private passenger vehicles, and it conducts detailed origin-destination studies that measure traffic flows of both private and collective vehicles that illustrate the high degree of the agency's infrastructural capacity. The CMTC was also known to have a relatively high degree of bureaucratic capacity among skilled staff, though a large segment of its human resources was in its corps of relatively unskilled bus drivers and ticket collectors.

Erundina saw transportation as a critical sector for realizing her "inversion of priorities," whereby the city would focus on extending public goods to its most excluded parts. She selected as the transportation secretary Tereza Lajolo, a human rights activist and city councillor for the PT. While Lajolo was considered to have a political constituency as a result of her activist past, she did not have prior links or foster credibility with the CMTC in order to develop any kind of plan for improving the service directly under municipal control. The CMTC's internal coherence, shaped by a strong cadre of trained and loyal career staff, was not particularly open to a new secretary who did not have preexisting connections to these professionals. And by the end of Erundina's first year in office, she moved to reshuffle her cabinet, giving Lúcio Gregori a dual portfolio, adding transportation to his existing role leading the secretariat of public works.

Gregori was a young engineer with little experience in political activism who had supported leftist intellectual Plínio de Arruda Sampaio in the PT's internal election to be the party's candidate for mayor. While the dual portfolio was new for him, his shared strong professional identity with the engineering officials in the CMTC gave him room to credibly introduce reforms to the transportation sector.

In 1990, Gregori was interviewed by journalists about efforts to reorganize the transportation sector. During the interview, he made an unplanned comment about a "free tariff" (*tarifa zero*). With Erundina's encouragement, he would eventually come to propose a policy that would reverberate through to Brazil's more contemporary political crises.

Even now, there is still a cost for almost all users to ride public transportation in São Paulo. But the structure of remuneration for bus operators and the cost for users have undergone significant changes since Gregori instigated debates about a free tariff. The free tariff proposal created an enduring link between activist demands for a right to urban collective transportation and the institutional focus of reforms to achieve it. At the time of writing, mayoral platforms for the 2024 municipal election are being debated. And both the right-wing incumbent, Ricardo Nunes, and the likely left-wing challenger, housing movement leader Guilherme Boulos, are proposing versions of a free tariff (Santini 2023). The interplay between social organization in the street and the formal bureaucratic sphere continues to draw on the ideas that first animated the Erundina administration's early efforts to reform the sector.

São Paulo: Building a Single Bus System and Breaking It Apart

When Erundina came to office in 1989, a strong contingent of her cabinet, including Tereza Lajolo, was focused on realizing an ideological commitment to make the management and delivery of all public goods in the city "state-owned," or in Portuguese, *estatizar*. At the same time as the new administration was trying to make all bus operations part of the public sector, the existing public services were contending with a poor reputation. With only 30 percent of the overall bus service provided in the city, most city residents—and especially private bus operators—did not see the CMTC as the dominant stakeholder in the sector. Furthermore, the number of buses CMTC operated had not increased in the past decade, which administrators from this period described to me as a clear indication of persistently precarious fiscal capacity.

In this context, Lajolo's attempts to reorganize the largely private bus operators into the publicly run system were viewed as a major affront to private actors. According to Gregori, the private bus sector engaged the administration with the position that it had long negotiated concessionary contracts with the municipality. Private bus companies were therefore not willing to negotiate over the question of whether or not they should be operating contracts on behalf of the municipality.

Gregori realized that the key to reorganizing institutional roles was to negotiate over the user bus fare. And that is where he started after taking over the transportation portfolio from Lajolo. Francisco Christovam, the president of SPUrbanuss, the "syndicate"[1] that represents the larger private bus operators in the city, described the strategy as follows:

> [Erundina] changed the relationship between the private operator and the concessionary authority. The method was as follows: "The tariff that you collect—it's not yours. It's mine, and then I will pay you for the quantity of service that you provide." You understand? So the companies moved from having their revenue based on tariff payment to provision of service to the municipality. I transport the passengers, and everything that the passengers pay, I put in the public account. And afterward the municipality pays me for the quantity of service.[2]

In essence, Gregori's focus on the tariff brought together the perspectives of both users and operators. The user would pay, the bus company would operate, and the municipality would have a new effective tool for regulation. The 1991 reform, which Gregori's team referred to as "municipalization," centralized the collection of the tariff throughout the city, providing a mechanism for creating lines of accountability for the provision of services.[3]

In order to bring the bus companies on board with the new arrangement, the municipality agreed to terms for remunerating private bus operators that many considered to be overly favorable to the companies. The Erundina administration agreed to pay bus companies on the basis of the distance they traveled as opposed to the number of passengers that each bus carried. On the one hand, this rooted institutional reform in a redistributive impulse because bus services were no longer tied to the tariff that users paid. In essence, while each passenger paid the same price, those traveling shorter distances were subsidizing the cost of transporting riders who rode for longer distances. As a result, rides from the periphery to the center were being subsidized by rides within the city center. And such spatial coordinates had clear socioeconomic ramifications. Even though the tariff was still levied, this approach drew on the same redistributive principle as Gregori's "free tariff" proposal, and in a 1990 interview, he emphasized that his new proposal was to be funded by an increase in the municipal property tax. "This is not about a free bus," he noted, "but about a redistribution of income" (*Estado de São Paulo* 1990).

The reform also put limits on critical elements of illicit activity tied to the bus sector. I am not aware of any systematic research on the role of organized crime in São Paulo's bus sector. However, my informants both in local government bureaucratic positions and, with much more circumspection, in the private bus sector consistently suggested that the cash basis of the system had made the sector advantageous for laundering money made through illicit drug sales. By conceding that tariff collection should go to the centralized municipal authorities and then be returned to private bus operators on the basis of services offered, however, companies faced new limits in terms of the extent to which they could serve this laundering function.

Gregori is now retired, and when I interviewed him at his home in the suburban municipality of Jundiaí, he readily acknowledged that his approach introduced new forms of instability into the provision of bus service. On the one hand, the approach incentivized additional buses to enter the service because companies were effectively guaranteed a return on the provision of the service. Paulo Sandroni, the president of the CMTC during this period, echoed this sentiment. "With 'municipalization,'" he noted, "it was said that [a bus company] would not generate revenue from the tariff but would generate revenue from the service provided. So instead of using five buses, he would provide twelve. Of course it is better for everyday people, but it also cost a lot."[4]

In addition to these direct cost implications, the "municipalization" reform encouraged inefficiencies that grew to become debilitating to the overall bus system. Because they were paid according to the distance traveled, buses often were serviced and parked at garages farther away than was economical so as to be able to charge a higher rate to the municipality. By the time Erundina was due to leave office at the end of 1992, the informal perua minibus taxis had mushroomed to such a high quantity that they threatened to undercut the formal bus system. Because the formal buses were not as interested in protecting their routes due to the fact that their income would be guaranteed regardless of passenger numbers, informal buses would show up shortly before or after the formal buses at bus stops in São Paulo's peripheries and charge a lower fare than formal buses subject to municipal price regulation. The lower price and, often, the perception of added convenience led these buses to establish a new foothold in the city's peripheral neighborhoods. In response, laws passed at the very end of the Erundina administration and during the Maluf and Pitta administrations progressively pushed the formal bus sector toward a structure of remuneration based on the number of passengers transported.[5] But the rise of the informal sector continued to undercut the financial sustainability of the "municipalized" formal bus sector.

Erundina's reorganization of the fare collection system introduced a redistributive impulse to public transportation while unintentionally encouraging the growth of informality. As the Maluf and Pitta administrations pursued privatization reforms in the sector, the growth of informal peruas continued to undermine the functionality of the system for users. Ideological debates over the public or private management of the bus sector were moot. The Maluf administration was intent on privatizing as much as possible, to limit the drain of the inefficient system on a municipal balance sheet that was increasingly under strain. In 1995, the Maluf administration spun off the CMTC into a municipal-owned entity with its own private board, now known as SPTrans. This "new public management" reform ensured that the municipality's commitment to public transportation would be on the basis of revenue neutrality. As a result, under SPTrans, 27,000 employees of the CMTC were reduced to 1,200.

The privatization effort created a corps of former public employees—bus drivers and ticket collectors—with intimate, tacit knowledge of the routes and behavior patterns of bus users, and many of these ex–public employees populated the growing operations of the peruas. Some degree of informal collective transport had been a constant in the city for decades. But after the 1995 privatization reform, the ranks of the peruas took off. According to a representative of one of the largest cooperatives of former perua operators, by 1997, there were 23,000 informal peruas on the streets of São Paulo. These buses mostly served the peripheries of the city, which were facing the brunt of increased economic recession and monetary inflation. As he stated:

> This economic crisis of unemployment led people in different social and economic niches—bank tellers, grocery workers—man, they started sorting

garbage and recycling. These people from various economic niches needed to work. So what they did is started to make transportation routes that took passengers to train stations. And afterward, these routes continued to extend, going from street corners in the peripheries, in the *favelas*—the peripheries that were farther from the center of the city where there was a huge lack of collective transport. So we began to expand the number of options.[6]

One of the few empirical studies available on this period of collective transportation in the city reports the testimony of an operator of a perua (known as a *perueiro*) who began working during this time. After being laid off from the CMTC, this perueiro considered becoming a driver of a passenger taxi car but felt that he understood the needs of his neighbors enough to provide a more comprehensive service beyond an individual passenger vehicle. He sought out an informal group of local bus operators in order to coordinate service in the farthest peripheries of the southern zone of the city, stretching all the way to the Guarapiranga Reservoir, approximately twenty-five kilometers outside the city center (Hirata 2011).

The privatizing drive of the Maluf and subsequent Pitta administrations gave renewed impetus to attempts to install new electronic card technology, which Erundina had also proposed. This was a direct affront to a key interest group, the ticket collectors, known as *cobradores*, who saw themselves as most vulnerable to any effort to cut labor costs in the transportation sector. As the frontline agents handling cash, cobradores were the primary link for organized crime to the bus sector, and gang organizations were often said to provide support for their hiring and firing. The cobradores fought back. In September 1998, *Folha de São Paulo* reported an agreement that pitted politics against the economics of change in the sector: "To avoid layoffs, which according to bus company owners and the municipality itself, are inevitable, Mayor Celso Pitta signed a decree ensuring that all *cobradores* would retain their employment status" (*Folha de São Paulo* 1998). The role of the cobradores would remain central to the bus sector's institutional reforms, especially in the subsequent mayoral administration of the PT's Marta Suplicy.

São Paulo: From Fragmentation to Integration

When Suplicy took the mayoral seat at the beginning of 2001, she expressed a clear intention to take on the "perueiro mafia" that she argued was holding back public transportation in the city. By the end of her first year in office, her administration successfully passed the first major legal reorganization of the public transport sector to do just that. Officials pursued a harsh demonization of the perueiros in public. In private, these officials worked to build relationships of trust so as to reorganize the sector so that it could be integrated into a single city-wide system of buses. As Nivaldo Azevedo, a former perueiro and long-standing operator of a legal "cooperative" of buses in the southern zone of the city, put it to me, "[Suplicy] created a revolution in public transportation in the city of São Paulo."[7] What he described as a "revolution" was built on the incremental foundations of the Erundina-era reforms of fare collection, known as *municipalização*.

Recall that these efforts were focused on ensuring that all fares from various bus operators went to a central municipal account. Other aspects of the Erundina reforms were less successful and were subsequently worsened by the privatization efforts under Maluf and Pitta. But even under the Maluf and Pitta administrations, Erundina's reforms of the modality for fare collection persisted. And they made possible a meaningful redistributive fare policy reform: A single fare paid could now cover transfers across multiple legs of the same trip, no matter the operator. Because the municipality was committed to remunerating bus companies, and bus companies had the experience of trustworthy remuneration by the municipality, the municipality could assume the function of distributing the costs paid by the user. This "single ticket" (*bilhete único*) was only functional within the municipal bus service when it was first introduced in 2004.

Soon after Suplicy assumed office, her newly appointed leadership in SPTrans assumed responsibility for developing the capacity to manage fare collection. While there were meaningful technological constraints to be overcome, my informants in SPTrans minimized these and invariably emphasized the negotiations with bus operators to get buy-in to the new approach.

From the administrators' perspective, there were three intertwined problems. First, the peruas had to be brought into a more coherent and formalized arrangement so that user fees from these informal vehicles could contribute to the centralized remuneration system. Second, the basis for remuneration for services provided by operators had to be renegotiated with both operators already in the formal system and the perueiros. And finally, the technology for enabling ease of travel for the user had to not threaten the employment of the ticket collectors (*cobradores*) in order to sidestep a key potential source of resistance to reform.

These three problems had to be tackled in order. In essence, any technological change in the bus system's operation would have to be preceded by a social and institutional reform. The peruas were the critical first step. In 2001, Secretary of Transport Carlos Zarratini led the passage of the first in a series of laws that empowered the city to reorganize the bus sector through the São Paulo city council.[8] However, Zarratini himself was perceived by perueiros as being unable to negotiate with the formal and informal bus operators who were critical to the law's implementation.

Despite Zarratini's lack of credibility with the perueiros, the staff of SPTrans began to hold meetings with perueiros to explore ways of reorganizing the informal sector. Vanderley Pezzotta, a nearly forty-year veteran of SPTrans, described the situation that faced the agency at that time:

> The regulated system regulated badly. The large bus companies operated badly—only thought about profit. And this opened the space for the informal system to emerge. They realized this niche and began to provide *perua* service on top of some of the profitable routes. They made connections that had the characteristic of being structural, which the public sector did not perceive. These were connections that were internal to various neighborhoods. And they could make these connections in part because they were using smaller vehicles, they had lower operational costs. We didn't have an electronic ticket at that time, and the *peruas* proliferated throughout the city of São Paulo. We ended up with about fifteen thousand *peruas* on the roads.[9]

As this quote suggests, in retrospect, the introduction of an integrated electronic ticket was understood as a game changer in the governance of the collective transport sector. But during this period, the goal was first to shift all operators onto a single regulated playing field. While many of the peruas operated to cannibalize formally recognized bus routes, they also operated many complementary routes that effectively extended service deep into neighborhoods in the city's periphery that were otherwise without access to collective transportation.

SPTrans staff began to convene perua operators for a series of negotiations ahead of the planned issue of a tender—a request for proposals—in 2003 for bus operation in the city. SPTrans officials and bus operators recalled this period as extraordinarily tense, with multiple informants noting the presence of individuals who were openly displaying guns at many of these meetings. Pezzotta described the process as follows:

> First, we had to understand which routes they were operating and what connections they were making. Many of the *perua* operators were working as individuals, only focused on one route, often on top of a regulated route. From there, we started to create a set of criteria for further talks to determine, "No, you can't operate that line. There is no reason for you to operate on top of a regulated line. You are going to have to choose another." From there, we began to get to know these guys, talking to them. And that's how we began. "Look, you operate a route that is similar to another one, so why don't you get together?" From there, we began to organize these guys into formal routes.[10]

Azevedo, of the cooperative for former perua operators, said that at least in the South Zone of the city, violence related to the consolidation of perua routes occasionally resulted in deaths. Even so, he suggested that the experience with the Suplicy administration stood in contrast to previous engagements with the municipality during the prior Pitta administration: "He [Pitta] was very bad in the sense that he was totally oriented toward the large bus companies. It was extremely difficult for smaller operators to come together and get formal recognition."[11]

Especially under Suplicy's second secretary of transportation, Jilmar Tatto, perua operators felt more confident that the municipality was prepared to treat them fairly. Tatto was appointed as secretary of transportation in November 2002, shortly after the passage of enabling legislation to begin the transition to an electronic ticket.[12] Azevedo described a sense among perueiros that Tatto was committed to an agenda of "social inclusion":

> It was his vision, even though we still have in Brazil this story that political parties are perceived the same, more or less, as football teams. If you are from the Left, then you are from the Left; if you are from the Right, then you are from the Right. So this business makes it difficult to resolve problems when you look at it as a general proposition. I would say that [the issue of formalizing the peruas] was not seen in this way. The secretary aimed to include everyone and resolve the problem.[13]

Despite Azevedo's insistence on a nonpartisan approach to formalizing the peruas, Tatto's activist history in the South Zone suggests that politics actually were quite important. When I asked Tatto why he got involved in the policy sphere of transportation, he relished describing his upbringing in the "liberation theology" tradition of the Catholic Church in the South Zone of the city and his history in the PT. Tatto had been a senior aide during Erundina's failed reelection bid in 1992. In this role, he came to see the crisis in the organization of public transportation of the city as one of the main challenges for a PT administration to solve. In fact, it was a major distributive issue for a political party that made addressing urban inequality one of its core ideological commitments.

Tatto described a rather interpersonal mode of negotiation with both established formal bus companies and perua operators to set up a new formalized system. The key, he argued, was to engage with the younger generation of these largely family-owned businesses. "Every previous secretary [of transportation] who had come to speak with them found that they were the type, you know—the 'bam-bam-bam,'" he told me, referring to what he saw as a relatively formalistic mode of negotiation in which city officials had to either take or leave what bus company executives were willing to offer. "The first thing I did was to say, 'I don't want to speak anymore with you. Truthfully, the city is grateful. And now I would like to speak with your sons, the new generation.'"[14]

The validity of this generational argument is hard to assess systematically, but it was a constant refrain among the politicians, bureaucrats, and private bus operators I interviewed.[15] Tatto's point about the importance of generational hierarchy and change in this sector also resonates with ethnographic observations from my own fieldwork. Private bus companies were the most difficult to access of any of the groups I interviewed for this book. When I did finally manage to arrange interviews, I would often be introduced to multiple generations of family ownership, and I would always be taken to greet a founder-patriarch before speaking with a son who was in charge of operations. Tatto's argument suggests that he saw building bridges to a newer generation of leadership within the bus sector as critical for implementing reforms. In turn, this indicates the sensitivity and familiarity that he had regarding the social and interpersonal realities of how the sector functioned.

The negotiations that Tatto led with both informal and formal bus operators soon established a split method for operating the bus system. The established formal bus operators, with fleets of large buses, would control "structural routes" along main avenues and in the center of the city. The previously informal peruas were organized into cooperatives that would control "local routes" in the city's peripheral neighborhoods. The cooperative organization structure made it possible for the municipality to have a legally recognizable entity with which to negotiate remuneration of fares collected through the electronic ticket.

Dividing the system in this way, which corresponded strongly to the core-periphery dynamic of residential settlement, made possible a dual system of corporate organization in the bus sector: cooperatives for the small operators who were formerly perueiros and formal business organization for the large operators who were previously part of the regulated system. And because the "Single Ticket" enabled fare payment to carry across both types of routes, this operational division further facilitated integration of the payment system.

These operational changes required technological changes. But, as always in the case of São Paulo, technological reforms were preceded by institutional change. The new ticket integration also required retrofitting of old buses and the introduction of new buses that ensured that all passengers could board and swipe an electronic ticket. It also meant that all riders could be tracked by municipal authorities as they traveled across the city (Campos 2018). Ana Odila, an advisor to the municipal secretary of transportation during the Suplicy administration, oversaw the implementation of the "Single Ticket" system:

With the "Single Ticket," we could transform the bus network because an individual could travel and use the network as they wished. This was the fundamental step for us to be able to demarcate routes and make a "structural" system. This first part was the most difficult, because I had to get involved with the method of accounts in the bus system.[16]

While this was and is universally described as the "Single Ticket" reform—that is, a technological solution—both public officials and private operators saw its significance in planning and institutional terms: a reorganization of the bus route system and an increased centralization of the system's finances. And as both municipal officials and bus operators attested, the set of interpersonal negotiations about institutional arrangements made possible the technological innovation.

The technological innovation had an institutional appeal for both the municipality and the range of incumbent operators. For the municipality, it offered a mechanism for increased planning authority to expand service and redistribution through the fare structure. For former perueiros, being incorporated into a formal system offered predictability of revenues and reduced operational risk. For the larger bus operators, becoming more deeply incorporated into the formal system offered the assurance of user enthusiasm for the bus system due to cheaper fares.

Christovam of the association of larger bus operators in the "structural" system, described the role of the "Single Ticket" as follows:

> The "Single Ticket" was an innovation of the Marta [Suplicy] administration. It was fantastic from the planning perspective because one of the key obstacles to strong integration was the payment of more than one tariff. For the love of god, if I go from an origin to a destination, I should pay one tariff! Do you want me to disembark, go to a terminal, pay another fare? I won't do it, I don't want to. So the "Single Ticket" said, "No, the public authority will pay the cost, and the user, you will pay a single fare from the origin to the destination. You can take three hours and up to four transfers for free." So then you have countered the argument of everybody who had to pay more if they had a multisegment trip.[17]

This sense of user confidence in the system was critical after years of increasing fragmentation and informalization. The Suplicy administration's "Single Ticket" reform effectively switched the institutional trajectory of the bus system. While private operators maintained many privileges, the "Single Ticket" implanted a fundamental principle: Users were riding on a single system.

When Suplicy lost her reelection campaign in October 2003, the bus system was on its way toward increased integration and formalization. A process of institutional reform that had begun haltingly under Erundina was now flowering into a system that ordinary users could easily recognize as cheaper and more functional, with more extensive service.

The subsequent center-right Serra and Kassab administrations produced a vertical alignment across scales of government that pushed the bus system's integration even deeper: the comparatively small subway "Metrô" system that served the center of the city. While the bus system remained the dominant mode of service used by *paulistanos*, deeper integration with the Metrô created a stronger cross-class investment in the use of collective transportation in a context of middle-class preference for the private car. Again, the principle established by the "Single Ticket" reforms under Suplicy was in play: The user sees a single ticketing process across modes. Because the Metrô was—and is— primarily located in wealthier parts of the city, its integration with the more extensive and popular bus system meant that the "Single Ticket" was integrating the collection of fares across the geography of class in the city.

The most significant roadblock to integrating the bus system with the Metrô appeared to be party politics. While the municipality controlled the provision of bus service, the state government controlled the Metrô. The PT governed in municipalities across the São Paulo metropolitan region. But the more conservative heartland of the rural municipalities in the state's coffee-growing regions had prevented the party from achieving statewide majorities. Coordinating with the state government, led by the center-right Governor Geraldo Alckmin of the Social Democratic Party of Brazil (PSDB), remained elusive.

When José Serra, a key power broker in the PSDB, entered mayoral office in 2004, most observers expected that his sights would shift to challenging Lula for the presidency in the 2006 election. Much of the day-to-day of his administration was left to his vice-mayor, Gilberto Kassab, a figure of the traditional politics of the center keen to be seen as a modernizer in his own right. The gains of the Suplicy administration were understood as useful building blocks for realizing this goal, especially in the transportation sector.

The new secretary of transportation, Frederico Bussinger, could not have cut a more different figure than Tatto. A veteran transportation planner and consultant, he had none of the activist nous of Tatto, a "son of the Zona Sul." It was Tatto's streetwise sensibility, built on strong links to informal operators in São Paulo peripheries, that helped facilitate the bus sector's institutional reorganization. But Bussinger carried the swagger of an experienced bureaucrat, skilled in the behind-the-scenes lubrication of highly formalized institutional settings such as São Paulo's interscalar municipal-state relationship. And though he was an appointee of Serra, he had previously consulted with his immediate predecessors, both Zarratini and Tatto.

Bussinger described the Suplicy reforms as indispensable to bridging the missing gap of interscalar governing coordination:

> It was all an evolution. Marta implemented a plan. She built a network. What was missing was a ticket, which was the last thing to be done. But

it was done without institutional definition. . . . It was all done in a very rushed way. It was electoral marketing. So much so that even up until today it is considered a banner for Marta [Suplicy].[18]

When Bussinger described a ticket as "missing," he was referring to the fact that the "Single Ticket" electronic pass only became available to users at the very end of Suplicy's term, due to her administration's prioritization of the institutional reorganization of the bus sector. Only under Serra did the municipality issue a formal decree regulating the "Single Ticket."

Tatto's leadership of the transportation department had ensured close ties with the needs of both users and previously informal bus operators in the peripheries of the city. Bussinger can be understood as a key municipal bureaucratic figure who could consolidate coordinating capacity across scales of government. The alignment of PSDB-led administrations in both the municipal and state governments made it possible to integrate the bus ticket with the state-run Metrô, which operates only within municipal borders, and a metropolitan rail line known by its Portuguese acronym CPTM, which operates across the much bigger metropolitan region.

> So as the municipality had implemented the "Single Ticket" system within the municipality for the bus, and the bus, from a quantitative perspective, transported more [people], we then proposed [the integration with the Metrô and CPTM]. What made it work was the fact of having Serra as the mayor and [Geraldo] Alckmin as the governor.[19]

From the perspective of an ordinary user, this made perfect sense. The interoperability of the subway and the bus systems was a straightforwardly rational idea. But from an institutional perspective, this was not so simple. Odila, the key advisor to Suplicy's transportation department on the initial "Single Ticket" program design, said to me that she had been seen as "crazy" for being wary about jumping into further integration.[20] This was because integration would further complicate the delicate balance of fare-sharing across various operators. The financial implications included more difficult cross-subsidization for the bus and subway systems down the line. The subway itself is a complex public-private partnership, with different operators responsible for each of the four lines.

But the state and municipal governments were now ruled by the same party, a useful (though by no means determinative) ingredient to increased coordinating capacity across scales of government, which I call "vertical cohesion." This meant that both governments were eager to produce an electorally popular win. The extension of integrated public transportation services across the city, which began under the center-left PT, had effectively crossed party lines to include the center-right PSDB and its political allies. This institutional layering had been kick-started by a view of collective transportation as a public good that municipal government could and should provide on a truly city-wide scale. And now this view had sprouted deep roots across both the municipal and state scales of government.

São Paulo: From Negotiating Ownership to Challenging Private Space

By the time Haddad's administration returned the PT to São Paulo's mayoral seat in 2013, the terrain of political debate had shifted considerably. The operational integration and regulation of the service were no longer in question. Now, the price of the fare and the space allocated for private transportation would produce a political clash with historic ramifications not only for the city but for the entire country.

The period of reform during the Suplicy, Serra, and Kassab administrations was focused on the operational integration of services that had been previously separated. The Suplicy administration drew on the PT's capacity to negotiate with the informal perueiros through its activist links in the far peripheries of the city. The Serra and Kassab administrations were then able to build on the formalized institutional arrangements of the Suplicy reforms and construct a broader interscalar cohesion in the system through the alignment of state and municipal policies. These institutional reforms delivered clear distributional benefits through the lower price of collective transportation services, with residents of the peripheries benefiting the most. This is because residents of the peripheries were the most likely to require trips with multiple legs, so the free transfer enabled by a single-fare ticket helped them the most.

However, the prior reforms still did not directly confront the broader context for transportation policy in the city: the dominance of the private car. As Brazil experienced historic economic growth and social inclusion in the 2000s, the middle classes also grew. The much-vaunted *classe C* in the five-class income division (A through E) commonly used by Brazilian researchers and policymakers bulged.[21] The growing capacity for consumption, bolstered by the expansion of credit to lower rungs of the income ladder, encouraged the purchase of private cars. About equal populations in the city drive a private car or use public transportation, but the roads were dominated—and increasingly congested—by the private car. In 2014, there was approximately one private vehicle for every three city residents on São Paulo's roads (World Bank 2014).

When Haddad took office, he was faced with a number of loose ends from the previous period of reform of the bus sector. The tender for operating buses in the city was up for renewal, and Haddad had committed to completing this task. Furthermore, transportation officials had long been calling for a review of the tariff, arguing that absent additional new revenues from either an increase in municipal property taxes or federal transfers, a fare hike would be necessary to keep the system operational. Haddad, who had made general commitments to fiscal probity during the 2012 election cycle, was keen to set the city on a more sustainable path. When I interviewed him, he defended his administration against what he saw as a set of unfair critiques that arose in the 2013 "June Days" protests, which called for the elimination of transport fares: "I think I solved the two primary problems of the city, which were the debt and the master plan. Because everything else depends on this. If you don't solve this, you don't solve anything."[22]

While the Kassab administration had declined to contemplate fare hikes in line with inflation in the lead-up to the 2012 election, Haddad faced pressure to adjust public transportation fares to help balance the city's books. This emphasis on fiscal balance was, on the one hand, consistent with the PT's municipal legacy of pushing the boundaries of redistributive policy within the space of orthodox fiscal management. On the other hand, a fare hike ran counter to the PT's legacy in pushing redistributive policy in the sphere of public transportation. A fare hike would hit the city's poorest residents most acutely.

The method for financing the public transportation system revealed the extent to which the Haddad administration saw its power at the city level as constrained. The Erundina administration's exploration of a "Free Tariff" proposal in the early 1990s was predicated on a proposal to raise municipal property taxes, known by its Portuguese initials as IPTU (Imposto Predial e Territorial Urbano, or Urban Land and Building Tax), but this was prevented by the municipal courts. Now, Haddad did not even contemplate a hike in the Urban Land and Building Tax, instead making a direct appeal to President Dilma Rousseff to use some of the national gasoline tax, known as the Contribuição de Intervenção no Dominio Econômico (Contribution for Intervention in the Economic Domain), to help fund the city's public transportation system. Tatto, who returned as transportation secretary under Haddad, described the dilemma as a distinct irony of PT administrations in São Paulo:

> Kassab had delayed a fare hike. He had the problem of being unable to act and did not raise the fare. Haddad came to office, looked at the accounts, and said, "Look, the municipality doesn't have anywhere to get the money. Either you put everyone into transportation and you don't have anything to do the minimum in other sectors. You have to get the money from somewhere." And it was from that logic that he raised the fare, which is, for a mayor, one of the most difficult things you can do. At the same time, we began a debate about who should finance public transportation, focused on the CIDE [Contribution for Intervention in the Economic Domain].[23]

Tatto, perhaps unsurprisingly given his role as a politician, suggested a unified PT position on the question of bus fares and how collective transportation should be funded.

But key bureaucrats tasked with overseeing the Haddad administration's public transportation policies revealed an internal divide. Ciro Biderman, one of Brazil's leading economists of public transportation and administration, served as the chief of staff for SPTrans from 2013 until 2015 under Haddad. He argued that though Haddad and Erundina were both PT members, Haddad's approach to the public transit fare was very different from that of the earlier mayor: "They had the idea that bus service is a public good. And it is not. It is a public utility. They are two distinct things. . . . It is not a public good, but it is a public utility for which you have to guarantee universal access."[24]

In effect, Biderman was suggesting that the Haddad administration was willing to push against what had once been the PT's dominant position on public transportation in the city. The emphasis on collective transportation as a public good under prior PT administrations had produced a set of reforms aimed at extending service and reducing price. This meant that there was a persistent focus on finding ways to cross-subsidize fares; the most obvious success in this regard was the integration of all operators in a single system and through a single ticket, so that shorter trips subsidized longer ones. The PT had also persistently proposed using local property taxes to fund the bus system, arguing that this would be justified because the political economy of land undergirded the spatial distribution of residents in the city.

The Haddad administration's "public utility" approach, as Biderman put it to me, suggested an important distinction. The goal was to ensure the service's financial viability, an issue that had been avoided for more than a decade, largely within the established strictures. The service could be improved in terms of trip speed (through dedicated bus corridors), vehicle quality, and upgraded ticketing technology. But the more redistributive elements associated with the "public good" approach of earlier administrations were not part of the political agenda articulated around collective transportation policy. Whether by ideological design or practical necessity, the new administration made its first move in the sector to implement a fare hike of twenty centavos, or 6.67 percent.

The effect was a tsunami of social protest that took on national implications. The June Days (Jornadas de Junho) of 2013 first exploded on June 17. The initial protests were organized by a movement that called itself the "Free Tariff Movement," explicitly inspired by Gregori's proposal during the Erundina administration. The MPL protests burst forth into more generalized protests after the state police—notably, not the municipal forces—brutally put down the initial protests, which was captured in vivid detail on nightly newscasts and in the pages of the country's leading newspapers.

Whereas prior PT administrations in the city had been quite open to social protests about the distribution of public goods, the Haddad administration responded to the MPL unrest in two ways that suggested a mode of operation that was closed to subaltern protest. In order to understand these attitudes, it is useful to compare how Haddad and Tatto each reacted when I asked about the role of these protests. While Haddad saw a clear threat from protest in the streets, Tatto saw an opportunity.

Tatto, with an activist background in the city's southern peripheries, was relatively sanguine about the upsurge in social protest during a PT administration. "The fact is that when you raise a transport tariff, it's always a moment of tension. That same social movement—those youths—they are always more courageous when it is a PT government. When it is another government from the Right, generally they retreat. They have more difficulty."[25]

Haddad, however, argued for a distinction between previous movements and what emerged in 2013. I interviewed him in the week following the publication of his first major statement on his mayoral administration since he lost his reelection campaign, a lengthy essay in *Revista Piauí*, a monthly magazine modeled on *The New Yorker*. The essay had been making waves among left activists, with a torrent of commentary in a WhatsApp group of housing activist leaders, PT intellectuals, and former Haddad administration officials. In the essay, Haddad contrasted prior movements to the 2013 protests, describing the latter as "without connections to political parties nor having electoral goals outside of a specific agenda that is difficult to contest. . . . They were very critical of any relationship to politics and traditional forms of negotiation" (2017, 34).

On the one hand, this analysis reflects the distance between the Haddad administration and the PT's traditional social movement allies, which we have already seen were critical in the housing sector in particular. Haddad's argument emphasizes the distance of the MPL's claims from the existing formal policy debate. On the other hand, Haddad saw the MPL as symptomatic of a broader social malaise devoid of distinct political claims altogether. He describes the transformation of the MPL's complaints into broad anti-corruption protests nationwide as at once akin to the pre-political patrimonialism described by the Brazilian historian Raymundo Faoro in his 1958 classic *Os donos do Poder* (*The Owners of Power*) and the "post-political" movements against neoliberalism that began in the 1999 protests against the World Trade Organization. The MPL, according to Haddad, was therefore not a harbinger of any kind of ideological break other than a break with distinct ideological foundations for politics altogether.

While at a theoretical level, these arguments are quite provocative, as a matter of governance, they seem questionable. Haddad himself described to me a "socio-environmental coalition" that he hoped to inaugurate with his administration. In an interview, for example, he highlighted the role of middle-class cyclist organizations in supporting his program to build bicycle lanes throughout the city. In contrast, he did not cite a specific organizational base that had been pushing for the more consequential policies for the bus sectors. These included expanding hundreds of miles of bus lanes on road space previously available to private vehicles.

The weak political coordination of these policies emerged during Haddad's losing reelection campaign in 2016. The bike lanes generally received strong approval in polls. A Datafolha poll in 2014 found that 80 percent of city residents supported them, though only 4 percent of respondents said that they used a bike on a daily basis. In contrast, 91 percent of city residents approved of the expansion of exclusive lanes for public buses, which account for three-quarters of all trips taken on public transportation (Johnson and Jelmayer 2015). Haddad's image was associated much more closely with the bike lanes than with the bus lanes. For example, photos of him riding a bike in urban street scenes were frequent in publicity materials.

The bus lanes fit awkwardly into the reelection campaign. Tatto noted to me that Lula, a strong backer of Haddad within the PT, came from the automobile sector—he led the autoworkers' union in the 1970s—and was not as comfortable talking about collective transport. Yet, at a kickoff rally for Haddad's reelection campaign, it was Lula who spoke about the value of the bus lanes. I managed to find my way close to the speakers' platform and noticed Lula looking back frequently to Haddad as he spoke about the bus lanes, a topic Haddad hardly mentioned in his own speech. Lula appealed to the raucous crowd: "They've cut your travel times, haven't they?" Afterward, those in attendance rushed to a podium that extended deep into the crowd to hug Lula. Many were in tears. Haddad followed Lula down the podium extension with much more reserve, waving politely to those transfixed by Lula.

In my interviews with bus company representatives, they all described the expanded reservation of bus lanes on the road as a help but not a major structural shift for their business. Instead, they focused on Haddad's attempts to negotiate a new contract and reorganize the bus system itself. This was ultimately left to Haddad's successors, as he continued to negotiate emergency extensions to the existing contract, which was held over from the Suplicy administration.

Ultimately, the extension of bus lanes represented a major theoretical affront to the structure of transportation in the city, relativizing the absolute right of middle-class private car owners to the roads. However, the lack of strong political mobilization for this policy reform transformed the project into a technocratic enterprise. The focus on bike lanes as the political leading edge of transportation policy gave Haddad a middle-class sheen of respectability. But he did not excite the PT's traditional bases of support, which overwhelmingly rely on the city's bus service and could have made his reelection campaign viable. An institutional—and politicized—project of transportation reform had transformed into a much more technocratic redesign of the built environment.

This managerial turn under Haddad stood in sharp contrast to the larger story in São Paulo in transportation policy. The city has achieved remarkable outcomes in overcoming some of the primary constraints to integrating informal transport into an extensive city-wide formal system. It did so by focusing on institutional constraints prior to introducing technological and design reforms. Redistribution through the provision of collective transportation as a public good had long been a political and not only technocratic project. The priority of the peripheries was given political voice through the alliance of housing movements and the PT, including party activists from the peripheries like former municipal Transportation Secretary Jilmar Tatto. In transportation, the organizational basis for this political voice was never as clear-cut as with housing movements, which had cut out a highly legible place in the city's civil society and political firmament.

The priority of the peripheries was clear, but the organizational actor to "embed" transportation policymaking in civil society was less so. The result was that the city's first attempt in the early 1990s to pursue redistribution-oriented policy to ease access to this public good was a "free tariff," which failed without a clear constituency. But it produced a mechanism for reform that enabled subsequent intermediation between PT political principles and the shadowy world of informal bus operators—the perueiros. In the early 2000s, PT politicians like Tatto had clear activist links in the peripheries and credibility. They drew on prior policy reforms that had been aimed at de-linking fare collection from individual legs of a trip by a single user. The result was ultimately the "Single Ticket," which not only resulted in convenience but effectively created a fare collection system in which shorter trips subsidized longer trips and enabled a bureaucratic mandate within municipal government to strip the responsibility for fare collection from private operators. Instead, the municipality could assert meaningful control over the planning and design of the bus system by centralizing fare collection and guaranteeing remuneration to operators. This was further entrenched by reforms under a center-right coalition government in the late 2000s that integrated the bus ticketing system with the state-run subway system. A broad political and social embeddedness became the basis for growing bureaucratic cohesion to administer a collective transportation system that was increasingly available as a public good.

Johannesburg: Leading with Technology

By 1989, South Africa was on its way to a negotiated settlement that would lead to the country's first direct democratic elections. But at that time, Nelson Mandela had not been released from prison; many political parties, including the ANC, were still banned; and "rolling mass action" under the banner of the United Democratic Front roiled urban townships across the country. And in the transportation sector, for much of the 1980s, the informal minibus, or *kombi*, had grown to displace formal collective transport funded by public authorities.

In 1986, the National Party's new president, F. W. De Klerk, appointed a new minister of transportation, Eli Louw, who immediately set about negotiating a program of "deregulation" to incorporate the wholly informal black-owned taxi sector. The newly formed South African Black Taxi Association was soon pleased with commitments by the national government to legalize the operations of most of their members and cited two key challenges for a broad "deregulation" policy: "giving the commuter the best choice in terms of having completion on the one hand; and flooding the market and making the industry unprofitable for everybody" (McCaull 1990, 57). The former was the goal; the latter, the fear—both potentially associated with an increase in the stock of minibus taxis on the road, hence the need for some institutionalized form of regulation.

The goals for the taxi sector articulated during the last days of the Apartheid regime would cast a long shadow over the development of policy for collective transportation in Johannesburg as the country moved into an era of political democracy. The São Paulo experience helps to contextualize why "deregulation" was not as simple as the South African Black Taxi Association made it seem. It is not clear at all, for example, that consumer "choice" is a particularly useful metric for considering the distributional questions at stake in the provision of collective transportation. The price and timing of transportation were even more extreme to begin with in Johannesburg in comparison with São Paulo, despite the sprawled and highly stratified spatial structure of both cities.

Darko Skrbinsek, a leading consultant to the taxi industry in Johannesburg and neighboring cities for two decades, worked as a senior advisor to the taxi sector on its negotiations with the city of Johannesburg during this period. He described the initial post-Apartheid relationship between the government and the taxi sector as one of profound ignorance:

> Especially twenty years ago or so, there were very skeptical government observations. Especially given the history of South Africa and [the taxi sector] being a black economic sector during the Apartheid regime. Obviously, there was quite a remote, distant relationship between the government and them. Except that they get licenses through the government. But as far as [taxi operators] being controlled or [government] having any information about them, there was basically nothing. Government didn't know anything about them, except that they see them on the road. So this was the whole concept of the minibus taxi industry development conceived during the Apartheid period and the regulation of public transport. . . .

That is where they opened the doors for the informal sector and, if I can say, illegal from a licensing point of view. Anybody who knows somebody can have any type of vehicle in a black township. It is obviously a tool to earning income.[26]

The role of informality as a defining characteristic of the minibus taxi sector meant that it was perceived as fundamentally outside of the realm of meaningful formal regulation. While less-used formal bus systems and a commuter train continued to operate, the dominant role of minibus taxis in transporting the city's residents meant that most residents were only able to access a transit service in which the state was absent.

As the city began investing in black township areas in the mid- to late 1990s, the taxi sector was stuck in a dangerous spiral of incentives. There was no way to stop new entrants, other than a very thin government licensing regime that focused on the quality of the vehicles used (and even then, it was not considered to be very stringent). This licensing regime enabled a linear, growing trend of unplanned deregulation: Competing taxi cartels continued to expand their fleets in order to capture ever thinner slices of a captive market (Sekhonyane and Dugard 2004). The need for collective transportation was growing as the city's new employment centers sprawled further into the northern and western suburbs, while black townships in the southern and eastern parts of the city likewise mushroomed.

Unlike neighborhood civic associations focused on rights to housing and basic services, taxi associations in Johannesburg were less explicitly political organizations. To a large extent, this has significant parallels with the sector of perueiros in São Paulo, who likewise formed cooperatives that had informal personal ties to politics but never articulated a programmatic political agenda. And as in São Paulo, a decline in formal employment increased pressure for informal employment in the collective transport sector. Even so, in Johannesburg, the regulatory environment for taxi drivers and especially owners had quickly become much less structured.

Furthermore, post-Apartheid efforts at reforming the transportation sector had been preempted by the broader deregulatory actions of the late Apartheid era. Eric Motshwane, a former taxi driver and taxi association leader, also described the entrenched interests of legacy leadership in the taxi sector: "The industry operates almost like the mafia. Remember that there is power that these guys have got. If you have leadership, you have power. You have absolute power."[27]

When I asked Motshwane how this power was exercised, he responded in stark terms:

I can take it to the extreme. I have absolute power almost equal to God, because you can decide who dies and who lives. You make the call. You want Ben killed, you just decree. Then he is killed. That is how much power they have. They collect monies. They exercise authority—who can operate where, who cannot operate where. So they wanted to cling to those traditional tactics, because they saw democratization of the industry as a threat. It was going to dilute their power.[28]

The result was increasingly brazen and deadly violence. The so-called taxi wars that began in the late 1980s were national in scope, imbricated in the dividing lines of internecine violence that had threatened to plunge South Africa into civil war in the 1980s. The *New York Times* would later refer to these "taxi wars" as "one of the strangest guerrilla wars to bedevil any nation" (Wines 2006), replete with opaque informants, spies, and double agents. Police associated with the National Party government—the party of Apartheid—were frequently accused of fomenting divisions, and central Johannesburg, Soweto, and the adjacent municipality of Ekurhuleni were among the flash points across the country (Sekhonyane and Dugard 2004). In one of the most comprehensive and early analyses of these taxi wars, Dugard attributes the violence to a decline in formal governing capacity, finding that "as the state's control over the economy and society has weakened in the course of South Africa's transition, taxi associations have developed as informal agents of regulation, protection and extortion" (2001, 3).

The national government aimed to get some modicum of control over the taxi sector by proposing a "recapitalization" program that would replace the fleet of vehicles operated by taxi owners. Taxi owners, organized into associations with frequently contested legitimacy, were resistant, insisting on much higher subsidies for replacing their vehicles. This had a powerful logic. The taxi sector had never received any meaningful public subsidy. And the offer on the table offered no guarantees for the sector's operational costs, which is where operators and owners saw the most pressure, given the oversupply of service providers.

To a significant degree, the unruliness of the dominant mode of collective transportation in Johannesburg's peripheries resembled the rise of the perueiros in São Paulo. In both cities, there was an increase in structural informality and economic recession, which produced pressure for the expansion of employment opportunities in the sector. Both cities also saw an uncontrolled expansion of routes, leading to turf wars, and an increasing role of organized crime and violence.

Despite these similar contexts, however, beginning in the late 1990s, we can make out distinctly divergent paths in the two cities' approaches to governing the dominant mode of collective transportation. As we saw in previous sections, São Paulo pursued an "institutional" path, focusing on reforming the governance of the transportation sector to enable better service. This later enabled subsequent reforms to the built environment and fare collection technologies used in the provision of collective, road-based transportation. The result was a bus system that retained and grew its user base and which extended deeper into the most excluded parts of the city. In Johannesburg, municipal authorities took the fateful path of pursuing changes in the built environment and fare collection technologies first. This produced a new formal bus system that was largely irrelevant to users of collective transportation in the city.

Even with basic conflicts of the taxi sector still largely unresolved, the city of Johannesburg began to develop plans for the introduction of a brand-new transportation system, anchored by bus rapid transit. This would reserve lanes of the road exclusively for the use of new buses, with new stations located on the sides or medians of roads, and would use an all-electric ticketing system that would not require human ticket collectors.

The origins of these plans were not in the desire to emulate the city-building standards of rich world cities, despite the increasing association over time of the BRT project to Johannesburg's marketing tagline, "a world-class African city." Rather, the roots of the BRT project were in the confluence of two lines of pressure, one homegrown and one a matter of south-south policy transfer.

As the city of Johannesburg was consolidated into a single metropolitan municipality at the end of the 1990s, the National Land Transport Act gave cities a mandate to develop their own transportation plans, as well as providing funds for "recapitalization" of the minibus taxis used in the sector. The city was furthermore reorganized through the iGoli 2002 project in the wake of the fiscal crisis of the late 1990s. This led to the creation of a new department, the Department of Transport Infrastructure. Bob Stanway, who became the first executive director of this department in 2003, told me that when he began his job, the taxi sector immediately began putting pressure on the department to provide lifetime operating permits. Taxi owners and operators felt that this was their right under laws instituted during the chaos of drawing up regulations amid the transition to democracy in the mid-1990s. "They had to be consulted with and convinced that, you know, that things have changed. Regulated competition has come in rather than competition by the barrel of a gun. That they have to start moving towards providing services that people need rather than what they think," Stanway said. "Very difficult times. Very, very difficult times."[29]

Under the leadership of Mayor Amos Masondo, the city used the transportation portfolio to move beyond its traditional hands-off approach to the taxi sector. With the provincial government increasingly taking on responsibilities for the taxi permitting process, the municipal government's role in transportation had largely been confined to the city-owned, self-governed entity of MetroBus. This was an Apartheid-era holdover of a small bus system that was designed to serve designated white areas of the city.

In 2002 and 2003, the city's Department of Transport Infrastructure spearheaded the Strategic Public Transport Network (SPTN) as part of its Integrated Transport Plan, the first municipal transportation plan in the country to take up the mandate of the National Land Transport Act. According to Stanway, the primary goal of this plan was to develop road-based infrastructure "to serve the existing users. In other words, to serve the existing taxis and buses."[30] In transportation planning lingo, this was the first "demand-driven" (Harber and Bryer 2020) approach to collective transportation in the city since the end of Apartheid.

The SPTN coupled this approach with a spatial planning emphasis, through an intention to focus on land development—both residential and commercial—along transportation corridors and to link transportation policy to a broader land use policy. In theory, this would signal a significant degree of cohesion across line departments to plan comprehensively for the city.

The SPTN framework included dedicated lanes for taxis and buses, new traffic light signaling protocols, and new sidewalk and median infrastructure. Masondo's successor as mayor, Parks Tau, was a member of Masondo's mayoral cabinet when the framework was developed and said to me that implicit in the SPTN approach was that much of the regulation of the taxi sector, including the issuance of operating licenses, would also be devolved to the city level. While the SPTN did not include any operational subsidy for the taxi sector, Stanway emphasized that the national government had begun subsidizing capital costs through its "recapitalization" program. Recapitalization was designed to upgrade the existing fifteen-seat "combo" vehicles that would be granted operating licenses. "We actually got budget, and we were already a year down the track with implementation on the Strategic Public Transport Network, and then came that quasi BRT thing."[31]

Johannesburg: Shifting to BRT

While there are competing narratives about why "that quasi BRT thing" emerged onto the policy agenda in the city, what is clear is that it was structured by a distinct case of international policy transfer. What was being transferred was the technology. The assumption of what Mkandawire (2009) has referred to as "institutional monocropping"—the transfer of institutional models across highly different contexts without contextual adaptations—was not far behind. What Johannesburg's experience with the adoption of bus rapid transit illustrates is that "context" is not merely the "soft" social ephemera that surrounds hard technological change. Rather, "context" is precisely the socio-institutional interface that preceded efforts at technological reform in São Paulo and which was treated so often as an afterthought in Johannesburg.

Masondo's first mayoral term began at the end of 2000, at the beginning of the unified, "unicity" Johannesburg municipal government. His administration was marked by planning for international events that he hoped to use as catalysts for major urban development projects. Reforming the transportation system was a priority, which he indicated by making the transportation portfolio a stand-alone in his cabinet, separate from both environment and development planning.

Rehana Moosajee was the ANC city councillor whom Masondo nominated to the transportation portfolio in his mayoral cabinet. She described entering into the portfolio after the city had encountered major resistance from the taxi industry to attempts by the local government to introduce MetroBus service into Soweto. This meant that one of her first tasks was to build a rapport with a notoriously prickly taxi industry that had just been in conflict with the city of Johannesburg. And new pressures were emerging.

At the annual South African Transportation Conference in 2005, two international consultants presented examples of BRT in Quito, Ecuador, and Bogotá, Colombia. As Johannesburg was preparing to be the epicenter of the country's FIFA World Cup showpiece in 2010, the municipal government was looking to fast-track transportation upgrades in anticipation of an avalanche of tourists and media attention.

As a result, Moosajee helped coordinate a "study tour" to South American cities for the leading organizations in the taxi sector—known informally as the "Top Six"—and the Gauteng Regional Taxi Council, as well as officials in the municipal Department of Transport and those responsible for coordinating the city's World Cup hosting responsibilities. Such a trip held the promise of integrating the concerns of the taxi sector with government efforts to introduce a brand-new design of public transportation in the city. As Moosajee described it to me,

> Pretty much from that trip, I think the sense was that this is doable for South Africa and it's doable for Johannesburg. Yes it's not going to be easy, but it's an interesting model in terms of moving the industry in relation to their transformation. So in November 2006 the city council took the decision to, at least for the first corridors of the SPTN, to then look at fully fledged bus rapid transit.[32]

This framing of the rationale for BRT emphasizes that the institutional challenges associated with the taxi sector were perceived as the key problem with moving to this technological framework for public transportation. The whole project was understood quite clearly as being about "moving the industry in relation to [its] transformation," in the sense of how it operated organizationally. But the solution to this "transformation" was framed in terms of a technological shift to BRT, not in terms of integrating the incumbent taxi sector into the "transformation."

I followed up with Moosajee two years after our initial interview, and she further described the rationale driving city politics in pursuit of the BRT model:

> Mayor Masondo was very clear that what we were driving as a city was transformation in the interest of the commuter, which we could only get through relationship with the minibus taxi sector. So almost I would say, his thinking and vision was, I mean, not using them per se, but they are means to a bigger end. That they're not the end in itself.[33]

This second interview puts a finer point on the nature of thinking around the move to BRT. The vision was all about what worked best for bus riders.

On one level, this is wholly understandable. Why shouldn't the user of the service be the first priority? But this thinking represented a mode of policy-making that aimed to bypass organizational realities. As Skrbinsek put it, "The key risk factor has been identified as how to approach or how to incorporate the taxi industry into this new system. Now, they didn't provide any solution to it. They didn't provide any suggestion to it."[34]

For decades, the taxi sector had been pushing either to keep working in the shadows of formal regulation or to be further incorporated on the basis of meaningful operational support, not just onetime subsidies for capital costs. An operational subsidy would have put the sector on a path similar to that of São Paulo, where a public agency managed the remuneration of profits to operators.

At the same time, this sector had proved its capacity to respond to user demand, which we can observe by dint of its sustained popularity. Local government, increasingly distant and at loggerheads with the taxi operators, surely understood the sector's structural importance. But it lacked both the will and the capacity to build the kinds of ties that might enable informed policy to bring the sector into a formal organizational relationship with the city *at the city scale*.

Ultimately, the introduction of BRT as the primary transportation priority in the city came to be seen as a reversal of the priorities embedded in the SPTN approach. Lisa Seftel, who served as the executive director of the transportation department, was a critical voice regarding BRT despite having presided over the department charged with leading the implementation of key components of the policy. She argued that the single-minded view of politicians and government toward the taxi sector, focusing on the capital component of transportation policy, blinded them to the potential operational risks of BRT.

> The compelling things about the BRT were the speed, the so-called price— so long as you put in the capital infrastructure, the operations can pay for themselves, which is a lot of absolute hogwash, as we have found out—and,

thirdly, the transformation process. You know, it was very compelling to say that you can make minibus taxi operators public transport operators.[35]

Realizing this third point—taxi operators becoming public transport operators—became a critical impediment. The taxi sector had barely bought into the since-abandoned SPTN approach and was dead set against the introduction of competition in the form of BRT.

As Motshwane put it to me, "We didn't even take them seriously. Because remember there was no history between us and local government, and we didn't see them having any teeth to bite, unless they came along with the provincial government."[36] This was because operational licenses, as well as capital recapitalization subsidies, were being granted through provincial government.

It was therefore a meaningful innovation that a negotiation structure emerged between the city government and taxi operators. These negotiations arrived at a model that bypassed the question of operations altogether. Instead, taxi operators were offered shares in a new public bus company. This suggested a degree of financial security, but it was also predicated on an insistence that taxis remove their vehicles from the road. Taxi owners and operators would have diminished power in the operations of transportation in the city.

In theory, this may have seemed attractive. But it relied on the basic assumption that running an untested public transportation technology would necessarily operate at a meaningful profit. Public transportation systems across the globe are rarely profitable. Moreover, the spatial structure of Johannesburg was particularly forbidding for the economics of BRT operations. In order to be profitable, BRT systems typically require what are called "origin-destination" trips, across all or at least most stops on a given route. The distance of historically black townships to economic centers meant that origin-destination trips were much longer and more concentrated on a few specific stops at the very beginning and end of a given route. For example, few people ever have a need to get off a bus when traveling from Soweto to Johannesburg's central business district, as there is little business activity or employment between the two locations. As Seftel described it to me in 2015, "[In Johannesburg], there is hardly a public transport corridor that is servicing more than six thousand people in the peak. You should not be introducing BRT unless you can get ten thousand people in the peak."[37]

The priority of technological change over institutional reform created its own path dependency. In September 2009, less than a year before the World Cup was due to begin in South Africa, the country's leading business daily newspaper, *Business Day*, published an account that illustrates the mainstream framing of the relationship between the taxi sector and the BRT:

The Rea Vaya Bus Rapid Transit (BRT) project hit a wall from the start, with the taxi industry doing almost everything possible to stop its launch. . . .

The system—modelled on Bogotá, Colombia's TransMilenio rapid bus network—so far runs services between Ellis Park, Soweto and the inner ring of
the Johannesburg CBD. The nearly 1500 Bogota buses carry over 1m people
a day. Though this is a far cry from the 8000 daily passengers Rea Vaya is
transporting, the SA [South Africa] system is but an infant. (Hill 2009)

These kinds of accounts juxtapose the twin imperatives of institutional change
and technological change without ever acknowledging their potential contradiction. In essence, readers are being told that BRT should work in Johannesburg but for the taxi industry's intransigence. The institutional challenges
that precede a technological shift become an afterthought.

As the BRT system began to roll out, however, these contradictions continued to deepen. The pressure to have at least some part of the BRT operational
prior to the World Cup in 2010 meant that negotiations with the taxi sector had
additional pressure. While some, like Motshwane, became integrated into the
BRT operations as both a shareholder and the manager of a bus depot for the
Rea Vaya system, the taxi sector as a whole was largely excluded from the new
formal service that was being introduced. The first BRT line to begin operating
was between the CBD and the newly remade "Soccer City" stadium in Soweto.
This was primarily serving match attendees and little else. The Rea Vaya's focus
on ordinary commuters from the city's peripheries would only come later.

The divided spatial structure of Johannesburg made the distinctive roles
of "trunk" and "feeder" routes in bus lines particularly important. "Trunk"
describes longer-distance trips, such as those between Soweto and the CBD,
while "feeder" describes trips between neighborhoods in the same part of the
city. Yolisa Kani, who managed the BRT project in the lead-up to the World
Cup, described the thinking within the city on how taxis might fit into the
operational model of the BRT overall:

> The buses were meant to replace the taxis, even though people will not
> confess as such. Because we talked about the trunk line and we talked about
> the feeder routes, which are still meant to be the smaller buses. But we
> realized we can't afford that. Then we went back to [the idea that] maybe
> the feeder can also be a taxi.[38]

Ultimately, this idea—where taxi operators would be incorporated into a
hybrid system that included both formal buses and more informal vehicles—
was overtaken by the need to get the system functioning and servicing customers with its primary technology—the bus—as the sole operational mode.

Block grants from the national government were complemented by user fees
and municipal block grants to the operations of the BRT. Kani told me that she
proposed an additional municipal gas tax to generate a dedicated revenue stream
outside of ticket sales. However, there was no political appetite for this, let alone

a more redistributive financial model, such as a dedicated portion of property tax, as was often debated in São Paulo for its public transportation system. The upshot of all this was that the operational side of the BRT was going to depend on user fees without having a clear path to capturing meaningful user demand.

Irrespective of whether we interpret the lack of incorporation of the taxi sector into the operational dimension of the BRT in Johannesburg as due to disinterest, lack of capacity, or something else entirely, the limited scope for negotiation produced a distinct dynamic. Skrbinsek described the logic that often prevailed in taxi associations: "Traditionally, the associations are territorial organizations. I'm just here to protect the territory of my members, of my routes. I can even talk to a rival taxi association's chairman and say, 'Let's create the conflict.'"[39] The prevalence of unlicensed taxi operators produced revenue streams that heads of taxi associations were unable to claim in negotiations with city authorities. While taxi associations saw their operations largely in terms of defined territories of the city, the municipality saw their operations in terms of physical vehicles and was only concerned with getting those vehicles off the road to make way for BRT routes.

The comparison with São Paulo's negotiations with the perueiros is again instructive. In São Paulo, perueiros were organized into formalized cooperatives that largely preserved existing territorial monopolies. In Johannesburg, the goal was to integrate taxi owners and operators into newly defined routes and technologies that bore little resemblance to the existing institutional arrangements of the taxi sector. When the World Cup was over, the BRT had not expanded beyond the lines to be used to get to and from soccer stadiums. By 2012, the municipality had negotiated stakes of ownership in the BRT system for only a limited group of taxi-sector leaders.

Motshwane was one of them. As he ascended the ranks of the leadership of the regional taxi sector, he became frustrated with the industry's political economy. The provincial government issued operating licenses with seeming abandon, flooding the streets with new vehicles and putting ever more pressure on the margins of individual taxi operations. This, in turn, underpinned the ever-present threat of violence in the sector. "This flouting of the rules . . . causes all these problems," he told me, referring to the overly permissive licensing regime of provincial government. "Where there is a discussion about taxi violence—no one, but no one will allude to flooding and saturation of the taxi industry as a catalyst."[40]

Sojane Modise, a veteran high-ranking official of the Gauteng provincial Department of Transport's registration and operation licensing division, emphasized that the provincial licensing practices had always been quite distinct from the Johannesburg municipality's BRT system. Taxi sector leaders, as well as leading officials in the provincial and municipal departments of transportation, all emphasized that the historic connection of the taxi sector to government was not through municipal leaders but, rather, through the provincial government's role in issuing operating licenses.

> Whatever has been happening with the bus rapid transit has not included province to any significant [extent]. It has just been more information to say, "This is what we'll be doing." The only little, you know, interaction has been to say, "Once we start with the bus rapid transit, we don't want to have competition on the route."[41]

Modise argued that this put the provincial government in a particularly weak intermediary role, without any sort of authority for planning routes.

Motshwane described his evolution as a deep skeptic of the role of local government in trying to make a deal with the taxi sector. "First of all I would be concerned about my power, my culture, then my safety. Although I am not guilty, even if you come across anything that is aligned with government, you just get killed." Given this degree of fear, Motshwane saw moving into the BRT program as effectively dropping one career and starting another; this was not about a gradual evolution within the same commercial space.

When I interviewed Motshwane in 2017, he insisted that BRT was fundamentally separate from the operations of the taxi sector. I include here the verbatim back-and-forth to give a sense of how this was rationalized:

> MOTSHWANE: Remember, the [Spatial Planning Transit Network] was not bringing any mass transit intervention. It wasn't bringing any mass transit intervention. It wasn't creating any job opportunities. It wasn't bringing any transformation as such. It was more to have dedicated clients where the taxis would travel much more faster. But it wasn't an intervention as far as the missions are concerned and cogency is concerned.
> BRADLOW: Yes. But when you say it wasn't a mass transit—
> MOTSHWANE: Intervention.
> BRADLOW: Intervention. I mean, two-thirds of the city that uses public transport was using taxis. Even today. Do you not consider taxis as mass transit?
> MOTSHWANE: Not in the sense of bus rapid transit.

This conceptual divide between "mass transit" and collective transportation would continue to bedevil transportation policy in Johannesburg. Mass transit came to be identified with a specific technology, the new BRT buses whose routes were being constructed around the city. Even Motshwane, a former leader in the taxi industry, came to view that previous life as wholly separate from his work for BRT.

The city would continue to roll out BRT lines haltingly in the wake of the 2010 World Cup. The initial phases of development after the tournament provided service into neighborhoods in Soweto, bringing users as far as Parktown, one of the historically established inner-ring suburbs in the northern part of the city. In 2016, as Mayor Parks Tau prepared for an ultimately unsuccessful reelection campaign, the city announced plans to extend the service to Sandton (Venter 2016).

In fact, the extension of the BRT lines through the northern suburbs of the city to Sandton had long been planned prior to 2016. But those plans faced resistance from ratepayers' associations, largely on the basis of NIMBY concerns. The story of the city improvement districts and strategic alliances between largely white neighborhood associations and property developers that we saw in the chapter on housing development highlights that this resistance had deep roots. Resistance to the BRT in the northern suburbs coalesced around preventing the installation of a BRT line on the Oxford Road corridor, which runs through some of the most established and well-heeled suburbs of the city and connects the main business districts of Sandton, Rosebank, and the historic CBD.

The municipality responded to this resistance by shifting its plans for expanding the BRT northward, moving the route from Oxford Road to Louis Botha Avenue. In October 2011, it set up a typical conflagration with the Alexandra Randburg Midrand Sandton Taxi Association, which was looking to protect its territory. In describing resistance to BRT extension, especially in the northern suburbs, Tau emphasized this connection between neighborhood associations and developers:

> It would have been those that felt they have the most to lose out of it, out of the implementation of the corridors of the initiative. Interestingly, the emergence of groups in the city that essentially would have wanted to maintain the status quo with a bit of cosmetic changes.[42]

The Alexandra Randburg Midrand Sandton Taxi Association claimed that it had not been consulted by the municipality prior to this decision. A newspaper report in the city's leading daily newspaper, *The Star*, underscores the continuing divide between the municipality and taxi associations:

> Mayoral committee member for transport Rehana Moosajee said the decision was made only recently, and consultations would start soon. She said Alexandra taxi association representatives had been involved in the planning of Rea Vaya since 2006 and had been taken on a tour of Bogota in Colombia to see the model on which the Rea Vaya system is based. "There will be further full consultation with them," she said. (Cox 2011)

By the time Tau ran for reelection, campaigning on the "corridors of freedom" mantra, which emphasized the role of the BRT in transforming the city, he faced persistent criticism that for all of the branding, little had been achieved with Johannesburg's mass transit system. Taxis remained the dominant player in providing collective transportation to most residents of the city, and the extent and nature of their regulation had barely budged. While the BRT had continued to extend northward, few were convinced that the emphasis on the new system had achieved goals around reducing the fundamental spatial and social distance between Johannesburg's peripheries. Tau described the persistence of debates within the ANC about how to use BRT as part of a broader redistribution-oriented political program:

> Its more than the BRT, it's more than human settlements, it's more than commercial settlements; it's about building an integrated city that's better functional, more urban efficiency, that enables efficiencies in the context of the white city paradigm that those residents of the city, those residents and users access to the amenities that cities are supposed to provide. So, it's a much more comprehensive, I think, contextualization of what we should do, as opposed to limiting ourselves to transit.[43]

Ultimately, the conceptualization of transit itself—as a system solely built around the new BRT lines instead of one incorporating existing infrastructure and operators—hindered a capacity to shape transit policy toward these broader objectives. Transportation came to be seen primarily through the lens of introducing a new technology with international cachet—the BRT. Taxi drivers, the historic social and organizational basis of collective transportation in the city, were held at arm's length. The perception of illegality and violence associated with the industry—perhaps correctly—meant that it was not treated as part of a broader tapestry of governing transportation in the city. Instead, it was a sector the city government needed to overcome and buy off. In turn, the taxi sector's deep-seated interests in territory and its wariness of public-sector involvement in its operations intensified its antagonism toward public policy reform. The loose, provincially run regulatory regime that flooded the roads with new entrants produced razor-thin operating margins and further raised the stakes of the changes introduced by city government. Matjila's enthusiastic claim in 1989 that "the taxi industry has reached the limit of its development as part of the informal sector" turned out to be wildly naive. Despite the transition to democracy, the dominant mode of collective transportation in Johannesburg would remain in the shadows.

Conclusion

Because the geographic distance between working-class neighborhoods and employment centers in São Paulo and Johannesburg is so vast, the importance of collective transportation to broader projects of urban transformation in these two cities cannot be overstated. It is also clear that the issues these cities have faced in terms of governing collective transportation are not unique. The growing peripheralization of poverty in large cities and metropolitan regions across the globe makes the transportation sector a critical focus for understanding contemporary urban inequalities.

By 2019, São Paulo's bus system carried 7.5 million people per day (Municipality of São Paulo Secretariat of Urban Development 2019, 6). Because Johannesburg's minibus taxi sector is largely informal, there are no official statistics on who uses it or how many people it transports; a widely cited report by a private business consultancy has estimated that 75 percent of people nationally use minibus taxis daily. And in Johannesburg, annual fare price rises for taxis regularly outpace those for every other mode of transport, including BRT (Transaction Capital 2019).

For a policy sector that is primarily subject to highly technical analysis, the contrasting trajectories of policy reform for collective transportation in São Paulo and Johannesburg carry important implications for how we think about institutions and history in this sector. Prioritizing reform of the institutions of the bus sector allowed São Paulo to develop ties to key actors in the sector that built trust that the public sector was not out to displace the interests of existing informal operators. In Johannesburg, a focus on technological change to a bus rapid transit system failed to build that trust.

And yet, this divergence was not inevitable. Johannesburg had begun developing a transportation planning framework—the SPTN—which we could easily imagine putting the city on a trajectory similar to that taken by São Paulo. The confluence of an international consultant–driven emphasis on the BRT technology and the rush to produce "world-class" infrastructural outputs in advance of the World Cup tournament certainly did not help matters. Especially given these pressures, the city lacked the capacity to mediate relationships with the dominant provider of collective transportation to conceive how taxi operations could fit into a formalized city-wide transportation network.

São Paulo also could have prioritized a technology-led direction. The city of Curitiba, a global "best practice" case of BRT implementation, was not an ocean away but, rather, a state away. When I would describe my research for this book to many of my informants in Johannesburg's transportation sector, invariably they would mention Curitiba. However, São Paulo took an approach that it had first developed in its housing sector reforms: a focus on directing resources and institutional attention to informal approaches that were being tested in peripheral neighborhoods.

São Paulo's capacity to first recognize the core organizational issues that impeded reform in the sector enabled it to then negotiate reforms that allowed the city to get control over fare collection and remuneration. This was made possible by the combination of politicians with long-standing ties to informal operators and a corps of technical bureaucrats who were willing to deploy their expertise behind the negotiations undertaken by their political principals. Only then was it possible to redesign the system itself, integrating informal perua operators in the far peripheries with central city bus operators into a single network. Embeddedness produced cohesion.

This development of institutional capacity rested on interpersonal ties between actors in the informal sector who were able to broker formal deals that focused on reforms in the operational sphere. Johannesburg, too, has brokered deals with the taxi sector. But these moves have all remained in the sphere of sporadic "recapitalization" and ownership agreements. To this day, there is no strong formal control over the operational conditions of the taxi sector.

In fact, Johannesburg attempted to sidestep these operational conditions altogether. It opted to introduce a new technology of collective transportation, hoping to entice taxi owners and operators into a brand-new relationship. All of its bureaucratic energy was dedicated to the creation of an entirely new system. There was no attempt to even try to wield coordinating capacity in the sector of public transportation that dominates daily life in the city. And the lack of engagement with the sector on its own terms produced a lack of embeddedness that could not generate any kind of subsequent cohesion along the lines of the São Paulo case.

Ultimately, the comparison of the priority on institutional reforms in São Paulo and the priority on technological reforms in Johannesburg suggests that these are aligned to distinct configurations of embeddedness and cohesion. A focus on institutional change in the bus sector in São Paulo was rooted in embedded ties between political elites and their base in the peripheries. This produced a series of attempted policy reforms that slowly built the bureaucratic cohesion to eventually implement reform. The focus on technological change in Johannesburg, by contrast, attempted to bypass the work of cultivating and deepening similar embedded ties to the informal taxi sector. The result was institutional fragmentation.

5

Sanitation

COHESION VERSUS COMPETITION

Both São Paulo and Johannesburg are landlocked cities. But their geography is shaped by water. São Paulo was built on the banks of the Tieté and Pinheiros rivers, which split the city vertically and nurture the coffee fields that first gave rise to the city's riches. Johannesburg has been sustained by the nearby Vaal River Basin, the primary runoff site of the Witwatersrand reef, home to the mines that give the city its isiZulu nickname, eGoli—the "Place of Gold."

If housing is the quintessential residential public good, and transportation is the quintessential networked public good, then sanitation occupies a complicated middle ground between the two. It is residential by virtue of it being a good that is ultimately delivered to individual homes. It is networked by virtue of its physical infrastructure—pipes that carry clean water to and dirty sewage away from homes.

On the other end of the delivery of the service lie the governing institutions responsible for those pipes. In both São Paulo and Johannesburg, new constitutional orders that came about as a process of democratization decentralized the final responsibility of delivering sanitation services to municipalities. In the wake of this change, the nature of sanitation as a networked good presented particular difficulties in navigating the institutional terrain of delivery. While municipalities were now responsible for the ultimate delivery of water, they also had to coordinate a range of agencies organized at scales above the municipal level, as well as multiple institutional combinations, including quasi-private governing arrangements. As we will see, sometimes this was due to choices made by city governments, and sometimes this was due to choices made beyond the city's control.

The divergent levels of success of São Paulo and Johannesburg in housing policy were largely due to the existence or absence of embedded ties between housing movements and local government bureaucrats. The residential component of housing made it a strong target for movement pressure. When it came to transportation policy, São Paulo's relative success and Johannesburg's relative failure were due to their respective priorities on institutional or technological change. As a network good, transportation was relatively more insulated from sustained social contestation, and the conceptualization of problems concerning how to coordinate the good within the bureaucracy mattered greatly.

Sanitation occupies a middle ground, in relative terms, in the degree to which it is open to social contestation. Of the three goods examined in this book, sanitation is well suited for disaggregating the coordinating dynamics—what I have called "cohesion"—that remain internal to state action. My core argument emphasizes that both embeddedness and cohesion are critical to generating urban power, the coordinating power necessary to realize more equal distributive outcomes in cities. This chapter recalls the fundamental lessons we first encountered in chapter 3. The extent to which both sanitation policy and housing and land use policy prioritize informal settlements in overall urban policy is rooted in the embeddedness of the local state in civil society.

As we will see, it is difficult to fully disentangle this chapter's focus on sanitation policy from chapter 3's focus on housing policy due to the land use laws that link the two. This means that as we look closely at issues of sanitation, the embeddedness of the local state in housing movements is never truly absent from the action. Even so, the institutional arrangements for delivering sanitation services—sewers, pipes, and toilets—are quite different from those involved in housing. In fact, one of the most distinctive aspects of this sector among the three analyzed in this book is the central role played by delivery agencies with vast degrees of autonomy. This autonomy produces a structural challenge for these delivery agencies to be accountable to municipal priorities—precisely those that emerge through embedded ties. As a consequence, the basic institutional conflict is how municipal governments can coordinate to ensure that the provision of sanitation services by independent delivery agencies reflects social embedded priorities. Cohesion, both vertical and horizontal, takes center stage.

This chapter examines the following question: How did São Paulo manage to generate downward, municipal accountability of a state-level sanitation company for slum upgrading, while Johannesburg struggled to generate the same type of higher-level support for its municipal sanitation priorities? I argue that São Paulo made institutional accountability to the municipal scale an explicitly political project, using new national mandates to strengthen the role of local government in directing the priorities of the state-owned sanitation company. In contrast, Johannesburg saw itself as being in competition with provincial and national mandates and therefore struggled to harness political demands for more equitable distribution of sanitation services.

São Paulo: "You Sign This Service Contract on Our Terms"

The sanitary conditions of São Paulo's favelas were truly dire as the country transitioned to democracy. In 1991, only a quarter of informal settlement households had access to a toilet, according to a recent analysis of the country's first post-transition census (Marques and Saraiva 2017). At the same time, the state of São Paulo was home to a crown jewel of the many state-level water and sanitation companies across the country, the Companhia de Saneamento Básico do Estado de São Paulo (Basic Sanitation Company of the State of São Paulo), known by its Portuguese acronym, SABESP. During the authoritarian era, a range of state-level institutions had been empowered with primary planning authority for infrastructure provision, often organized by the state-run São Paulo Company for Metropolitan Planning. These institutions aimed to rationalize large-scale urbanization through comprehensive metropolitan-scale planning (i.e., above and beyond the scale of municipal government).

The assumption of relatively centralized planning for sanitation was buttressed by the organizational culture of SABESP. The company has long been considered a prestigious post in the public sector for top civil engineering graduates. Additionally, the raft of economic reforms pursued under Fernando Henrique Cardoso's presidency (1995–2002) included the partial privatization of the company. In my interviews with a range of both senior executives and lower-ranking officials at SABESP's headquarters compound in the upscale Pinheiros neighborhood of São Paulo, invariably my informants would make a reference to the fact that 49.8 percent of the company's shares are traded on the New York Stock Exchange. This was to underscore the degree of market discipline to which SABESP officials felt accountable. The contrast was implicit but unmistakable: *Other water and sanitation agencies answer to a diffuse and perhaps even undefinable array of mandates. SABESP, due to its obligation to shareholders, is transparent and measurable.* The ethos of depoliticization and efficiency as a consequence of privatization has been common across a number of state-level sanitation companies across Brazil (Cruxen 2022). And it is of a piece with a broader set of trends toward privatization and decentralization in water and sanitation management across the developing world (Herrera and Post 2014).

The effect of SABESP's depoliticized attitude would shape its relationship as a state-level agency with the municipality of São Paulo. Mário Reali worked as a senior official in the city's municipal government and served as the mayor of Diadema, one of São Paulo's adjacent municipalities, between 2008 and 2012. In his description of the relationship between SABESP and municipalities, he focused on the almost coercive control the state exerted over the decisions that could be made at the city level: "The relationship that this company [SABESP] has with municipalities has been with a party line of 'Look, either you sign this service contract on our terms, or you won't have any investment [in sanitation services].'"[1] The state-level water and sanitation company would answer to its own internal priorities—and those of its shareholders.

This presented clear challenges for coordinating a more equal distribution of sanitation services across urban space. The deep sense of operational autonomy that characterized SABESP was a fundamental block to any kind of vertical cohesion in municipal coordinating authority. Even if the city wanted to make particular changes, those were beholden to the structural leverage that was controlled at the state level.

In 1988, once the Workers' Party won mayoral seats in São Paulo and a number of neighboring municipalities, the question of control over sanitation policy was a critical one. Effective upgrading of favelas seemed to require a significant reprioritization of management and planning. The neighboring municipalities of Santo André, São Bernardo do Campo, Diadema, and Mauá all established their own municipal sanitation companies. Reali, who ran Diadema's municipal sanitation company in the early 2000s, described why these were always a precarious administrative proposition, despite their seeming political advantages:

> Look at the contradiction. The municipal company bought water from SABESP—the state company. And the distribution and collection of sewage required paying a tax to SABESP. So why was this more expensive? Because there was no regulation of the price of bulk water. And the price of bulk water was huge. It accounted for half of the [Diadema municipal sanitation] company's revenue.[2]

To run a separate municipal sanitation company that was ultimately reliant on SABESP meant providing a service that was inevitably more expensive than having SABESP responsible for the municipal service.

When Erundina entered the mayoral office in São Paulo in 1989, her administration, like other PT administrations in the São Paulo metropolitan region, had a great degree of skepticism about the role of SABESP in supplying water and sanitation services to city residents. But while SABESP was relatively willing to accept the creation of municipal water companies that bought its services in smaller cities, losing direct control over water provision in the state's capital would have been a major blow to the company. From the perspective of the Erundina administration, the new mayor was also facing a number of concurrent challenges in service provision, such as those enumerated in the previous two chapters on housing and transportation. The risks of creating a new municipal company were great.

I interviewed Erundina's secretary of finance, Amir Khair, in his home office, where, directly behind his desk, he displayed a photo of himself with Erundina on the night she won the internal party primary to contest the mayoral seat in the 1988 elections. At the time, Khair was seen as a relatively orthodox financial manager within the PT, independent of the traditional corporatism associated with the party's union leadership but also not a leftist firebrand. He described to me how Erundina's administration, as it thought through its relationship with the state-level SABESP, pursued a middle-ground strategy in its approach to governing sanitation distribution. Unlike neighboring municipalities, the administration decided that the primary goal in São Paulo was to ensure that favela residents would be able to pay a heavily subsidized "social tariff" to SABESP, lower than the regular tariff paid by other city residents, instead of trying to take over the direct provision of services.[3]

At the same time, the emphasis of Erundina's administration was to find ways to upgrade and formalize favelas so that they could access SABESP services. And much of this work was not conducted through sanitation policy but, rather, through housing. As we saw in chapter 3, housing was largely an autonomous arena for local government, and the Erundina administration felt empowered to pursue its own policy agenda in that particular sector. But extending sanitation networks to favelas was a much thornier interscalar proposition, and it would still require the municipality to strike deals with a state-level agency in order to get anything done.

Erundina began with the Guarapiranga Reservoir, which would later become a focus of attention of housing policy during the Serra and Kassab administrations (2005–12). A program called "SOS—Dams" (SOS—Mananciais) was the result of an agreement between the São Paulo state government and the Municipal Housing Secretariat to provide sanitation infrastructure (Kfouri 1995). Begun in 1990, it established two key principles of action. First, the favelas near water reserves, especially in the south, were in particularly dire need of sanitation services. Second, the extension of services by a state-level agency such as SABESP would be done in conjunction with housing policy at the municipal level. The focus on extending services to the most excluded parts of the city was unequivocal. However, a World Bank report on the Guarapiranga upgrades argues that one of the deficiencies of the project was the "low level of cost consciousness and lack of an explicit cost recovery and subsidy strategy" (Imparato and Ruster 2003, 63). The World Bank report poses the orthodoxy of full cost recovery for an independent provision of service against the redistributive goals that animated the Erundina administration's efforts to extend sanitation services.

The willingness to work with the state-level SABESP, despite these tensions, was a legacy of the Erundina administration's divergence from her party's mayoral colleagues in neighboring municipalities. While neighboring municipalities opted to focus on creating a new set of institutional arrangements to escape the perceived strictures of SABESP's operations, the Erundina administration instead chose to carve out space for the city's peripheries within SABESP's existing operational approach. Given the lack of dedicated municipal funding for operating water and sanitation services, Erundina's administration could only hope to ensure that subsidy and cost-recovery arrangements were not overly onerous for favela residents.

As it was in the sphere of housing policy, we see how Erundina prioritized her administration's embeddedness in the demands of movements based in the favelas. But in terms of water and sanitation policy, her administration during this period lacked fiscal and legal authority to provide water and sanitation services directly. In a city as large as São Paulo, with massive, immediate needs, experimenting with an independent municipal service provider was much too risky. As a result, her administration deprioritized efforts at seizing direct implementing authority. The result was an administration that was largely a "mobilizational regime" of high embeddedness and low cohesion. While it was deeply engaged with the concerns of people on the ground in the favelas, it lacked a more institutionalized coordinating authority to deliver new services to them.

Constrained financial resources at all scales prevented the new program from achieving significant outcomes while Erundina was in office. But improvements to sanitation remained part of the public discourse around favelas throughout the years of the Maluf and Pitta administrations (1993–2000). Instead of the in situ slum-upgrading projects of the Erundina years, marked by self-build mutirão projects, the focus more generally shifted to new housing construction in the peripheries. The Maluf and Pitta–era "Cingapuras" focused primarily on new "greenfields" locations, often built near favelas. Sanitation conditions in these high-rise buildings were a marked improvement, at least for those able to move into the new developments.

For much of this decade, SABESP's work in the Guarapiranga Reservoir aimed to emulate aspects of the mutirão project approach pioneered by housing movements and municipal officials during the Erundina administration. This form of in situ upgrading combined improvements to dwellings with provision of basic services and often enabled new water and sanitation infrastructure to be built where people were already living. This is generally complicated by the frequent need to move housing structures in order to install pipes, which requires significant degrees of trust enabled by high community participation in mutirão projects. The need for "sociotechnical facilitation" was a critical element of project design, which was based on World

Bank–supported "best practices." Within the municipality, this expertise was located in the Department of Housing, drawing on the department's experiences in neighborhood-based slum-upgrading projects. Even so, SABESP operated with limited support for this kind of state-society interface. As the World Bank would later argue, "The motivation for community participation for Guarapiranga's sponsoring agencies was to ensure the feasibility of the project's implementation" (Imparato and Ruster 2003, 63). This soon fell by the wayside, and the municipality turned to a series of private-sector contractors to manage the vast majority of the work.

We can interpret SABESP's role during this period in two ways, which are not necessarily in contradiction. On the one hand, the internal bureaucratic coherence of SABESP, a state-level agency, allowed it to be a relatively effective administrator in a context of weak municipal authority. Service to existing residents connected to the water infrastructure network was reliable. On the other hand, its internal coherence shielded it from a broader state-society interface that could enable a more embedded form of institution-building. These two faces of SABESP's work on slum upgrading in the 1990s are telling, especially in light of the proof of concept for a more movement-driven approach to both the hard outputs of delivering residential public goods and the "soft" outputs of municipal institutional capacity.

Hélio Castro, who worked as an administrator at SABESP for twenty-five years, described the company's governing arrangements as having been traditionally focused on the water basins that it used to service its customers. Key water sources in the São Paulo metropolitan region were the reservoirs in Guarapiranga, Alto Tietê, and Cantareira, and SABESP's administrative organization was designed around these different water reserve systems. But it is critical to understand that, in the 1980s, this meant that the agency was not being organized around any clear principle of service delivery.

Castro described how SABESP's internal administration had shifted by the end of the 1990s. Now, in addition to it being organized around the geography of water reserves, additional divisions were made along the lines of service responsibilities, such as water treatment, water distribution, and sewage collection. The provision of different kinds of services was now a basic organizing principle of SABESP, as opposed to just managing different geographies. While this would have significant implications for realizing more equal distributional outcomes, it was seen within SABESP as a purely technical change: "There was a contract with a consultant who did an analysis and identified that a more efficient administration would be to divide on the basis of service processes."[4] It would take a major federal government reform to more effectively empower the dynamics of decentralization that would open up the municipal institutional sphere for more embedded forms of building sanitation capacity.

São Paulo: Central Action to Decentralize Control

From the perspective of delivering sanitation services, the administration of Marta Suplicy kept the city in a relative holding pattern. Echoing Erundina, her administration reengaged housing movements in a shared project of local institution-building. This was especially the case in housing policy, where the municipal government had clear roles, responsibilities, and funding. To the extent that housing policy alone could coordinate effective delivery of sanitation services, we can understand the Suplicy administration from 2001 to 2004 as a significant contributor to that project.

The more significant contributions during this era, however, came from the many São Paulo–based activists and bureaucrats who were involved in the project of building a set of federal urban policies that could cascade down to the municipal level. This project was set in motion once Lula's presidential administration inaugurated the Ministry of Cities upon coming to office in 2003. This new ministry was divided into three secretariats—housing, transportation, and sanitation—and each of them was designed to develop national legislation that could produce a new enabling environment for municipal government action. A national sanitation plan was deemed an urgent priority due to the dire state of sanitation services across the country. If the condition of favelas in the large, sprawling cities of Brazil's wealthy southeast was of concern, the situation was much worse in the cities, towns, and villages of the much poorer northeast. Even today, approximately half of all Brazilian households are not connected to a sewage network (Garcia 2020).

Many of the functionaries in the Ministry of Cities had experience in the experiments São Paulo's neighboring municipalities undertook to run their own municipal sanitation companies. These experiences underscored two issues: (1) the need for some modicum of municipal control in order to reprioritize sanitation investments in the most underserved areas and (2) the need for federal regulatory support in order to do so. The rationale for municipal control was relatively well established, if not unanimously agreed upon, but the need for regulatory support to realize this control was much less clear.

Brazil's City Statute of 2001, which was passed by the federal government soon after Suplicy assumed office in São Paulo, established the municipal master plan as a mechanism of asserting municipal authority over questions of the distribution of urban public goods. While many of Brazil's largest cities dragged their feet in producing master plans of their own, the Suplicy administration quickly made use of the City Statute to introduce planning tools that relativized the right to private property through the zoning tool of Zonas Especial de Interesse Social (ZEIS, or Zones of Special Social Interest). The São Paulo example showed that even very large cities could use the plan to begin realizing the goals of the "right to the city" intended to be regulated through statute.

The Ministry of Cities pursued a related strategy in its attempts to make the constitutional right to sanitation a reality. The National Sanitation Law of 2007, which was part of a broader delineation of the functional roles for different scales of government in providing basic sanitation, required municipalities to produce city-wide sanitation plans. To this day, the majority of municipalities in Brazil have not done so, but as it was with the City Statute's requirement that municipalities produce city-wide master plans, São Paulo was one of the first movers in producing a Municipal Sanitation Plan.

On June 18, 2009, the municipality passed a law requiring the development of a city-wide sanitation plan. The plan published the next year bore the general seal of the municipality—not the seal of an individual department within the municipality—thereby emphasizing its cross-departmental significance. The plan itself refers to a wide range of departments that were understood to take on essential roles in the delivery of sanitation in the city, including housing, urban development, social assistance, public works, environment, urban security, and the coordination of submunicipal governments.

In the document, the centrality of housing, and slum upgrading in particular, is unmistakable. They are listed as the first priorities in the plan, which refers to the range of preexisting programs intended to benefit from the additional planning authority of the municipality for sanitation. The upgrading of slums near water reserves, such as Guarapiranga, is described as being of particular importance, due to the intersection of its social and environmental consequences:

> The need to upgrade and regularize *favelas* in the areas near the reserves that supply the Billings and Guarapiranga dams is urgent and cannot be delayed. The Guarapiranga region is the most problematic. More than a million people live there, many of them in precarious conditions. Studies by several organizations focused on environmental preservation have highlighted the need for upgrading these basins, which, if neglected, will compromise the entire water supply in the city of São Paulo. With part of the resources coming from the World Bank and another part from the São Paulo municipality, the Program has already served thousands of families in the Guarapiranga reservoir basin and is now working at Billings. The Mananciais Program is considered strategic by the municipal government. The program is coordinated apart from the urbanization program, as it is an action developed jointly with the state government, with the central objective of restoring the water quality of the Guarapiranga basin and, now, in 2008, also of the Billings basin. (Municipality of São Paulo 2010, 45)

This emphasis is surprising for two reasons. First, while this plan directly linked housing and environmental concerns, housing activists and members of environmental movements have historically been estranged in São Paulo, owing in large part to the distinct class and racial profiles of these movements: Housing movements are largely working class and nonwhite; environmental activists tend to be educated professionals and white. Second, during a supply crisis four years later, the state government would use the scarcity of water in the city as the basis for highly unequal rationing of water distribution (Aldana Cohen 2016). This occurred despite a rhetorical insistence by the state government that such rationing was not, in fact, occurring (Millington 2018).

SABESP is generally considered to be sympathetic to the politics of São Paulo's state government, which the center-right Social Democratic Party of Brazil has controlled in every election since 1994. From the perspective of interscalar political alignment, the combined timing of the National Sanitation Law in 2007 and the passage of the city's sanitation plan in 2010 was fortuitous. The National Sanitation Law was passed in the third year of the PSDB coalition's mayoral rule in São Paulo, right in the heart of what I have described previously as São Paulo's "integrationist" regime of urban governance. By that point, many of the redistribution-oriented goals that had guided the administration of public goods had taken root beyond partisan boundaries.

This sequencing meant that by the time the municipality was preparing its own basic sanitation plan, it had significant hands-on experience with the urban upgrading programs that would become central to the plan. Maria Teresa Diniz, a deputy in the housing department led by Bete França, argued that the agency's work during the Serra and Kassab administrations ended up delivering sanitation infrastructure to many more people than during the previous PT administration of Suplicy. "When we began working in SEHAB [the Municipal Housing Secretariat], I began to work there while Bete França was the superintendent. There already existed a new housing plan that had been completed during Marta [Suplicy]'s administration," she told me. "This was in the beginning of the Serra administration. But it had been done in a way that we Brazilians call 'within the office.' Meaning that the team of the previous housing secretary had not participated in the production of the document."[5]

While I was not able to corroborate this claim with officials from the Suplicy administration, the key point was that the entrepreneurial team of bureaucrats that surrounded França had a distinctly protective sense of ownership over policies that would otherwise have been associated with their predecessors. França, who had experience with the World Bank's involvement in Guarapiranga in the late 1990s, moved quickly to make the extension of sanitation infrastructure to slums, particularly in and around the Guarapiranga Reservoir, a centerpiece of her department's approach.

França spearheaded some of the most difficult slum-upgrading projects in the city's history, focusing on a number of the largest contiguous zones of informal settlements in the city's southern zone, near the Guarapiranga Dam. These projects were particularly problematic because of the technical challenges in delivering new water and sewer infrastructure in extremely dense, low-lying neighborhoods right next to a body of water. Upgrading informal settlements in the Guarapiranga Reservoir had previously been deprioritized in SABESP's work. The company, which maintained sole control over planning for the extension of new infrastructure, had instead focused exclusively on preserving water quality in the dam itself.

Now, however, the city's Basic Sanitation Plan linked the two as equal priorities. The plan continued to emphasize the priority of water quality but placed this in the context of upgrading the informal settlements in the reserve. In effect, the plan provided a bureaucratic administrative mechanism for linking SABESP's long-standing work in the area to a revived focus on the residential conditions of those living in the city's most excluded neighborhoods.

The focus on slum upgrading in the Guarapiranga Reservoir had been broached since the Erundina administration. And it had a renewed emphasis under Suplicy. But with the combination of new funds through the Ministry of Cities established in 2003 and regulatory power from the National Sanitation Law of 2007, França was able to act. Her housing department focused on incorporating informal settlements into the city's formal infrastructure. The National Sanitation Law and the city's Basic Sanitation Plan were significant enablers. The housing department could now push SABESP more effectively to deliver services to what were some of the most marginalized informal settlements anywhere in the city. França also oversaw the establishment of a new geospatial data management system within the municipality, which created a mechanism for prioritizing informal settlements by vulnerability on a systematic basis.

In addition, new funding streams for this upgrading work were part of the changing institutional alignment between SABESP and the municipality. The city's Basic Sanitation Plan drew on the provisions for municipal authority for sanitation planning to ensure that this happened. Importantly, the city established a new slum-upgrading fund that would be seeded with 7.5 percent of SABESP's gross revenue from operations in the municipality. This new fund, called the Fundo Municipal de Saneamento Ambiental e Infraestrutura (FMSAI, or Municipal Fund for Environmental Sanitation and Infrastructure), was designated for use by the housing department, thereby ensuring that the new funding mechanism would bind sanitation planning to the broader residential upgrading remit of the housing department (Municipality of São Paulo 2010, 220–21). The logic of the FMSAI built on that for the fund for urban development, which had relied on dedicated funding streams from local property taxes for slum upgrading and had been established as far back as Bonduki's leadership during the Erundina administration. In both cases, new funds for slum upgrading within the municipal housing department relied on capturing the profits of urban public goods delivered by the state-level SABESP on market principles.

In 2009, the federal Minha Casa, Minha Vida (My House, My Life) program was inaugurated. The program subsidized private contractors to develop affordable homes. Due to pressure by housing movements, a smaller carve out of this program enabled federal housing subsidies to go directly to housing movements and cooperatives. As funding streams directly to municipal governments became less flexible, the FMSAI provided a much-needed source of municipally held funds for residential upgrading. It ensured a downward flow of funds to the municipal scale that enhanced local government coordinating capacity. After the PT's Haddad took office at the beginning of 2013, a regular drumbeat of press releases emerged from the municipality, touting its work in areas with large informal settlement populations. A typical press release announcing the construction of 492 new houses for favela residents in the southern slum of Heliópolis trumpets, "In six months, the Sanitation Fund invests 36 million (reals) in works in Heliópolis." The text emphasizes that FMSAI funds were critical to augmenting the existing funds the municipality used for urban development (Municipality of São Paulo Municipal Housing Secretariat 2013).

In the case of FMSAI, this new fund could have become a one-way resource grab by the housing department, which might have de-emphasized slum upgrading for greenfields housing development. But the Basic Sanitation Plan furthermore required that the housing department produce a plan, known by its Portuguese acronym PARFMSAI, for the use of these funds. The plan was approved by a committee composed of representatives from sectoral participatory councils made up of civil society representatives. One with consistent representation in the governance of the FMSAI has been the Municipal Housing Council, which has had the regular participation of housing movements. Furthermore, this plan was to be shared in a new institutional forum made up of representatives from both the municipality and SABESP, called simply the Management Committee.

Taken together, the reforms associated with the FMSAI contributions created new lines of accountability in a relationship that had been perceived by both sides—the municipal government and SABESP—as largely unaccountable. The internal coherence of SABESP had shielded it from the priority-setting procedures of municipalities across the São Paulo metropolitan region. This autonomy had long generated resentment and incapacity in upgrading sanitation conditions in the most vulnerable parts of São Paulo. The Management Committee created a space for joint planning for the extension of water and sanitation services. Furthermore, the National Sanitation Law had established, for the first time, an independent regulatory authority that would govern SABESP's actions.

The evolution of these two institutions, FMSAI and the Management Committee, is a useful window into the extent to which federal legal reform from above created the space for downward accountability. At the same time, it is worth underscoring the extent to which SABESP, an agency with high technical capacity and a strong corporate culture, could push back against this new bureaucratic system of accountability. In large part, this power imbalance can be chalked up to the fact that SABESP was managing a relationship with a municipality with comparatively more diffuse technical capacities and only new institutions with which to engage with it. SABESP, by contrast, had built up years of institutional coherence and bureaucratic savvy on the details of administering water and sanitation services.

The Management Committee established through the municipality's Basic Sanitation Plan was composed of voting representatives from both the municipal and state governments. SABESP representatives sat in on all of the meetings, though it did not have any voting power on the committee. Sandra Gianella, who represented SABESP in these meetings for the vast majority of their existence, was emphatic about this division of responsibilities: "SABESP is a service provider for the municipality. So it doesn't vote on decisions. It has a voice. It expresses its opinion. But it doesn't vote. The state and the municipality decide all strategic questions regarding the investments of this committee."[6]

Embedded in Gianella's characterization is the notion that SABESP, despite not having a formal vote, was still able to express its priorities. Informants from both the state and municipal government who participated in these meetings told me that this informal influence remained substantial. SABESP's technical advantage meant that, as the municipality's service provider, it was able to frame conversations about what was and was not possible to achieve in terms of extending services to the most difficult-to-reach areas. Furthermore, the historic political alignment of the state government and SABESP meant that municipal officials perceived that the state government was particularly favorable to the views of SABESP in these Management Committee meetings. For example, a set of internal documents from the Management Committee in 2017, which were shared with me by a SABESP participant in the meetings, included an organogram of subcommittees that would deal with technical issues. Each of the four subcommittees was made up of one member from the municipality and one member from SABESP; representatives of the state government were not involved.[7]

While state officials provided a buffer from the persistent power of SABESP, it was incomplete. Denise Lopez de Souza, who served as the executive secretary of the FMSAI in the municipality during the Haddad administration, described an example of the type of conflict that could arise between the city government and SABESP:

There are certain interventions that we [the municipality] need, and sometimes, say, it will require the removal of a sewer pipe. I am channeling a stream and then I have an existing pipe that I need to relocate. Only this pipe is already an existing asset for SABESP, which SABESP had installed. So this is an investment that will burden SABESP right now, and they had not scheduled or prepared to deal with it, or planned to make an investment in this area. But without removing this pipe, the municipality's work is not viable. So we have a planning conflict, right? And we need a solution. So this solution can produce delays, which will impact related contracts that one or the other party has.[8]

Lopez de Souza's description illuminates why the creation of new lines of accountability through the redefinition of SABESP's role as a service provider to the municipality was so important. Coordinating plans creates the opportunity to align investment priorities. The case that she described seems rather quotidian, and seemingly something that all parties should want to resolve, but without an alignment of investment planning and decision-making, one can easily imagine how independent bureaucracies would be unable to overcome a potential failure of institutional collective action.

Lopez de Souza further described a form of "vertical cohesion" as central to the operational innovations in the management committee model. "The meetings of the Management Committee are an opportunity for the state, municipality, and SABESP to be seated where many issues that were previously dealt with in isolation in SABESP's regional offices, and which did not have a solution," she told me.

Previously, if the regional office [of SABESP] says something is not possible in order to meet a specific need of the city, it was not possible—period. Now this need is articulated at a higher level, which has the power to deliberate and even to say, "SABESP must plan and will respond."[9]

Lopez de Souza's portrayal of the municipal government as being a "higher level" of accountability is telling. This suggests that the reorganization of institutional roles, first envisioned in the National Sanitation Law, created a sense of municipal authority over SABESP that did not previously exist. Castro described the precise nature of this authority in his similar account of how the Management Committee functioned:

The Management Committee for the contract is made up of representatives of the contracting authorities, which are the state and the municipality, and representatives of SABESP. So, today, the representatives of the contracting authorities, the state and the municipality, define what should be done. And SABESP does what has been defined. It is logical that [SABESP] participates in the definition of what should be done because it has the expertise to say, "Look, it's important to install a sewer line here." *But at the end of the day, it's the municipality of São Paulo who says, "Look, I want you to first install a sewer line here."* So SABESP comes to the municipality of São Paulo and responds, "Look, in order to install a sewer line there, I need the municipality to remove these houses that are in the way because I don't have the legal authority to do that." It's the municipality that has it. In this way, they deliberate together to define what should be done in each area.[10]

In both Lopez de Suza's and Castro's descriptions, we clearly see a recognition of the mutual interdependence of the institutions involved. At the same time, we get two different takes on where power lay. According to Lopez de Souza, SABESP had to be responsive to the municipality's planning and normative goals. But according to Castro, SABESP's technical goals were the overriding concern. In this sense, it was not only the legal assignment of roles envisioned in national law that redrew lines of accountability to the municipality. Rather, it was the creation of shared institutional spaces such as the Management Committee of the municipal contract with SABESP, as well as civil society participation in the oversight of the FMSAI, that made it possible to link formal lines of accountability to practical institutional action.

An additional dimension of institutional reorganization, which the National Sanitation Law enabled, was the independent regulation of SABESP. Prior to the passage of the National Sanitation Law, SABESP set its own prices and monitored its own service quality through an in-house department. This arrangement was viewed as presenting natural conflicts of interest. SABESP was frequently subject to concerns that its services were overpriced, and this view only grew as SABESP was subjected to the profit discipline of international markets after its partial privatization and listing on the New York Stock Exchange in the early 2000s.

Shortly after the passage of the 2007 law, a new regulatory authority for the state of São Paulo was established. This authority, the Agência Reguladora de Serviços Públicos do Estado de São Paulo (Regulatory Agency of Public Services São Paulo, known by its Portuguese initials ARSESP), was grafted onto the Public Service Commission for Energy, which the state had established ten years earlier. Castro, the SABESP veteran who would become the director of ARSESP, described the evolution of utility regulation as follows:

SABESP was the institution that did the planning, it self-regulated, it did its own fiscal oversight. With the Sanitation Law of 2007, the law began to insist on a contractual relationship, in which contracts were executed through a service solicitation and a service delivery provider. This clarified roles. The granting authority is responsible for planning. *So it is the municipality that says, "Look, I want my city to universalize water and sewage by 2030." And it [the municipality] decides who will provide services in the city.* Or it can go to the state government and say, "State, I am delegating to you the delivery of services in my municipality." And the state has an executive arm, which is SABESP. So it says, "SABESP, you go to this municipality to provide a service." And then it has a regulatory arm, which is CSPE [the Public Service Commission for Energy].[11]

Using the Public Service Commission for Energy as a precursor meant that ARSESP was modeled on the basis of the national electricity regulator. However, ARSESP had an additional responsibility of managing contracts, which placed it much closer to the operational side of utility delivery than is often the case in utility regulation.

While this new arrangement was designed to establish an arm's-length regulatory institution, the creation of ARSESP helps explain the weaknesses of the reforms that the National Sanitation Law brought about. Along with ARSESP's close involvement in the administration of contracts, its upper echelons were perceived to be dominated by ex-SABESP officials. Castro's own trajectory to the leadership of the regulator is an exemplary case in point. Informants in both the municipal and state governments reported that this meant that contract oversight was not perceived to be entirely independent.

Even with these obstacles, the new degrees of planning autonomy that the National Sanitation Law ensured for municipalities dovetailed with the range of reforms and growing planning capacity. These had enabled housing policy innovations like the ZEIS, which accelerated efforts to upgrade slums. A recent comparative study of eighteen municipal sanitation plans by large and medium-sized cities in Brazil found that São Paulo was one of three cities (along with Belo Horizonte and Blumenau) to rank the most comprehensive in the range of sanitation interventions envisioned in its sanitation plan. São Paulo was also one of six municipalities in the sample to have approved a municipal legal framework to govern sanitation policy. And it was the only city to have created an institutional setting for civil society participation in sanitation policy—the council dedicated to oversight of the FMSAI funds used for slum upgrading (Pereira and Heller 2015).

The Erundina administration's early attempts to pursue slum upgrading that would extend the distribution of sanitation services to vulnerable, informal areas of the city relied on extremely circumscribed authority and resources. In contrast, PT mayors in neighboring municipalities attempted to assert new authority over sanitation planning without the resources and institutional cohesion to put that authority into effective practice.

The São Paulo case suggests that building vertical cohesion has been particularly important for generating meaningful coordinating authority. A legal route for institutional reform tends to emphasize the assignment of authority as the critical determinant for delivery. This was the route taken by some of São Paulo's municipal neighbors, to ambiguous effect. The practical challenge of governance, especially for the complex delivery of public goods such as sanitation, is not just the assignment of authority but the coordination of it. In São Paulo, legal reforms to assign new responsibilities to the municipality were not actually the proximate source of its authority. Rather, it was the fact that these reforms enabled the creation of new institutional spaces for deliberation and planning that, in turn, made this authority real and practicable. In other words, cohesion required embeddedness in order to generate meaningful coordinating authority—urban power.

Johannesburg: Autonomy without Authority

In South Africa, the experiences of colonialism and Apartheid bequeathed a behemoth of centralized delivery of water and sanitation in Johannesburg. Before democratization and the end of Apartheid, the city was planned on the explicit basis of both segregation and population control, with weak and divided local authorities split between white and black areas of what is now the single Johannesburg Metropolitan Municipality. But during that same time, the delivery of water infrastructure was under the full control of the Rand Water Board, an independently governed public entity that had managed the Vaal River Basin since 1903.

The push to decentralize much of basic service delivery was first broached in the "Water Supply and Sanitation Policy" White Paper of 1994 (Republic of South Africa Department of Water Affairs and Forestry 1994), as part of the range of service delivery white papers produced during the transition to democracy. This white paper placed a strong emphasis on cost recovery, which resulted in an operational model that often conflicted with the goals of universalizing access to water and sanitation services. The self-sustainability of financing water and sanitation delivery was potentially in conflict with the imperative to universalize access, which implied a strong need for subsidies to poor urban residents with little capacity to pay (Millington and Scheba 2021). The eventual legislation based on the white paper, the Water Services Act of 1997, specified the relationship between water boards and municipalities along lines that were comparable to the relationship between the state-level sanitation companies and the municipalities in Brazil. According to the act, water boards such as the Rand Water Board were designated as "Tier 1" institutions, which described their role as the primary provider of bulk water supply. Notably, the role of municipalities in providing household-level services was much greater than that envisioned in the design of Brazilian institutions. From the outset of democracy, municipalities in South Africa were to be the primary supplier to end users.

While it took until 2007 in Brazil for municipalities to gain clear responsibility for planning the delivery of water and sanitation services, from the beginning of democracy in South Africa, the new constitutional dispensation envisioned this responsibility to lie with municipalities. The role of the Rand Water Board in driving policy change was therefore much more passive than SABESP's. The new constitution made clear that water boards in South Africa were providers of bulk services for plans that would be developed and implemented at the more decentralized scale of the municipality.

At first glance, this appears as though it would have put Johannesburg in a more advantageous position than São Paulo to overcome similar obstacles in the provision of sanitation services in informal settlements. If municipalities are more attuned to the needs of informal settlements, then presumably a municipal responsibility for providing sanitation services would be more likely to prioritize those needs. However, mere institutional responsibility is not the same as strong coordinating capacity in practice. The latter requires configurations of external embeddedness and internal cohesion that can wield the planning and implementation apparatus of the municipality toward universalizing the service. Here, I document how Johannesburg's relative autonomy was undercut by a series of management reforms that splintered lines of accountability and ultimately made it more difficult for local government to coordinate effective implementation. As a result, even today, Johannesburg's capacity to deliver sanitation services to the city's most excluded parts remains remarkably stunted.

The early 1990s were a period of large-scale delivery, especially of the services that were easily visible and easy to deliver. The early focus on road paving and the electrification of Soweto, for example, drove significant capital outlays. These were counterbalanced by the strategies of elites to "ring-fence" property taxes, made possible by the fragmented nature of transitional arrangements of municipal governance, particularly the municipal substructures.

The fiscal crisis of the late 1990s became a crucible for urban management that created path dependencies to which the municipality would continue to respond throughout the period under examination here. Jay Bhagwan, a veteran senior researcher in the national Department of Water and Sanitation, described the pressures of the settlement patterns of urbanization that dovetailed with these capital investments in historically underserved areas in the city's far reaches:

> What happens is that because you now have a fairly new population that is poorer, that is informal, that is starting to occupy your peripheries, servicing them is expensive. Because now you need a lot of cash to build infrastructure that is not closely connected to all the other stuff.[12]

Public officials were not only contending with the capital needs of overcoming Apartheid-era segregation in access to basic services. They also had to contend with the growth in new peripheral settlements due to the end of Apartheid laws governing population controls. The challenge for water and sanitation delivery, therefore, became more broadly about the challenge of managing exclusion in a context of informality. Apartheid had actively excluded. Now, the inability to keep pace with informal urbanization produced a further, new layer of exclusion.

Abri Vermulen, who worked as an engineer in the national Department of Water Affairs and in the city of Johannesburg, described a typical view of this period from the perspective of water and sanitation professionals in the public sector:

> The townships were built sort of as a temporary residence, although it became permanent. But I think due to the control that was there, there was not that much, it was very controlled. So really sort of from the nineties the informal settlements really started because this whole urbanization thing was very tightly controlled on racial lines. Until all that went away. Then we suddenly started experiencing very rapid urbanization and particularly informal settlements.[13]

This understanding of growing urbanization and informality in the post-Apartheid period would frame the sense of urgency within much of the public sector throughout the period under examination.

As Kathy Eales, who managed the program of water infrastructure in the city of Johannesburg's Department of Infrastructure and Services in the mid-2000s, put it, "The key point about the informal settlements is that the government was counting backlogs. The pressure was on to reduce the backlogs."[14] In this sense, local government was keenly aware of the exclusions of informality in the city. These were articulated as "backlogs": in essence, a waiting list for water and sanitation infrastructure.

This all should seem quite logical as a matter of political priorities. But the capacity to integrate these priorities into the institutional arrangements for delivery was quite a different story. In fact, this pressure was being counter-vailed by substantial alternate forces—in particular, concerns of fiscal sustain-ability. While Johannesburg's municipal government was indeed concerned about backlogs, it did not have a very simple way to push out funding for new sanitation infrastructure (let alone maintenance) to informal settlements.

Johannesburg: Fragmented Vertical Cohesion

The Reconstruction and Development Program of 1994, which framed the national government's housing subsidy program, structured a persistent inter-scalar tension in the coordination of housing and sanitation delivery. While municipalities were responsible for delivering water and sanitation services, the housing subsidy was managed through the provincial government, which also had the primary responsibility for planning housing projects. This meant that municipal authorities were effectively chasing new housing projects that were being planned by provincial authorities as opposed to being able to integrate the delivery of these services themselves. RDP was the primary mode of delivering houses to people living in informal settlements; it was not a program to improve those informal settlements. And municipal government's efforts at providing sanitation to informal settlements were rarely aligned to provincial plans for the delivery of houses. Therefore, spatially targeted planning was particularly weak for water and sanitation delivery to the most excluded parts of the city.

Furthermore, area-based delivery strategies were not part of Johannesburg's approach to managing the water sector, which meant that sanitation provisioning was not coordinated across the geography of the city. The fragmentation of eleven submunicipalities in the transitional period after 1994 meant that responsibilities for delivering water and sanitation services were split across multiple departments. Plans for capital investment in one area of the city were not necessarily tied to a broader city-wide spatial planning approach, which meant that Johannesburg's financial planning was not aligned to a city-wide capital investment strategy.

As the fiscal crisis of the late 1990s became acute, the municipal government found itself in a situation where reforms to separate the administration of water and sanitation delivery into an independently governed entity looked particularly attractive. This meant establishing a series of municipal-owned entities that were supposed to have a separate governance structure. Along with City Power (electricity) and Pikitup (refuse removal), other MOEs involved in the delivery of public utilities, Joburg Water was established. While each of these MOEs was supposed to have a separate governing board, "the CEO of each of these entities was supposed to report through the board to the city," said Roland Hunter, Johannesburg's chief finance officer from 1999 to 2000. "The idea was that through these boards, the focused service delivery mandate would jack up performance."[15]

As the national government pressured the city to reorganize in response to the growing fiscal crisis, Khetso Gordhan was brought on as city manager in the municipality of Johannesburg to oversee the process that would result in the iGoli 2002 plan. This plan emerged through the so-called Committee of Ten of national and local government officials, which was headed by City Councillor Kenny Fihla as the political principal. According to the national Treasury's David Savage, the Committee of Ten looked to cases such as New York City's fiscal crisis in the 1970s as object lessons for city reorganization. As Savage told me, the MOE model "was pretty unique at the time, and it was quite deeply influenced by the kind of global narratives around New Public Management."[16] This referred to a set of principles for public administration designed to make public agencies run on private-sector tenets, such as being self-financed, performance-based contracting, and being subject to competition (see Kaboolian 1998).

Roland Hunter was hired by Gordhan to help drive this reorganization. The delivery of water and sanitation was given an additional reform dimension beyond those of the other MOEs: a service contract with a private contractor. A joint British-French firm called Suez secured a deal as a consultant to manage this contract, and Jean-Pierre Mas, a principal in the firm, became the temporary executive to oversee the service contract. According to Pascal Moloi, Johannesburg's city manager at the time, this arrangement was approved prior to the 2000 local elections, though it was only announced after the elections were held and Amos Masondo's victory as mayor was confirmed. This approval made Joburg Water the first MOE to have been formed as part of the municipality's restructuring process.[17]

The turn toward the MOE model had significant implications both for the distributional effects of water and sanitation policy and for governing capacity. The distributional effects were twofold. First, they helped spur the organization of a new, if short-lived, grassroots movement called the Anti-privatization Forum. The Anti-privatization Forum was born out of attempts to cut services in black township areas, especially Soweto, on the stricter cost-recovery administration of Joburg Water, as well as City Power. Second, the transition to an MOE-administered system raised the ire of the South African Municipal Workers' Union, whose members feared that the MOE's more privatized structure would reduce their bargaining power as public employees.

When I interviewed Mas, I asked him about Joburg Water's approach to planning for the extension of services to informal settlements. He quickly pivoted to the question of cost recovery from existing services:

> Another issue—and obviously that took us a lot of time—most of all was the revenue issue, the Soweto issue. That took a lot of time out of us. So when we saw the housing was that amount and the city didn't want to change anything. Obviously we didn't try to rock the boat on that issue, but we were not very happy with what was going on.[18]

Mas's reference to "housing" here refers to the widespread conceptualization within government of a backlog in housing delivery as the main contributor to the growth of informal settlements—because the city could not keep up with housing demands, residents were taking it upon themselves to erect their own houses. The key point is that informal settlements were largely outside the purview of Mas's early efforts to steady the finances of Joburg Water through a focus on its operational revenue streams. His emphasis on the "Soweto issue" referred to ongoing battles to recover rate payments from township residents for water delivery.

Even as Joburg Water was placing its focus on recovering operational costs, when it came to delivering sanitation services to informal settlements, the municipality was still aiming to extend services. Though the MOE was not directly answerable to the planning apparatus within the municipality, Joburg Water staff met regularly with their counterparts in the municipality's infrastructure and services department. Or at least that was the idea. "There was a meeting that was supposed to happen monthly, which I then said needed to happen fortnightly because it is never bloody happening. So let's give us two opportunities to not meet rather than one opportunity per month," said Eales.[19] Absent a tractable planning tool—such as the city-wide sanitation plan that helped organize the delivery of services in São Paulo—the authority between relevant departments for slum upgrading remained diffuse. This led to situations where housing projects were planned entirely separately from the extension of sanitation services. This resulted in situations such as that described by Eales in Orange Farm.

> EALES: Orange Farm was a big informal settlement—it is a big informal settlement in the south—and an area that has now been formalized is Stretford. That was the first place in Jo'burg to have prepaid [water] meters. It was a pilot site for a number of new technologies. Stretford was an area which, for me, it was just a constant nightmare. There were always sewer spills there. There were always, it was just disgusting, and it didn't take too much effort to find out the problem was that the housing contractor, I can't remember whether—yes, in fact there was one section where basically people's sewerage pipes just went into the ground and then it was a dead end.
>
> BRADLOW: So the shit was just going into the ground?
>
> EALES: Ja, and so basically it was a classic thing of somebody ate the money. They covered over the ground and they left. Now Joburg Water comes in and realizes they've got to do several cases of re-reticulation, who is going to pay? So it would be those kinds of issues.[20]

The case that Eales described highlights both the inability of the housing department to effectively manage its own contractors and the challenges posed by housing and Joburg Water working in an uncoordinated fashion. In this, Joburg Water's installation of bulk water and sewer infrastructure was not planned in concert with the city's plans for house construction. We can reasonably expect that a more coordinated project design would have more oversight over project management.

According to Eales, the lack of oversight in housing proved to be an endemic challenge for preventing petty corruption at the project level as well as coordinated planning for the municipality's infrastructure department and Joburg Water. As a result, the timing of house construction and water and sewer pipe installation was rarely in sync:

The housing manager—a nice person, impeccable [anti-Apartheid] struggle credentials—but just, she couldn't get her team to deliver. So always, Joburg Water was under pressure of, "How come services in this area are so disgusting in this informal settlement?" It is because we were told that the houses would be on stream by X date and we planned accordingly.[21]

The upshot here is that the planning and implementation of delivery for water and sanitation in the city lacked cohesion in both dimensions. The interscalar, or "vertical," dimension was fragmented due to the relationship between the Rand Water Board (responsible for bulk services), the city of Johannesburg (responsible for regulation and planning), and Joburg Water (responsible for service delivery). Each of these entities had its own separate governing structure, and they could not plan together. While Joburg Water was seen across the municipality as being effective in generating a cost-recovery model that was internally rational, it was not responsive to the municipality's broader planning apparatus for the extension of service.

Roland Hunter described a governance breakdown that enabled political appointees on the Mayoral Committee (effectively the mayor's cabinet) to bypass the independent governance structures of MOEs:

> The CEO of these [municipal-owned] entities was supposed to report through the board to the city. But the [member of the Mayoral Committee] just phones the CEO and bypasses the board, and they very quickly understood—the CEOs—that their real boss was the [member of the Mayoral Committee] and the board is actually fluff. That happened in all cases. Then all the good people started leaving the boards.[22]

Mas, the Suez executive who became the first CEO of Joburg Water, described a context of internal governance at the MOE that shifted significantly in the company's first five years:

> At the beginning, there was a big, I would say, a real partnership with the [Joburg Water] board. And they told us, "You have the responsibility of the management, you know the management better than us. Obviously we have got the political vision, whatever the strategy vision." Which is totally normal. At the end of the day, at the end of five years, I was seeing that the board was micromanaging far more. Far too much.[23]

The quick deterioration in independent governance can be seen as a response to the lack of political buy-in to the lines of planning accountability. The lack of cohesion in the water and sanitation sector created increasing fissures that could be broken wide open by political discontent. Hunter argued that the increasing conflict with the South African Municipal Workers' Union created pressure within the African National Congress to jettison the team in the city of Johannesburg that had led the iGoli 2002 reforms. Furthermore, while Joburg Water had formal governing independence, it could not bill for its services independently. Despite a separation of billing procedures for each consumer-facing MOE anticipated in the iGoli 2002 plan, the city of Johannesburg continued to collect a consolidated bill from consumers for water, electricity, and other city services. This incomplete independence paved the way for an incremental political weakening of Joburg Water's autonomy.

According to Hunter, Kenny Fihla, the leading elected official who was part of the core team, faced significant internal pressure that led him to not seek reelection as a city councillor. Likewise, Ketso Gordhan and Hunter himself were sidelined and left. Anthony Still, who would replace Mas as Joburg Water CEO, lamented this chronology, particularly the loss of Gordhan, who had championed the MOE model as city manager, the top-ranking executive bureaucrat in the municipality.

> When Ketso left at the end of 2000, he should have ideally been able to stay on another year. But once he'd sort of done his job and he gave birth to a baby without suckling it, you know. The politicians got a bit more powerful after. As the years went on they started rearing their heads again because they'd all been put on the back foot a bit. And they slowly got to rear their heads again, and so they were quite keen to get rid of Ketso because he was too powerful for them.[24]

The team that had spearheaded the reorganization of key service delivery functions of the city into independently governed MOEs had little staying power within the structures of the city government. The political pushback against the reform further undermined the independence of the intended governing structure of MOEs like Joburg Water.

It is worth pausing here to underscore how this situation varied from the São Paulo case. In Brazil, the municipality encountered a situation in which SABESP, the primary service delivery agency, was not accountable at all to a planning apparatus located within the municipality. Unlike Joburg Water, SABESP also had a strong internal bureaucratic culture and system of governance. And unlike the city of Johannesburg, the São Paulo municipality had a cohesive planning apparatus that was tied to a wide base of political support in broader society, particularly in the sphere of housing movements and their associated activist professionals. So while sanitation policy reform in São Paulo created lines of accountability from the service delivery agency to the municipality that helped build coordination and planning capacity within the municipal government, reforms in Johannesburg separated the delivery of sanitation services from the city's broader planning goals, thereby creating incentives for increasingly fragmented and captured governance. The key point here is that while sanitation policy appears to be a relatively insulated sphere of policymaking, the broader embeddedness of the local state in civil society was critical to the variations in the cities' cohesion within this specific policy arena.

The division between responding to political demands from below and administrative capacity was well understood within Johannesburg's city administration. Pascal Moloi, the city manager during Amos Masondo's first term as mayor, used the image of the "hourglass" to describe this division:

> MOLOI: We drew an hourglass between myself and Masondo. That he would deal with the superstructure, I'll deal with the substructure, with the infrastructure, okay. And—
>
> BRADLOW: The superstructure being?
>
> MOLOI: Being the body politic. And where the hourglass meets, that's my point of interaction with him, intersection with him. So no one in the administration would dare go through and deal with politics not through me, okay.[25]

Moloi alluded to a similar breakdown in the independent governance of MOEs, and Joburg Water in particular, as Hunter and Mas. However, his emphasis on the division between politics and administration underscores a critical missing element of the MOE structure. He described a situation in which department heads—top bureaucratic officials—frequently tried to develop direct ties with administrators of MOEs. In addition, at the time, court cases were pending regarding the illegal use of private consulting services to influence these relationships. My informants suggested that these allegations concerned irregularities that they understood to be quite likely true.[26] Likewise, members of the Mayoral Committee—political principals—were seen to be packing MOE boards with their own choices. This created incentives for petty patronage ties, as well as foreclosing pathways for broader social input. The mayor, whom Moloi described as the opposite end of the "hourglass," may have intermediated with society at a macro-level. But the broader institutional surface of local state-society relations was being shrunk through the fragmentation of administrative governance.

While the fragmented relationship between Joburg Water and the city of Johannesburg persisted into the 2000s, the national policy environment for extending services to informal settlements began to shift. The original Reconstruction and Development Program housing subsidy, which began in 1994, was seen as having created a fragmented governing arrangement, due to the fact that housing projects were conducted through provincial administrations, while municipalities were responsible for connecting houses to basic services such as water and sanitation. It also put a strain on capital budgets. The incentive structure of the individual capital subsidy model for housing meant that building on the cheapest land was most desirable. This produced a large number of housing projects—most of them poorly located and badly constructed—in peripheral areas of the city that often entailed the costly extension of basic service infrastructure, a cost ultimately borne by municipal governments (see Bradlow et al. 2011).

An alternative approach to slum upgrading, whether via the in situ approaches commonly used in São Paulo or via the "site-and-service" approach favored by World Bank programs in a number of African and Latin American contexts in the 1970s (Gulyani and Bassett 2007), was not part of the policy mix. Both the "brownfields," in situ approach and the greenfields, "site-and-service" approach rest on delivery principles of incrementalism. In the former, existing neighborhoods are upgraded where they are, progressively being drawn into the formal infrastructural networks of the city. In the latter, basic services are provided by the government, often without a "top-structure" house, on the assumption that new residents will build their own dwellings. In both modalities, a fully upgraded house with all basic services and individual land tenure is delivered over a period of time, as opposed to all at once. And as we have seen in the São Paulo case, the ability to deliver services to informal settlements without formalized, individual tenure rights has been a critical dimension of expanding options for the delivery of water and sanitation infrastructure. In Johannesburg, such an approach never took hold.

Johannesburg: Fragmented Horizontal Cohesion

By the mid-2000s, South Africa's national government reformed housing policy to enable more incremental approaches to upgrading informal settlements and improving basic services such as water and sanitation. The Breaking New Ground policy framework, promulgated through the national Department of Housing in 2005, aimed to create a policy environment that would enable incremental slum upgrading, with a focus on providing basic services on "greenfields" sites often prior to the delivery of an individual tenured house (Tomlinson 2006). The formal approach to in situ upgrading is delineated in the Upgrading of Informal Settlements Program, or UISP, which is contained within chapter 3 of the *National Housing Code* (Republic of South Africa Department of Human Settlements 2009). The UISP established a legal pathway for progressively formalizing informal settlements, with the goal of enabling the delivery of basic services.

However, informants in Johannesburg's housing department consistently emphasized that the project planning apparatus in the city remained focused on a housing-first mode of operation. Manny Sotomi, for example, a former director of housing in the city government, described an internal incentive structure whereby officials were evaluated on the number of housing projects that they "packaged," or conceptualized and managed, and the national government subsidies that they secured for those projects. Taken together, there is no clear incentive for prioritizing the delivery of services without first establishing the tenure rights that would enable the individual housing subsidy to be released. It is therefore unsurprising that by the end of my fieldwork for this book in 2018, nobody could point me to a completed project in Johannesburg that could be said to have used the provisions of the UISP. The upshot is that housing policy—which was focused on delivering completed houses that were also fully tied into the city's sanitation infrastructure—prevented the city from prioritizing incremental upgrading and delivery of basic services.

Instead, the focus on basic service delivery in Johannesburg moved to particularly lax targets set by the national government. Eales described an emphasis on the delivery of "chemical toilets," a form of porta-potties, or "VIP" toilets, which are slightly more permanent in structure and have better ventilation: "Government was counting backlogs, and backlogs were—you know, the pressure was on to reduce the numbers. Now how do you do that in an informal settlement? What we decided, the idea of what was better than all these ghastly chemical toilets was wherever possible put in VIP toilets."[27]

While there were cases where the city tried to install flush toilets inside homes in dense settlements in both Soweto and Diepsloot, Eales noted that the municipal government was unable to continue to invest in their maintenance. As a result, they quickly became inoperable. A similar issue prevented the effective delivery of communal toilet blocks—rows of toilets in a location near dwellings—in informal settlements, which has been implemented in a number of cases in other parts of the world, notably in Indian cities such as Pune and Mumbai (Burra, Patel, and Kerr 2003).

The result was not only a lack of vertical cohesion across scales of government that prevented delivery; this was compounded by the fragmentation that also existed across agencies within the local government—a lack of horizontal cohesion. Describing the fundamental disconnect between two agencies within local government, Eales pointed out, "If it is everybody's responsibility, it is nobody's responsibility, and public flush toilets simply don't work unless you have adequate maintenance capacity. Housing said, 'We've done our job. We're not in the business of service provision. Joburg Water must take it on.'" This meant that the initial high costs of building the infrastructure only led to further situations where that infrastructure became unusable due to lack of maintenance. As Eales suggested,

> So, Joburg Water got assigned this absolute horror of trying to keep these settlements going and they were disgusting, the facilities. I mean, what it takes and they didn't have that budget, so they said there is no ways they put in additional of these. The infrastructure was expensive, and far more than that it was the [operating expenditure].[28]

When I cited figures about in-household toilet access in informal settlements in Johannesburg, Eales argued that the city's approach to delivering sanitation services to informal settlements was shaped by national government directives.

> Do you mean a private toilet, or do you mean a toilet within ten meters or a toilet within one hundred meters? What do you mean? That's the key issue. Because what national policy targets set is what incentivizes the politicians to respond, so if the goal is X, you can't say, "Oh, you're bad people, you didn't achieve Y." They were trying to, okay. So I can scratch up the definitions for you, but I am pretty sure it would be something within 200 meters, which, if you have diarrhea, it is like cold comfort.[29]

Ultimately, these directives for delivering toilets at relatively large distances from individual homes meant that even the delivery that was happening in informal settlements was not likely to be socially meaningful, even if it did fulfill bureaucratic imperatives.

In fact, municipal standards changed over time. As a World Bank report from 2011 acknowledges, "High settlement densities, insecurity of tenure and complex community dynamics make planning and implementing standard infrastructure solutions difficult, if not impossible" (Water and Sanitation Program 2011). There has been no consistent standard in Johannesburg, which appears to be largely driven by the lack of a city-wide policy for upgrading informal settlements.

One of the only supports for municipal inputs into shaping delivery standards for toilets emerged through a Constitutional Court case that concerned an informal settlement in Ekurhuleni, a large metropolitan municipality on Johannesburg's eastern border. The Harry Gwala community, named after a trade union activist and military recruiter for the ANC during Apartheid, took the municipal government to court to insist on its responsibility to deliver toilets, which were largely absent from the informal settlement. The case was brought in the name of the Nokotyana family, who resided in Harry Gwala and was the primary complainant in the case. In 2009, the pressure from the litigation led the municipality to promise to deliver at least one "chemical toilet" for every ten households. The Harry Gwala community objected, saying that this number was too low, and the national and provincial governments stepped in to offer funding for one chemical toilet for every four households in the community. The larger Ekurhuleni municipality then rejected the offer, arguing that it would amount to prejudicing the prioritization of service provision to other informal settlements. In essence, this was a logic of saying that the Harry Gwala community could not jump the line for toilets.

In November 2009, having let the various scales of government try and fail to negotiate a remedy, the Constitutional Court rejected the Harry Gwala community's case. In doing so, the court argued that because the tenure status of the informal settlement was "in limbo," the municipality could not be compelled to provide it with services. Critics in the academic and nongovernmental organization sectors have argued that this meant that "the court was attempting to use all the tools it had to avoid giving definitive content to socio-economic rights" (Tissington 2011, 45). In essence, the lack of clearly assigned property rights overrode constitutional commitments to universalize access to sanitation.

Other Constitutional Court rulings on housing and basic services are often seen in another light. The case of *Republic of South Africa v. Grootboom*, which was heard and decided in 2000, is a global landmark in jurisprudence affirming the right to housing. But the salient point from the Nokotyana case is that neither the legislative process nor the judiciary has delineated a clear process for actually generating clear standards for delivering sanitation to informal settlements.

The onus, therefore, lies in the bureaucratic capacities of local governments to both set standards and realize constitutional rights in practice. Officials in Johannesburg's local government were primarily responding to the directives of the national government's Free Basic Services program, which were designed to address "indigents." This program pulled together a range of legislative actions in the first decade of South Africa's democratic government. In 2001, parliament passed "Regulations Relating to Compulsory National Standards and Measures to Conserve Water." The purpose was to create "minimum standards" for the realization of the rights to water and sanitation enumerated in the Water Services Act, which had been passed four years earlier in 1997.

However, none of these regulations addressed informal settlements, and the policy framework for providing sanitation services in the upgrading of informal settlements was largely left to housing policy in the second half of the 2000s. This was punctuated by the introduction of the UISP. Not only did the UISP have implementation bottlenecks that largely prevented it from being used, but it still did not delineate a clear set of standards by which implementation agencies could be measured.

If the national policy framework could not provide a clear road map for local governments to provide toilets to informal settlements, the lack of local authority over the direct providing agency made it doubly hard. Joburg Water lacked an independent regulator, and as David Savage of the national Department of Treasury argued, this situation further fragmented the broader coordination of delivery of services.

These are monopoly providers, essentially, of these services. So from an economic perspective one needed to keep a handle on performance and price and so forth. The kind of standard for the monopoly industries. But there is also a kind of coordination challenge where all of these services are landing in space and you are wanting to make sure that you are managing the urban environment in a more integrated way and that you have the cities—that their spatial governance is coherent.[30]

It is unclear whether an autonomous regulator overseeing an MOE like Joburg Water could have helped improve the coordination between quasi-independent agencies as well as municipal and provincial departments. As we have seen, governance challenges within Joburg Water, the priority of property rights over the need to extend services, and the lack of clear standards for service delivery had all prevented the MOE from planning in concert with municipal authorities. Nevertheless, Savage underscored that the mere existence of Joburg Water as an independent MOE made it ill-suited to the kinds of coordination functions that are associated with delivering urban public goods "to get a particular spatial outcome."

While movement-based protest in Johannesburg remained relatively isolated to, at most, a few individual settlements, the precipitous rise in relatively atomized "service delivery protests" was a clear response to both the gaps in and nature of delivery (see Paret 2022). The issue of toilets became a frequent flash point, and residents increasingly took to the streets. While the rise in "service delivery protests" since the mid-2000s has been a national phenomenon, Johannesburg has always been home to either the first- or the second-largest share of protests of any city, depending on the year. The most systematic longitudinal analysis of these protests has found that there has been a persistent increase in both their frequency and the incidents of violence involved with them (Alexander et al. 2018). On occasion, these protests have even included demonstrators wielding buckets of feces taken from overflowing publicly installed toilets in their neighborhoods. Paret (2018) has documented how these protests have produced collective actors in marginalized neighborhoods while also stirring up new tensions between residents that have limited their ability to link collectivities beyond individual neighborhoods.

With both national housing policy reforms and urban governance reforms unable to yield lasting results in improving the distributive consequences of the built environment, the national Treasury took on an increasingly hands-on role. In the post-Apartheid period, the Treasury has been seen as an "island of excellence" within the South African bureaucracy. Its willingness to intervene more directly in city administrations was understood by the range of my informants in national, provincial, and local government as a sign of the seriousness of the urban governance challenge. In 2011, the Treasury established the City Support Program in order to facilitate a unified focus on "spatial transformation," with an emphasis on the largest metropolitan municipalities in the country, including Johannesburg.

The policy proposals to emerge from the City Support Program focused on building planning and coordination capacity in these municipalities. This was to occur through a process of "accreditation," by which competencies that rested with provincial government, such as the financial control of subsidized housing projects, would be assigned to municipalities. As Savage put it,

> There certainly was a push from the Treasury side that goes quite far back, to say, "Listen, the metros are already playing a kind of contractual role in the delivery of these programs, but we are still not getting the spatial location. So we just transfer the function to them effectively." There is a political economy around house delivery in South Africa which makes it kind of third rail of our politics. It has got a whole lot of invested interested clustered around it now. So it has been very difficult to really shift that.[31]

One of the new planning tools proposed by Treasury to South Africa's large cities was called a Built Environment Performance Plan. According to Samantha Naidoo, a senior staffer in the Treasury's City Support Program, this tool was supposed to align existing spatial development plans, in particular the Integrated Development Plan that all cities are required by law to produce, with a financial plan tied to infrastructure investments articulated in the plan.[32]

If this sounds like an alphabet soup of plans upon plans, then you are not just imagining things. As Naidoo acknowledged, the Built Environment Performance Plans were not a statutory planning tool, meaning that they established no additional line of legal accountability.

The Johannesburg case illustrates just how much the absence of internal coordinating capacity—cohesion—defined the city's inability to get anywhere close to universal provision of sanitation in informal settlements. The independent governance of Joburg Water did not necessarily mean that the municipality would be unable to coordinate delivery with such an entity. In fact, as we saw in São Paulo, municipalities *can* generate significant capacity to coordinate with independently governed water companies, even when they function at a larger, state-wide scale. But local government in Johannesburg lacked a clear conceptualization of the problem, in part due to its distance from an increasingly oppositional social movement sphere within informal settlements, and often lacked national policy backing to align Joburg Water's actions with its own planning priorities. And even when local government did have nationally determined policy tools at its disposal, it was not able to use them to align Joburg Water's priorities with those of the local government.

Conclusion

Perhaps even more than housing or transportation, the question of delivering sanitation in São Paulo and Johannesburg has revolved around establishing meaningful relationships of accountability *within* the bureaucratic sphere. Cohesion is the more obvious deciding factor in this policy arena compared with embeddedness. In large part, this is due to a common feature of both cities. In both São Paulo and Johannesburg, the agency responsible for delivering water and sanitation services to city residents has existed, in varying ways, outside of the direct control of the municipal government. In both cities, this created significant hurdles for effective planning and the ability to then deliver on those plans. Critical to the varying levels of success in the two cities was the degree to which they could generate coordinating capacity between municipal government and these independent agencies for the delivery of water and sanitation services. What mattered was the capacity to coordinate with other parts of municipal government, especially plans for land use and housing, along with the capacity to insist that an independent agency be accountable to municipal priorities.

In São Paulo, the independent, state-level agency of SABESP was brought into a deliberative institutional arrangement in which the municipality gained legal authority to insist on its own planning principles. These new lines of accountability were facilitated by national legislation, while the city's planning principles for the delivery of sanitation to favelas were incubated in the progressive focus on slum upgrading that began during the Erundina administration and had taken root in the design and execution of housing policies in subsequent administrations of both the PT and a center-right coalition led by the PSDB.

In Johannesburg, by contrast, the creation of a new independent municipal-level agency, Joburg Water, failed to facilitate the same kind of institutional cohesion that São Paulo was able to achieve. The agency was not designed to respond to planning principles other than operational financial sustainability. And in the absence of a comprehensive planning context, the breakdown in the agency's independence was precipitated by ham-fisted attempts by individual politicians to gain control of aspects of the agency's governance. National policies likewise were unable to facilitate an integration of planning and delivery, as they provided no mechanism for ensuring that municipal plans drove Joburg Water's priorities. Housing policy persistently failed to encourage the kinds of slum-upgrading programs that had scaled up in São Paulo, as land use policy insisted on fully assigned individual land titles in order to intervene effectively in the infrastructure of informal settlements. The continued emphasis on new, greenfields housing delivery cultivated competition between municipal and provincial authorities and sidelined the implementing agency, Joburg Water, in the process of planning for extended services.

While embeddedness may take a secondary role in explaining divergent outcomes in this sector, we can still clearly make out its influence. The relationship between sanitation delivery and the policy sphere of housing and land use makes clear that the social embeddedness of the policymaking process will result in a more actionable policy apparatus for addressing informal settlements. By the time Brazil's federal government had introduced a National

Sanitation Law empowering municipalities in 2007, São Paulo had a clear land use policy arsenal to relativize the property rights of informal settlements in order to authorize the delivery of new infrastructure to these areas. In contrast, even though national policy in South Africa continuously aimed to enable the upgrading of informal settlements, without a clear assessment of property rights, the municipal provision of sanitation was hamstrung by an inability to deliver. The Constitutional Court case of the Harry Gwala informal settlement in 2009 and its resolution illustrate this clearly.

The degree of institutional cohesion in these two cities settled the fate of improving the sanitation conditions of their informal settlements. The horizontal dimension of cohesion—coordinating across line departments—required a degree of vertical cohesion that was either facilitated or stalled by national policy change. But ultimately, each city's capacity to draw on national policy change to force lines of accountability to the municipal scale became critical for ensuring coordinating power across line agencies in the city.

6

Conclusion

In 2017, just one year after the period of time under review in this study, Marielle Franco wrote a brief essay about the right-wing political wave growing in Brazil. Franco—black, gay, female, and from the favela of Maré in Rio de Janeiro—had been elected in Rio's 2016 municipal elections as a city councillor representing the Socialism and Liberty Party, which had broken away from the Workers' Party in 2004 in the wake of a corruption scandal. In this urgent, prescient essay, she describes a "conjuncture, which favours Bonapartism or the rise of conservative authoritarianism" (2018). She wrote with a clear-eyed view from the social peripheries of a city increasingly governed in practice by a combination of illicit crime organizations, elements of formal political institutions, and police. She placed the inclusion of favelas and their residents at the center of her writing and activism.

Three months after the essay was published, Franco was found dead in her car, shot in an apparent targeted assassination. She was on her way home after participating in a public roundtable discussion about "young black women moving power structures," and in recent months, she had become increasingly outspoken about the murders of young black people in favelas at the hands of police and shadowy "militias." Her assassination highlighted the extent to which the sociological promise of democracy—political equality—is largely mediated through a dense web of inequalities of identity in place.

Franco's murder and the subsequent election of Jair Bolsonaro in 2018 underscored the possibility of a coherent conservative authoritarianism in Brazil that crossed cultural, social, and economic dimensions of political life. Franco's view from the periphery illuminated something more like a narrow Bonapartism—a charismatic authoritarian style marked by selective appeals for order. Bolsonaro, an exemplar of this characterization, was often cast in the role of "Trump of the Tropics," a quintessential political figure of "law and order." But, both on the campaign trail and in office, the Bolsonaro phenomenon represented a yearning for an impersonal order of law. Instead, his rise came to personify the social, economic, and spatial orders of the past. These are the same spatial orders of inequality that São Paulo has struggled to overcome, with a success that has been substantial, if incomplete, since its first direct mayoral elections in 1989.

Meanwhile, South Africa remains fraught with protest, but unlike many comparable middle-income countries across the Global South, it has not seen an authoritarian figurehead à la Bolsonaro take power through elected office. However, similar authoritarian forces are growing. From 2016 to 2019 in Johannesburg, for example, a short-lived ruling coalition of the center-right Democratic Alliance and the nominally populist left-wing Economic Freedom Fighters took power. The coalition's mayor, Herman Mashaba, frequently railed against undocumented foreigners from other African countries as the key impediment to his efforts to upgrade the inner city and peripheral townships. Within the African National Congress, which continues to rule at the national level, demagoguery that distinguishes the deserving "native" poor and the undeserving "criminal" foreigner continues to gain traction, occasionally fueling deadly riots like those that swept many neighborhoods across the city in 2008. Amid the fragmentation and fracturing of social movements in South Africa's urban "shacklands," especially in Johannesburg, a turn to anti-foreigner organizing continues to grow (see Paret 2022), which may be laying the groundwork for a more authoritarian government in the future.

In Brazil, the PT and a diverse range of social movements and unions helped build a relatively durable political basis for the achievements of the country's welfare state. Today, political parties and social movements are adjusting to the reality of a new political climate. Though Bolsonaro was defeated by Lula in 2022's presidential election, his allies remain powerful both in electoral politics and in broader Brazilian society. But the longer-term path forward is clear. São Paulo's sporadic progress over the last three decades has illustrated that a project to undo the now-deepening inequalities of both social power and material resources will need to be one with an "urban power." It will have to be capable of wielding public institutions of the state that can channel popular movements to overcome the peripheries that define Brazilian political life. Over the past three decades, the democratic project in Brazil has enabled São Paulo to haltingly, and unevenly, overcome these political peripheries. The rise of Bolsonaro and his allies aimed to restore them.

In Johannesburg, a democratic project with very similar roots as that of São Paulo has not led to the same levels of success. The structure of segregation in the built environment has largely been left intact from the Apartheid period. Even so, the intraparty politics of the ANC have, until now, contained the more authoritarian populist impulses that have emerged. It may be precisely that the relatively closed formal party political space has helped foreclose possibilities for a reordering of Johannesburg's spatial landscape.

Urban institutions in both cities have not operated with total independence from larger forces. In fact, each of the factors I have proposed to explain the redistributive regimes of public goods in these cities incorporates structural forces that are often global and transnational. Dynamics of urban neoliberal restructuring under conditions of the contemporary global integration of markets are undoubtedly part of the story. The persistent prevalence of informal settlements in both cities, as in most cities in the world, is a testament to this. Further, a key dimension of the concept of cohesion is the role of interscalar relationships, thereby emphasizing the interdependence of city, state, and national scales of political and social action.

One of the points of this study is to emphasize that cities, in terms of their economic and political structures, are not merely dependent on what happens at larger scales. In short, local governments *intervene*. And the sphere of local government institutions, in its own right, is a critical ground for understanding social conflict and change in cities. The question is to what extent local institutional interventions will achieve their desired aims and, furthermore, why those aims emerge in the first place. Not only do megacities such as São Paulo and Johannesburg face significant challenges of coordination, but processes of institutional change must contend with histories of fragmented and clientelistic administration.

The vastly different trajectories of São Paulo and Johannesburg in distributing three critical public goods—housing, transportation, and sanitation—suggest not only common themes but explanatory concepts that can help us identify important variation in the relationship between urban governance and redistribution. In this book, I have elaborated the key features of urban power—the coordination of the formal and informal social relationships that produce governing institutions to manage the distribution of public goods across the space of the city. The ties between local government and the sphere of social movements in civil society—embeddedness—and the coordinating capacity internal to the local state—cohesion—are what make urban power effective toward building a more equal city.

The histories documented here emphasize three key tensions in how local government institutions in these two cities have tried to grapple with profound inequalities in the distribution of the urban built environment. Why was it so important for housing and land use policy that in São Paulo, city-wide movements from below were mobilized, while in Johannesburg, similar movements were demobilized? Why was it so important for transportation policy that in São Paulo, local government prioritized reforming institutional relationships between informal bus owners and local government over introducing technological changes, while in Johannesburg, local government prioritized technological changes over institutional reforms? Why was it so important for sanitation policy that in São Paulo, local government was able to make an independent water and sanitation company accountable to its planning priorities, while in Johannesburg, an independent water and sanitation company maintained its formal independence?

These questions emphasize degrees of variation that require sociological theorization beyond that which has generally been used to explain trajectories of inequality in cities. I have therefore proposed concepts that address anomalies in the related research programs of "power-resources" theory in political sociology and "institutionalism" in the sociology of development: embeddedness and cohesion. The embeddedness of the local state in a sphere of movements in civil society helps to build the cohesion of the internal coordinating capacity of the local state.

In looking at the distribution of housing in each city, a key tension emerges in the role of social movements for housing in embedding local state institutions in a broader social sphere. This, in turn, explained, in São Paulo, the construction of internal coordinating capacity within the local bureaucracy and, in Johannesburg, its absence. Consequently, São Paulo was able to generate sufficient coordinating capacity to mediate the strong, organized interests of private real estate and pursue redistributive policies in housing and land use. These policies, in some critical cases, relativized private property rights and empowered housing movements as agents of both delivery—through self-build housing programs—and policy. Through a political project that fragmented city-wide movement organizations in Johannesburg, the ANC-led local government lost the social base with which to generate a similar kind of coordinating capacity that could rebuff reaction by traditional elites to redistributive policies.

Our examination of the governance of collective transportation highlights the tension between an embedded governing logic that prioritized institutional over technological change in São Paulo and an autonomous governing logic that prioritized technological over institutional change in Johannesburg. The institutional route in São Paulo drew on less organized but no less consequential forms of social embeddedness than in the case of housing and land use. Key bureaucratic officials and political principals used their embedded ties with peripheral neighborhood brokers to facilitate negotiations with private minibus operators to integrate them into a city-wide, formal system of bus-based collective transportation. The technological route in Johannesburg sidestepped such efforts, making these kinds of negotiations less central to the policymaking process. Only once new technological infrastructures were in place did the municipal government scramble to try to produce a new institutional alignment of private minibus operators and bus rapid transit infrastructure. To this day, BRT remains a largely marginal form of collective transportation in a city that is dominated by unsubsidized private minibus taxis.

In the area of sanitation, the tension of how to make insulated, independent water and sanitation agencies responsive to the priority of extending services in the city takes center stage. São Paulo was able to more deeply coordinate and align the internal accountabilities of semi-independent water companies to municipal sanitation planning priorities, while Johannesburg saw persistent competition in these accountabilities. Here, a sphere of policymaking was comparatively closed off to the social contestation that this book's concept of "embeddedness" emphasizes. Indeed, the challenge that both cities faced was precisely how to make a relatively independent government agency more responsive to some form of popular demand around the expansion of sanitation services to the city's most excluded territories. In São Paulo, this required the vertical cohesion—enabled by national legislation—of making a state agency that was effectively accountable to municipal priorities. It also required the horizontal cohesion of planning across the areas of land use, housing, and sanitation. Though institutional cohesion takes center stage in this story, the priority of the urban peripheries could only win out because of the broader embedded ties established in policy spheres that were more open to social contestation, notably, housing and land use. In Johannesburg, the city government faced a parallel challenge, but it struggled to similarly make an autonomously governed water agency accountable to municipal planning priorities. It could never draw on the same kind of national legislation that established similar lines of accountability in Brazil, but the city's own agencies also could not coordinate among themselves to present a coherent set of planning priorities in the first place. This cross-city comparison is illustrated in Table 6.1.

Each of these three tensions shows how configurations of embeddedness and cohesion explain how the cities have been able or not able to generate a more equal distribution of the associated urban public goods. This is so even though the policy areas of housing, transportation, and sanitation vary in terms of their explicit openness to social contestation. Taken together, this suggests a robustness of these concepts for explaining regimes of urban public goods distribution.

The Importance of Historical Sequence

The conceptual tools of embeddedness and cohesion make it possible to explain the variations between these cases by using a historical perspective that is sensitive to sequence. In the political conflicts associated with each public good, we can see how early decisions shaped subsequent trajectories. Sometimes, this produced an oppositional reaction. In São Paulo, the

TABLE 6.1. São Paulo's and Johannesburg's Sequential Process through Configurations of Embeddedness and Cohesion

		Embeddedness	
		Low	*High*
		Rentier	*Mobilizational*
Cohesion	*Low*	Narrow elite capture	Redistribution-oriented policies without financial and administrative capacity
		Johannesburg	
		Managerial	*Integrationist*
	High	Programmatic top-down administration, often growth-oriented	Effective administration of redistribution-oriented policies
			São Paulo

Erundina administration's reforms to encourage self-build housing projects managed by housing movements, for example, were followed by the top-down, rentier logic of the subsequent Maluf administration's "Cingapura" high-rise, low-income housing policy. But in other cases, this sequential logic of analysis produced a more linear path dependency. Johannesburg's largely white property owners and developers, for example, used relatively hidden tactics of organizing, which in turn reduced the capacity of the local state to implement redistributive reforms.

In São Paulo, we see a common trend across the three policy arenas of housing, transportation, and sanitation toward increased embeddedness and cohesion. But even this was ultimately unstable. In housing, the balance of national policy overwhelmed municipal policy, which pushed housing movements to move their focus away from programmatic policy engagement at the city scale. In transportation, the city's emphasis on bike and bus lanes distracted from the fundamental mobilizing question of the price of a bus ticket. And in sanitation, the role of regulators with close ties to the state-level water agency (the Basic Sanitation Company of the State of São Paulo) created limits to deeper bureaucratic cohesion.

A somewhat surprising thread runs through all of these limits to the stability of increased embeddedness and cohesion: The fact that these weaknesses were largely revealed during the mayoral term of the PT's Fernando Haddad. Earlier mayoral terms of the PT were absolutely critical to bringing allied movements into contact with the bureaucratic sphere. However, as Haddad's outsized impact illustrates, an alignment with a single party of the Left is clearly not a sufficient reason for success in building a more equitable govern-ing regime. In fact, across all three policy sectors, the "integrationist" configu-ration of embeddedness and cohesion in São Paulo stretched across PT and center-right mayoral administrations. Moreover, the trend in Johannesburg toward diminished embeddedness and cohesion—something approximating a "rentier" governing regime—occurred throughout ANC administrations.

Taken together, this suggests that party competition has been just as inte-gral to the emergence of embeddedness in São Paulo as the role of a party of the Left. To illustrate, if the PT's first mayoral term in São Paulo had not created a set of programmatic policy engagements between movements and bureaucrats at both senior and "street" levels, it is hard to see how embedded-ness could have emerged in the first place. But it is just as plausible to suggest that without the period of conservative reaction that followed in the latter part of the 1990s, the renewed mobilization by housing movements may never have come to pass. Such mobilization was critical to establishing a sphere of movements in which the second PT administration, of Marta Suplicy, could be embedded, thereby creating the conditions for broader internal coordinating capacity with local government—cohesion.

In Johannesburg, by contrast, it was absolutely critical that the ANC made the explicit decision that its allied social movements should demobilize. It was also critical that the ANC deprioritized the demands of movements in the rushed negotiation over municipal administrative boundaries, leading to the consequen-tial, if temporary, arrangement of submunicipal structures on the front line of local tax collection. As Paret (2022) has shown, what remains of the movement sphere in Johannesburg is largely neighborhood-based, with ineffective engage-ments in the electoral sphere and a total disengagement from any program-matic orientation. Instead, the focus of these neighborhood-based movements is largely about making particularistic demands for the provisioning of a road or water tap for their own neighborhoods outside of any policy-based demand. In transportation policy, Johannesburg's ANC-led government did not see itself as accountable to a broader social sphere, and thus it prioritized technological reforms associated with the BRT system and deprioritized institutional reforms that could have prevented resistance from minibus taxi owners and operators. In sanitation policy, city government officials had no ties to grassroots activists who could help them conceptualize an institutional strategy to leverage national laws and make an independent water agency accountable to municipal government priorities in informal settlements.

During South Africa's transition to democracy, the ANC's decisions to demobilize its social movement base would have been unthinkable in the con-text of a viable electoral alternative. The resulting absence in city government of embedded ties to a sphere of large-scale movements rooted in the urban peripheries meant that the interests of business and property could ultimately prevail in decisions over housing and land use in the city. And this could happen even without a coordinated project with municipal political elites. The turn toward piecemeal, unplanned, and narrow returns in Johannesburg was precisely due to the power of real estate elites in the city to pursue their own "rentier" projects (which involve low embeddedness and low cohesion) in the absence of a coordinated "managerial" growth machine (which would involve low embeddedness and high cohesion).

The distributional outcomes in the two cities, in comparative terms, should therefore be seen in this light. In São Paulo, the meaningful improvements the city made in housing, transportation, and sanitation are inextricable from the governing conditions that made these improvements possible. Johannesburg, which started from a similar or, arguably, even better position at the moment of democratization, failed to generate the same kinds of governing conditions. Its meaningfully poorer outcomes are, therefore, a consequence of these same dynamics.

Toward a Global Urban Sociology

By developing this theoretical apparatus and deploying it to explain three tensions in the histories of the distribution of public goods in São Paulo and Johannesburg, this book breaks new ground toward a truly global urban sociology. In recent years, we have seen increasing calls for concepts in the sociology of cities that have comparative implications (Garrido et al. 2021; Ren 2018) as well as those that focus on organizations and institutions in urban sociology (Marwell and Morrissey 2020). The sociology of cities has too often avoided questions of institutional change at the scale of the city. Either such changes are read off of national or global changes, or they are set aside in favor of analyzing urban social problems outside of their local political and institutional context. But public goods distribution in cities is subject to observable and not just hypothetical variation. We need to elaborate the conceptual tool kit more concretely for explaining these variations in cities and not assume that either aims or capacities to realize those aims are predetermined. If local governments do *intervene*—and the three case studies presented here clearly show that they do—then the regimes of urban public goods distribution that characterize *urban power* are constructed over time through sequential processes that can be traced empirically.

I have argued that configurations of "embeddedness" and "cohesion" can help us categorize and compare how local political power is coordinated across cities. The four possible configurations—"rentier," "mobilizational," "managerial," and "integrationist" (which are presented in Table 1.2)—make space for variation-finding approaches that emphasize patterns in contingency, as opposed to patterns in structure. In other words, embeddedness and cohesion draw our attention to the specific, contingent relationships among actors in key political and bureaucratic positions and their relationships with market and civil society actors. If São Paulo and Johannesburg were merely instances of "actually existing neoliberalism" (Peck, Brenner, and Theodore 2018), then we would expect that institutional conditions for uneven development would be overdetermined by what are essentially global flows of capitalism. As Parnell and Robinson (2012) have argued, however, Johannesburg urban policy is a useful starting point for theorizing beyond the "neoliberal" frame precisely because the city has the conditions of relatively strong state capacity and meaningful rights-based programmatic commitments. Researchers in Johannesburg continue to find that it is a case where the confluence of race in politics and commitments to redistribution eludes highly structural accounts about the overdetermining role of global markets in urban politics (Mosselson 2017). Marques (2023) has made similar arguments about São Paulo, positing that it illustrates degrees of incremental distribution that challenge more structural accounts of urban development.

The advantage of the historical approach I deploy here is that we can make sense of a consequential series of strategic attempts at reform, contention, and the reformulation of priorities in both cities. In fact, it is striking just how durable the political imperative to address spatial division has been in São Paulo and Johannesburg. Throughout the past three decades, each city has continued to push processes of institutional reform in order to alter its spatial trajectory. Individual instances of deal-cutting notwithstanding, the political mandate of these cities has always been to craft institutions that could redirect trajectories of the distribution of public goods across highly unequal geographies of urban settlement.

Variation in the coordination of power to distribute is at the core of a global urban sociology. Comparative work on the management of air pollution in Chinese and Indian cities (Ren 2020), ethnographic work on the transformation of urban boundaries and social distinction in Manila (Garrido 2019), and single case studies concerning the relationships between neighborhood movements, private developers, and the courts in Mumbai (Weinstein 2014) are all examples of how a global urban sociology finds both patterns and variation in the historical and relational analyses of power in distinctly urban conflicts. This book builds on that prior work to illustrate how structured comparison of cities can leverage variation for developing broader theory.

But we should not think of these tools as being limited to cities in the Global South or in the so-called developing world. They offer us a theoretical framework that can be applied broadly. I illustrate in Table 6.2 how the conceptual tools I have developed here can travel to a range of different urban contexts across the globe. Different cities have diverse levels of inclusion in aspects of the built environment of the city. For example, sanitation access

TABLE 6.2. Comparative Illustrations of "Embeddedness" and "Cohesion"

		Embeddedness	
		Low	*High*
		Rentier	*Mobilizational*
	Low	Narrow elite capture	Redistribution-oriented policies without financial and administrative capacity
		Indian cities, 2000s	*Washington, DC, 1979–91*
Cohesion		*Flint, MI, 2011–17*	*New Delhi, 2015–present*
		Managerial	*Integrationist*
	High	Programmatic top-down administration, often growth-oriented	Effective administration of redistribution-oriented policies
		Modal U.S. "growth machine"	*Chicago, IL, 1983–87*
		Chinese megacities, 2000s	*Amsterdam, 1990s*

is universal in most cities in the richest countries. But conflicts over public goods—struggles over consumption—are common to all of them. Of largely universal significance is the role of local government in investing in social housing. But the conflicts over sanitation that I examine in São Paulo and Johannesburg have functional equivalents in cities where sanitation might be universal, and the issue of water and sanitation infrastructure continues to drive political conflict even in cities in the world's wealthiest country, the United States. While I do not address sequential dynamics here, the role of time in urban politics underscores that no city is immutably in one configuration. For this reason, in this discussion, I delimit my invocation of specific cases to particular time periods.

> **Rentier (low embeddedness–low cohesion):** The informal, deregulated, and captured modes of urban planning in India have been found to be endemic (Roy 2009). In the United States, an illustrative example is the municipality of Flint, which has been under the receivership of the state of Michigan since 2011 and has subsequently been providing poisoned water to city residents for the past three years. Civil society has been rendered almost irrelevant to formal politics, while private holders of municipal bonds were paid in full (Fasenfest 2017).

Mobilizational (high embeddedness–low cohesion): Washington, D.C., under its first black mayor with strong links to the civil rights movement, Marion Barry, in the late 1970s and early 1980s, and New Delhi, India, under the Aam Aadmi Party since 2015, are two cases of new reform-minded, social movement–backed administrations. Both are capital cities and have been subject to national governments that have significant power to undermine municipal policy changes. Opposing right-wing parties have led each city's respective national/federal government. Despite attempts to introduce reforms, each city had only limited financial independence to reorient the delivery of public goods on a programmatic basis. In each case, the space of the city saw limited change in the distribution and quality of public goods such as housing (Diwakar 2016; Thompson 2006). In these cases, we see strong demand-side dynamics of social mobilization without interscalar—or "vertical"—cohesion.

Managerial (low embeddedness–high cohesion): As I have noted above, the managerial configuration is most evident in the literature on "growth machines," in which a relatively capable local government coordinates with business elites to pursue the programmatic goal of economic growth. Another important—though nondemocratic—case is large Chinese cities since economic reforms in the 1990s that decentralized borrowing authority to local governments. This has led to central government evaluations of local government capacity that focus largely on achieving economic growth objectives. (Lei 2023). The *hukou* system of internal migration, which limits access to public goods in cities on the basis of holding a residential pass, has produced extreme rationing of access to urban public goods along with a strong orientation to economic growth outcomes (Dreger, Wang, and Zhang 2015; Friedman 2022). Exclusions from the public provision of housing and education are particularly prominent examples. In both cases, the local state is cohesive enough to pursue a relatively programmatic project, but its managerial character does not guarantee human development objectives as the programmatic goal.

Integrationist (high embeddedness–high cohesion): Amsterdam, the Netherlands, has managed to maintain high levels of investment in public goods, especially housing, which Fainstein (2010) attributes to the legacy of squatters' movements in the city in the 1960s and 1970s, as well as continued commitments by the Dutch national government to invest in municipal services. Chicago, under its first black mayor, Harold Washington, from 1983 to 1987, is another example, though his untimely death shortly after he began his second term makes this harder to evaluate in terms of material outcomes. The social coalition of working- and middle-class black residents and liberal whites that backed his administration enabled it to reshape local politics to direct funds and bureaucratic administration toward the development of previously marginalized neighborhoods in the city (Clavel and Wiewel 1991).

These illustrations show how the concepts I develop to explain the variation between two cases—São Paulo and Johannesburg—might travel to a much broader range of cases across the developed and developing world. One of my primary aims in this study is to show why this kind of comparative theorizing "from the South" is critical for urbanizing political sociology and politicizing urban sociology across the globe. This comparative approach is also illuminating in the ways it points to future directions such research can take. First, our political sociology of development needs to bring cities back in, much as it brought "the state back in" more than three decades ago. The social actors that can impact institutional change in the political sphere are varied in the issues that animate their mobilization and in the alliances they form. Comparative studies of democratization and redistribution have, thus far, largely focused on the traditional actors of unions and parties. But at the urban scale, we can also make sense of the emergence of different types of influential organizations and actors, such as housing movements, that have been essential to driving outcomes that the role of political parties, on their own, cannot adequately explain. To "bring cities back in" means not only to focus on issues such as standard of living and collective consumption as driving forces of institutional change but to treat the sphere of local government institutions as varied and socially contested.

Our sociology of cities also needs to bring institutions of the state back in. Work on the structural foundations of urban change has identified undeniable shifts that characterize the realities of urban political economy. But the variable social world of urban politics continues to wield influence in changing the fates of the climate resilience, health, and social solidarities of city residents. By making institutional change central to our empirical analysis of cities, we can develop a conceptual tool kit for systematically analyzing the substantive variation of distributional outcomes across cities, which will go a long way toward determining humanity's urban future.

Taken together, both the in-depth paired comparison of São Paulo and Johannesburg and the brief comparisons in this chapter point toward the centrality of a focus on "urban power" for explaining why some cities are more effective at reducing inequality than others. The questions of social and bureaucratic coordination that frame the concept of urban power all point toward the democratic ideal of cities that American urbanist Jane Jacobs once invoked: "Cities have the capability of providing something for everybody, only because, and only when, they are created by everybody" (1961, 238). This may be a utopian ideal more than a realistic blueprint. But it points toward a project—both analytical and practical in scope—that lies ahead. To understand change in cities—to be able to distinguish between those institutional moves that increase equality and those that do not—we need research tools that can uncover the dynamics of who is involved in the work of city-making that determines the distribution of life chances of all who live there.

At first glance, this approach might be unsatisfying as a recipe for policy. Describing varying levels of "urban power" does not necessarily create a recipe of specific interventions policymakers can use to construct embeddedness and cohesion out of thin air. But as seasoned practitioners of many stripes know all too well, these relationships between individuals and the structures—both formal and informal—through which those relationships develop are the stuff of making policy. There do not exist any politicians, bureaucrats, movement organizers, or property developers who can merely bend any situation to their will. But they can cultivate dispositions toward the structures and institutions that are bequeathed to them through historical sequence.

This book's comparison of São Paulo and Johannesburg is designed precisely to help understand the extent to which key actors and organizations in the urban context can have agency in changing distributional outcomes. In other words, how can this concept help those in policy and organizing circles? This is a common question for analyses of state action that adopt a sociological "state-in-society" view, which suggests that change in government institutions cannot be separated from broader social structures. One way to approach this question is to follow Peter Evans's exploration of how this problem could be overcome through theorizing "constructability," defined as "the application of imaginative organizational arrangements or institutional 'soft technologies'" that can "produce synergy over relatively brief periods of time" (1995, 1124). The divergence between Johannesburg and São Paulo underscores how such meso-level interventions can alter the historical sequence of configuring embeddedness and cohesion.

These cases suggest that the "organizational arrangements" that Evans theorizes as potentially making a difference are not only within the state. Policymakers and organizers who want to take "urban power" forward in their work can use this framework to understand their own reflexivity in processes of policy reform. The trajectories of state institutions and grassroots movements are in a dynamic relationship. Social forces construct the urban state just as much as the urban state constructs these social forces.

"Urban power," then, provides a lens for interpreting these structures and institutions, as well as goals for practitioners. For example, bureaucratic actors can take this theoretical framework to think of their work as not only internal to the agency in which they are employed. They can seek out organizations in movements in civil society that can make their own work more effective. This is a form of what the political scientist Jessica Rich (2019) has called "state-sponsored activism." Likewise, movement strategists can organize for programmatic policy changes that can enable and strengthen their bureaucratic allies within government agencies. To put a spin on Rich's terminology, we can think of this as "activist-sponsored statecraft."

Both São Paulo and Johannesburg had very similar endowments of social mobilization, institutional capacity, and constitutional legitimacy. They also possessed a similarly unequal distribution of urban public goods. In São Paulo, the Erundina administration's early insistence on reinforcing its ties with housing movements laid the groundwork for cultivating a movement sphere oriented toward city-wide programmatic goals, as well as a corps of bureaucrats who could help construct a more cohesive form of local government in subsequent administrations. This was a policymaking choice with consequences both for government and for a broader sphere of social movement. In Johannesburg, by contrast, the ANC's early insistence on demobilizing housing movements laid the groundwork for an increasingly fragmented and nonprogrammatic movement sphere and a corps of bureaucrats without the social ties to confront the particularistic strategies of resistance used by property owners and developers. This was also a political choice—one that did not adequately account for its ramifications internally within local government as well as for the organization of movement allies. The "urban power" framework can help policymakers and organizers see how the strategic choices they make have deep effects that can set processes of policy reform on remarkably divergent paths.

We can imagine alternate pathways too. For example, if movements in Johannesburg were able to network and organize at the scale of the city, we would expect a more programmatic set of engagements with local government to emerge. In turn, we could reasonably expect that this could have substantial effects on the policies, organizational arrangements, and bureaucratic cultures that shape the local government. The challenge, however, would be overcoming the now-entrenched position within local government that strong social movements are largely an obstacle to policymaking and implementation, as opposed to a source of constructing the embedded ties required for cohesive, redistributive delivery of public goods. This is precisely the risk that the Haddad administration ran into in São Paulo, as it grew increasingly distant from the housing movements that had been critical to the coordinating power of previous PT-led administrations in the city. The Haddad administration's vulnerability to right-wing reaction is perhaps not so surprising in this light.

Seeing from the Slum

A lingering question of urban sociology has long been to what extent the subfield is concerned with social problems that happen to occur in urban space, as opposed to a distinctly "urban" set of questions. The latter perspective implicates the institutional and political setting of the city and not just its spatial coordinates. A focus on public goods such as housing, transportation, and sanitation, which I have termed here as "urban public goods," makes the process of urbanization itself the background driver of how we understand urban conflict. The governance—and seeming ungovernability—of patterns of urban settlement across the globe has made the distribution of urban public goods central to the human experience.

It is not the ungovernability of cities in most of the world that characterizes them. Instead, it is the multiple modes of governing these cities that matters. Exclusion from urban public goods is as much a form of governance as inclusion is. The notion that cities are ungovernable assumes that everything that occurs outside of the formal state is a sphere without governance.

One important approach to overcoming this view is to study the internal politics of slum neighborhoods themselves. A growing interdisciplinary literature in cities of the Global South undertakes precisely such an approach (see Auerbach 2020; Fahlberg 2023; Levenson 2022; Paller 2019; Paret 2022). This work has largely focused on the leadership of individual informal settlement communities and how that leadership interacts with government institutions. But the role of slums in a global urban sociology can also be understood at a scale above the neighborhood.

"Urban power"—the degree of local state embeddedness in civil society and internal bureaucratic cohesion—captures the way that fights over exclusion from urban public goods produce a wide range of distributional outcomes across the city as a whole. Though slums have historically been invisible in official maps and official politics in São Paulo, Johannesburg, and many major metropolises of the world, they can hardly be erased from our maps of the social conflicts that profoundly shape urban institutions. They are the physical territory that constructs politics in most of the world. For this reason, the increasing importance of urbanization and slums in the reports of the Intergovernmental Panel on Climate Change represents a significant advance for bringing some of the most excluded and climate-vulnerable populations into the interdisciplinary scientific frame.

To wish to erase slums is to wish away the terrain of social struggle. All struggles for "urban power"—and the distributional outcomes of these struggles across urban territory—are part and parcel of the rationed statecraft of all cities.

The centrality of life and politics not only in but also about slums to the social reality of the contexts where most people live makes this a critical site for contemporary research. The environmental, public health, and political issues of our time have their roots in precisely this territory. This has historical precedent. The nineteenth-century slums of London first entered mainstream political consciousness due to the spread of cholera (Davis 2006). In our time, and in the final years when I was finishing this book, the coronavirus pandemic became another stark reminder of the critical role the urban slum plays in the formation of public health and climate resilience.

As epicenters of the virus first began to emerge, they were concentrated in cities. Early press reports, therefore, concluded that cities were the key vector for the disease. We soon found, however, that the disease's epidemiological spread was as unequal as the cities in which it smoldered. In Brazil, the first deaths were of a doorman and a domestic worker, who contracted COVID from their employers. While the density of the urban built environment was initially thought to be a vector of spread, it soon became clear that this was not precisely the issue (Fang and Wahba 2020). Instead, it was the ability to "socially distance" that was the main territorial characteristic of urban spread of the disease.

The urban peripheries in countries such as Brazil and South Africa amplified the disease's reach. Why? The emerging research suggests that the primary factors included overcrowded housing, lack of water and sanitation, and collective transportation that is both densely packed and necessary to access even the most meager of livelihoods. Official numbers of COVID-related deaths worldwide are largely unreliable. Instead, models of "excess deaths" get us much closer to understanding the disease's true toll. Both Brazil and South Africa had among the highest "excess death" counts in the world. One of the most widely cited models, produced by *The Economist*, finds that Brazil had more than 750,000 excess deaths in the first two years of the pandemic, while South Africa had more than 250,000. On a per capita basis, both countries are well above similar estimates for the United States.

This was a disturbing window into the governing dynamics of climate resilience in contexts defined by pervasive informality. Each of these cities faced water shortages in the past decade due to conflicts between municipal governments and state—in the case of São Paulo—and provincial—in the case of Johannesburg—water agencies. In both instances, slums were the first areas of each city to face rationing of water supply, despite facing the greatest need. Perhaps unsurprisingly, given the analysis in earlier chapters in this book, São Paulo's favelas were able to put up much more of an organized fight that could reach local government bureaucrats to turn the taps back on more quickly (Aldana Cohen 2016) than Johannesburg's *mjondolos* (du Plessis 2023).

Furthermore, each country's democracy is under increasing strain. In 2021 in South Africa, poor urban neighborhoods across the country's largest cities exploded in riots egged on by allies of the ousted president, Jacob Zuma. In 2022, the urban peripheries of the large cities of Brazil's southeast, especially São Paulo, were key swing districts that sealed Bolsonaro's narrow loss to the PT's Lula. Notably, São Paulo's swing was not replicated in other large southeastern cities such as Rio de Janeiro, perhaps reflecting the more persistent roots of working-class organization and responsive urban policymaking in São Paulo. To wit, the most voted-for congressional representative in the entire state of São Paulo was Guilherme Boulos, leader of the Homeless Workers Movement, currently the city's most active housing movement.

Novelist and essayist Arundhati Roy wrote a particularly haunting essay just as the coronavirus was beginning to spread across the globe. The pandemic, she contended, was "a portal, a gateway between one world and the next" (2020). The mechanisms by which the pandemic spread are the quintessential urban terms of social conflict.

A global social scientific project of analyzing power, politics, and climate resilience in a twenty-first century beset by extreme inequalities of work, shelter, race, and caste is one that will necessarily locate the slum at the center of its conceptual outlook. These are the places of first arrival for migrants in a warming world and the crucibles of politics across the globe that increasingly challenge the basic foundations of representative democracy. The challenge of distributing public goods in cities will be central to the political demands and organization that emerge from these spaces.

Shortly before she was assassinated, Marielle Franco cast her gaze toward the favela as she concluded the essay with which I began this chapter. She wrote of the need to "center as social actors those from the margins and the favelas throughout Brazil. Building structures that help empower poor, black women to take on the role of active citizenship, aimed at winning a city of rights, is fundamental for the revolution the contemporary world requires" (2018).

The dreams of political equality that were so closely held in both Brazil and South Africa at the end of the twentieth century still appear on the horizon three decades later. The struggles for urban equality that once characterized those dreams persist in struggles to produce *urban power*. They are the struggles whose outcomes will pave the way to whatever world is to come.

Methodological Notes:
Biography, Reflexivity, and
Policy Translations

One of my earliest, fuzzy memories is of watching the U.S. broadcast of the PBS *NewsHour* as Jim Lehrer announced that Nelson Mandela would be released from jail in 1990. I was only four years old and can only recall that my parents must have made it quite clear how important this was to them. My father had left South Africa for the United States in 1977 to avoid mandatory conscription into the Apartheid military. My mother emigrated in 1981, and they were married two years later. As Apartheid fell and democracy prevailed in South Africa, the pull of return would continue to grow. By 2008, my parents had established new careers and a home back in their birthplace of Johannesburg. In annual visits to extended family in the city in the years following Mandela's release, I encountered degrees of inequality that jarred with the optimistic story that shaped my first awareness of politics as a child—Mandela's freedom, the first elections in 1994, and the sense that the end of formal civic inequality should necessarily entail fundamental material changes.

My relationship with South Africa shifted when I moved to Johannesburg shortly after graduating with an American undergraduate degree. I began work with a South African daily newspaper, covering a wide range of stories, including a feature report on the door-to-door canvassing campaigns of the three most competitive parties in the 2009 national election: the African National Congress, the Democratic Alliance, and the new ANC breakaway party called the Congress of the People.

This reporting took me to the informal settlements of the Apartheid-era southern peripheries and post-Apartheid northern peripheries of the city. In Alexandra, Klipspruit, and Kanana, a neighborhood of Soweto, I was struck by the deeply political claims that I heard from residents of the shacks who were being canvassed by each of these parties. These claims revolved around questions of the urban public goods that are the subject of this book, especially housing and water.

Later in 2009, once the ANC's Jacob Zuma had secured a resounding election to the presidency, I moved away from journalism and became a researcher in the coordinating secretariat of a network of community-based and professional nongovernmental organizations based in informal settlements across much of Africa and Asia, with some minimal presence in Brazil and Bolivia. This network, called Shack/Slum Dwellers International (SDI), introduced me to a wealth of knowledge about informal settlements and housing struggles across the globe. I was lucky enough to learn from many of these grassroots activists and visit their neighborhoods in Johannesburg, Cape Town, Nairobi, Kampala, Dar es Salaam, Accra, Freetown, Harare, La Paz, El Alto, Mumbai, and Bangkok, among other cities.

I had come to this work with a background in studying social and cultural history, so I was primed to seek out sources of agency in an unequal world. My work with SDI reinforced this sensibility, as I witnessed both the protests and the slum-upgrading projects that affiliated movements and organizations were pursuing across the globe.

I also met other kinds of actors involved in negotiations over these projects, especially local government politicians and bureaucrats. As a result, in the middle of my five years working with SDI, I pursued a professional degree in urban planning. I discovered readings in sociology and the intellectual tools to begin to put my comparative instincts into some kind of comparative structure.

I draw on this brief autobiographical interlude to explain why I sought out the questions that would come to motivate this study. Among other things, these questions had significant consequences for the particular tools of research that I would end up using to answer them.

I first had to reconcile my activist and professional sensibilities about urban inequalities with my scholarly ones. My practice-based sensibility was one of incremental success. A "win" is that which is better than what came before. As a matter of research method, this might suggest focusing on an individual project or neighborhood. As a practitioner, that was how I saw change.

But it was hard to know what it all added up to. Does a win at a project or neighborhood level constitute a change in institutions? Or a change in urban experience? Does it constitute a change in politics? What does it mean to realize change? By posing these kinds of questions in my new position as a researcher, I aimed to test—even falsify—the assumptions that I had brought to my experience in practice.

As a matter of case selection, this meant flipping on its head how I thought about South Africa. Because most of my practice-based work had focused there, I was very attuned to even the most minor of successes. A single water connection or toilet installed in an informal settlement was a victory. And I certainly do not want to downplay these real successes. For those who experience them, they are crucial. As a practitioner with SDI, I was also very focused on how movements relate to state institutions, and I often found myself as an observer in meetings with local, provincial, and national government officials in South Africa and occasionally in other countries in Africa. To get a meeting and especially a memorandum of understanding was understood to be a big win.

Now, I wanted to know whether a comparative perspective would confirm just how much of a success I perceived this to be. When I began my doctoral education, I knew that I wanted to compare South Africa—and Johannesburg— with somewhere else. As I read more about Brazil and São Paulo in the early months of my doctorate, two things stood out to me in relation to the case I knew best: similar degrees of inequality and similar political thematization of urban inequality in transitions to democracy. I had previously been somewhat skeptical of the Brazilian story under the Workers' Party. I had personally witnessed and documented the work of organizations based in slums struggling to get local governments to act in a number of poor and middle-income countries. How different could Brazil possibly be?

After conducting initial research trips to both countries in the summers of 2015 and 2016, I realized that, indeed, there were important differences. I began to analyze the quantitative outcomes that I present in chapter 2. These helped illustrate that this was not just a difference of institutional narratives but, rather, of real hard outcomes on the ground. My first steps down the road that would eventually lead to this book had upended many of the assumptions I had initially held about comparison and difference across the two countries.

And this not only made me rethink São Paulo and the Brazilian story. It also helped provide—to the extent possible in a cross-country, cross-city comparison—a compelling counterfactual for how to think about the Johannesburg story. I began to reflect on the paths not taken in this city I had known my whole life. Could the role of social movements have been different? What was the role of party politics? What was the role of the largely white middle-class suburbs that had been home to my own family for generations?

This last question framed the reflexive aspects of my research for this book in ways that I had to navigate throughout my field-based investigations. When conducting a field-based research project across multiple continents, in contexts riven with some of the deepest class- and race-based inequalities in the world, I was inevitably—and frequently—confronted with questions of my own positionality and how it might affect my findings. In both São Paulo and Johannesburg, the color of my skin created one set of reactions on the part of my informants; my language, another; my accent, yet another; and, finally, my relative familiarity with local networks, places, and experiences due to my family history, yet another.

In São Paulo, I was primarily coded as a stranger. To the exclusively white actors in the private sector whom I interviewed, my connections to an Ivy League institution in the United States may have opened some doors that local researcher colleagues informed me were normally hard to access. Often, such informants would want to tell me about a child, niece, or nephew who had attended an elite school in the United States or a time that they themselves had visited one of these schools. A mix of my race and my cultural habitus also led some of these actors to express very harsh opinions about the movement sector and PT politicians, even referring to some of the most radical movement actors, particularly the Movimento dos Trabalhadores Sem Teto, as a criminal element. It was clear that these views were being expressed with such vehemence because of a perceived racial and class solidarity. Similar kinds of comments have made it into the public sphere, particularly when the MTST's leader Guilherme Boulos made a surprisingly competitive run for São Paulo's mayoral seat in 2020.

For the largely mixed (*pardo*, in the Brazilian Portuguese racial classification system) or black actors in social movements, their degree of ease with my presence depended on the type of movement I was studying. Older movements, such as the União dos Movimentos de Moradia, have significant familiarity with working with international researchers. In fact, on a few occasions, I found myself at UMM meetings and conventions with other international researchers, from the United States, Europe, and Australia. On one occasion, I was enlisted as a translator at a public event that the UMM convened as a dialogue between housing activists and lawyers from South Africa and Brazil. Newer movements such as the Frente da Luta por Moradia and the MTST were also familiar with international researchers but had less established mechanisms for mediating such engagements. With these organizations, I had to broker access through multiple rounds of contacts and attend a number of meetings and events before I could be granted a sit-down interview with key leaders. These movements had a greater degree of wariness of how researchers would both use their time and represent them to the outside world. Finally, government officials—both politicians and bureaucrats—were often keen to engage with an outsider. They were familiar with the politics of being represented in academic work, and many of my informants in this sphere were connected to the academic circles in which I was engaged at the University of São Paulo's faculties of social sciences and urban planning.

To all of these actors, my ability to speak Portuguese was essential. Very few spoke much English, and even for those who did, I insisted on speaking in Portuguese. I had picked up the language through daily instruction in the second year of my Ph.D. While none of my interlocutors would have mistaken me for a native speaker, I could fluently engage in both technical and delicate political issues that were discussed in my interviews. I preferred to always conduct interviews in Portuguese because I felt that it was more important for my informants to be able to express themselves as precisely and comfortably as possible.

In contrast to São Paulo, where I was almost always coded as an outsider, in Johannesburg, I occupied a more ambiguous position. Many of my initial interviews were arranged by virtue of connections I had from my prior professional work. In those cases, I was understood to be somebody with prior background knowledge and, moreover, as somebody who had a relationship with other key actors. But subsequent interviews, with those recommended by my initial contacts, were in a relational context that initially coded me as a foreigner by virtue of my accent and institutional affiliation. During the course of an interview, my history in the city would often come up. For white interview subjects, this would invariably bring down their guard, and an air of confidence would rush into the room. For black interview subjects, this would also often be the case. But in a number of instances, the opposite would occur. In some key instances, I pursued multiple interview sessions with a subject. The goal in these cases was to use a second sitting to create a more familiar space for discussion.

The role of language was also critical in Johannesburg. All of my informants spoke some level of English, and I never had to use a translator. But for some of the social movement actors and some of the private-sector entrepreneurs I interviewed, English was clearly not the preferred language of communication. What surprised me, then, was that my experience conducting interviews across a range of classes, races, and institutional settings in São Paulo was more uniform and easier to predict than in Johannesburg. While I was conducting interviews in a second language in São Paulo, all of my informants were responding in their first language. I was struck by how relatively easy it was to speak with people in the poorest neighborhoods I visited in São Paulo, while in equivalent places in Johannesburg my limited knowledge of isiZulu or seSotho might present a challenge for communication. Though the vast majority of Johannesburg residents speak English, it is largely a second language.

So what does all of this mean for the reliability of my findings? It is clear that my own positionality as a researcher inevitably had an effect on how respondents comported themselves with me, in terms of their expectations of my social position and own associated biases. Most of my sixteen months in the field was spent conducting semistructured interviews with my informants. I had a set outline of questions with which I approached the interviews. These all lasted between thirty and 120 minutes, with most lasting approximately sixty minutes. Each of the interviews was recorded, though on some occasions my informants would ask me to stop recording for small portions. I do not report findings from notes taken during these pauses in recording, but I did use them to help me contextualize how to report quotes from interview transcripts that respondents did approve being recorded. Every interview was transcribed. While I did plenty of observation of movement meetings and public hearings, I do not primarily rely on observational ethnographic data to drive my analysis here. On a few occasions, I do describe some nonverbal cues of my informants while they were speaking, which I had included in my field notes.

Semistructured interviews of this nature are always subject to concerns of bias, which I aimed to limit in two ways. First, while my universe of respondents is certainly not a random sample in a typical quantitative understanding, it was designed to represent perspectives across the key relationships I analyze in this book. My goal in selecting interview subjects was to ensure that each group involved in conflicts over each of the three public goods studied here was interviewed. Some of this selection was deductive, because my reading before going into the field had made clear some of the key institutions, movements, and private actors with whom I would need to speak. I also conducted a form of relational snowball sampling. This meant that I was asking respondents for advice about others with whom I should speak. But it also meant that I was noting who was being described as adversaries or counterparts in conflicts across institutional divides. For example, if a private developer mentioned a certain movement or leader within a movement, then I targeted that person as an informant, even if the developer did not suggest this person as a subsequent contact. This allowed me to triangulate interview-based accounts across opposed perspectives.

Second, I aimed to limit bias by triangulating the accounts I was hearing in my interviews with the archival record. Much of this was done through consulting newspaper archives, as each city is home to multiple newspapers with complete online archives that date back into at least the 1990s. I collected hundreds of physical documents from municipal and political party archives during visits to offices in both cities. In Johannesburg, I consulted the archives of the South African History Association, which included a number of documents related to the negotiations over the transition to democracy. All of this archival research made it possible not merely to report what I was being told in interviews but to make sure that there was a recorded basis for my informants' accounts of the past.

Finally, I want to emphasize a particular task of comparative, historical, and qualitative sociological research on public policy. Though this was a multilingual research project, I found that one of the most difficult issues I encountered was translating not between Portuguese and English but, rather, between the languages of policy I encountered in São Paulo and Johannesburg. Public policy is a sphere of both technical knowledge and technical language, and these become embedded in very local cultures that are full of place- and institution-specific jargon. Because I conducted multiple field visits in both cities, I was able to triangulate how policymakers in São Paulo talked about policy in each of the three policy arenas of housing, transportation, and sanitation with how their counterparts did so in Johannesburg.

I discovered that the distinct language of policy in different places is an inevitable block to global, comparative analysis in practice. This was a source of some of my greatest confusion while in the field. I began to realize that even within the same country, policymakers at different scales may have different definitions of, for example, what adequate provision of sanitation should mean. This helped me understand that my role in comparative analysis of these two cities was to serve as a translator with a clear empirical benchmark. Unlike policymakers who respond to changing legal definitions of what is normatively "adequate" provision, my role was to adjudicate to what extent a particular public good had actually been provided compared with somewhere else. While this is very much a work of sociological analysis, my hope is that by analyzing policy debates and decisions in a common language across these two cities, this work can help model the translational task of comparative policy analysis.

List of Interviews

In Brazil

First Name	Last Name	Date(s)
Nazareno	Afonoso	9/30/17
Pedro	Algodoal	10/24/17
Ricardo	Araujo	4/19/17
Nivaldo	Azevedo	12/14/17
Dito	Barbosa	7/6/16
Percival	Barreto	10/20/17
Claudio	Bernardes	7/11/16
Ciro	Biderman	6/8/17
Nabil	Bonduki	6/21/16, 5/18/17
Ana Lúcia	Brasil	11/24/17
Ailton	Brasiliense	10/23/17
Frederico	Bussinger	11/13/17
Celso	Carvalho	10/17/17
Hélio	Castro	5/2/17
Francisco	Christovam	4/26/17
Eliene	Coelho	6/16/16
Companhia de Desenvolvimento Habitacional e Urban do Estado de São Paulo group interview		7/11/16
Mylene	Comploier	6/1/17
Marcel	Costa Sanches	9/18/17
Ronaldo	Cury	6/6/17
Frederico	da Silveira Barbosa	6/16/17
Carmen Silvia	de Carvalho Bueno	6/5/17
Fernando	de Mello Franco	5/25/17
Eduardo	Della Mana	9/29/17
Maria Teresa	Diniz	10/17/17
Adriano	Diogo	11/17/17

Rosilda	Domingues	9/28/17
Mariza	Dutra Alves	6/12/17
Sérgio	Ejzenberg	9/26/17
Ângelo	Fede	9/21/17
Gonzalo	Fernandez	9/26/17
Daniela	Ferrari	10/4/17
Ângelo	Filardo	5/23/17
Elisabete	França	7/4/16

Frente da Luta por Moradia
(Front for the Housing Struggle)
group interview   6/5/17

Ricardo	Gaboni	11/29/17
Sandra	Gianella	6/7/17
André	Gonçalves	6/23/17
Lúcio	Gregori	4/26/17
Beth	Grimberg	11/21/17
Eduardo	Grisotto	11/30/17
Ester	Guimarães	5/2/17
Fernando	Haddad	6/5/17
Tereza	Herling	5/15/17
Geraldo	Juncal	5/24/17
Mamoro	Kanzawa	6/1/17
Jorge	Kayano	4/18/17
Amir	Khair	6/9/17
Luiz	Kohara	4/24/17
Violeta	Krubusly	6/10/17
Marta	Lagreca	10/5/17
Esther	Leblanc	5/4/17
Hamilton	Leite	5/23/17
Ricardo	Leite	5/4/17
Mariza	Leste	6/12/17
Bartiria	Lima da Costa	7/7/16
Denise	Lopez de Souza	9/26/17
Rodrigo	Luna	9/21/17
Antonio Luiz	Marchioni (Padre Ticão)	10/10/17
Erminia	Maricato	6/21/16
Júlio	Marques	11/30/17
Paulo	Massoto	5/9/17
Margarete	Matiko	9/27/17
Sônia	Mistrello	10/18/17

Paula	Motta	6/20/16
Ana	Odila	4/21/17
Marco Antônio	Palermo	10/17/17, 10/25/17
Paulo	Pavani	9/21/17
Simão	Pedro	11/16/17
Carlos	Pelarim	6/13/17
Ricardo	Pereira	5/4/17
Úrsula	Perez	5/15/17
Vanderley	Pezzotta	10/3/17
Roberta	Primasi	6/8/17
Mário	Reali	10/4/17
Miguel	Reis	9/29/17
Evaniza	Rodrigues	5/8/17, 6/6/17
Sérgio	Rodrigues	10/26/17
Raquel	Rolnik	10/2/17
Ana Claudia	Rossbach	4/19/17
Américo	Sampaio	10/25/17
Celso	Sampaio	6/29/16, 4/24/17
Marcello	Sampaio	9/28/17
Paulo	Sandroni	5/11/17
Antônio	Santana	10/30/17

| São Paulo Company for Metropolitan Planning group interview | | 6/16/16 |
| Afonso | Silva | 6/12/17 |

| Sindicato das Empresas de Compra, Venda e Administração de Imóveis (Syndicate of Purchases, Sales, and Administration of Property of São Paulo) group interview | | 7/11/16 |

Weber	Sutti	7/14/16, 6/14/17
Jilmar	Tatto	12/12/17
Paulo	Teixeira	5/24/17
Márcia	Terlizzi	6/9/17
Ricardo	Toledo	5/10/17
Fernando	Tulio	5/15/17
Eduardo	Vasconcelos	5/11/17
Ney	Vaz	4/24/17
Chico	Whitaker	6/13/17
João	Whittaker	6/14/16

Graça	Xavier	6/27/16
Ricardo	Yazbek	12/6/17
Luis	Zamperlini	9/15/17
Muna	Zeyn	9/20/17
Mauro	Zilbovicius	6/14/17

In South Africa

First Name	Last Name	Date(s)
Gemey	Abrhams	7/7/15
Ashraf	Adam	7/27/17
Taffy	Adler	6/24/15
Nellie	Agingu-Lester	7/22/15
Richard	Bennet	8/10/17
Lael	Bethlehem	7/1/15
Jay	Bhagwan	7/27/17
Estee	Campher	7/11/17
Clive	Chipkin	7/10/15
Richard	Cottrill	7/23/15
Cedric	DeBeer	7/27/15
Lloyd	Druce	7/22/15
Kathy	Eales	6/22/18
Tiaan	Ehlers	7/21/15
Jan	Erasmus	6/12/15
Kenny	Fihla	7/15/15
Charl	Fitzgerald	6/26/15
Rory	Gallocher	7/9/15
Neil	Gopal	7/10/18
Ros	Gordon	8/2/17
Graeme	Götz	7/13/15
Philip	Harrison	6/8/15
Yael	Horowitz	7/13/15
Etienne	Hugo	6/25/18
Roland	Hunter	7/28/17
Paul	Jackson	7/20/15
Zunaid	Kahn	6/22/15
Yolisa	Kani	7/25/17
Paul	Kollenberg	7/27/15
Jak	Kossef	7/17/15
Mzisi	Kuhlane	7/24/17
Gerald	Leissner	7/21/15

Jonathan	Liebmann	7/7/15
Josiah	Lodi	7/11/17
John	Loos	6/15/15
Peter	Magni	6/26/15
Antonino	Manus	8/2/17
Jean-Pierre	Mas	8/28/17
Collen	Masango	8/14/17
Freeman	Masuku	7/17/17
Imelda	Matlawe	8/24/17
Lekgolo	Mayatula	7/23/15
Simon Sizwe	Mayson	6/15/15
Sithole	Mbanga	8/8/17
Leila	Mckenna	6/15/15, 7/15/17
Ishmael	Mkhabela	6/22/15, 7/21/15
Imogene	Mncwango	8/17/17
Sojane	Modise	8/24/17
Pascal	Moloi	8/4/17
Rehana	Moosajee	7/9/15, 7/12/17
Blake	Mosely	7/13/15
Eric	Motshwane	7/8/17, 7/25/17
Helgard	Muller	8/16/17
Ravi	Naidoo	7/22/15
Samantha	Naidoo	7/20/15
Monty	Narsoo	7/12/17
Stephen	Narsoo	7/11/15
Matthew	Nell	6/8/15
Jeff	Ngcobo	6/29/18
Malijeng	Ngqaleni	7/14/15
Trevor	Ngwane	7/20/15
Thulani	Nkosi	8/11/17
Gerald	Olitzky	6/11/15
Chippy	Olver	8/28/17
Anthony	Orelowitz	6/18/15
Li	Pernegger	6/16/15
Brian	Phalloh	7/8/15
Patrick	Phophi	8/30/17
Herman	Pienaar	7/21/15, 8/8/17
Kamini	Pillay	8/23/17
Renney	Plit	7/9/15
Giuseppe	Plumari	7/13/15
Mala	Ramana	7/28/17
Henning	Rasmuss	6/22/15

Tobie	Roux	8/16/17
Lauren	Royston	6/22/15
Kecia	Rust	8/22/17
Greg	Sacks	7/22/15
David	Savage	8/11/17
Geci	Sebina	7/10/15
Rashid	Seedat	6/22/15
Lisa	Seftel	6/25/15
Julius	Sello	8/28/17
Yondela	Silimela	7/6/15
Darko	Skrbinsek	7/18/17, 7/21/17
Manny	Sotomi	8/18/17, 8/23/17
Bob	Stanway	7/18/17
Anne	Stephny	7/20/15
Anthony	Still	8/28/17
Mike	Sutcliffe	8/15/17
Josef	Talotta	6/7/15
Parks	Tau	8/10/17
Johan	Van Der Merwe	7/22/15
David	Van Niekerk	7/14/15
Ahmedi	Vawda	8/25/17
Abri	Vermulen	8/16/17
Dylan	Weakley	8/4/17
Mel	Wilkinson	8/4/17
Erky	Wood	7/7/15
Tanya	Zack	6/8/15
Gina	Zanti	7/7/15

1. Theorizing Power, Public Goods, and the City

1. Mariza Dutra Alves, interview with the author, June 12, 2017. Unless otherwise noted, all translations are mine.

2. The term *slum* has a highly varied political meaning across the world. In South Africa, it is sometimes seen as having a pejorative or stigmatizing connotation. In other contexts, it is extremely common. Beyond the political meaning of the term, it encapsulates a range of housing realities, from dense high-rise tenements to sprawling low-rise peri-urban settlements. In this book, I use the terms *slum* and *informal settlement* both. Notwithstanding the sometimes stigmatizing connotation in South Africa, *slum* is a term with a global valence and the most commonly used, for example, in United Nations research and documentation.

3. As key examples in the sociological literature on "modernization" and development, see Bellah 1958; Germani 1969; Inkeles 1969; Lerner 1958; Portes 1976; Rostow 1959. Likewise, as key examples in the sociological literature on urbanism and urbanization, see Burgess 1982; Mckenzie 1924; Park 1936; Wirth 1938. While the former are global and comparative in orientation, the latter are largely concerned with the United States.

4. See Ball 1986 for a review of how work in urban studies has developed this approach.

5. This latter conceptual approach—of the city as a commons—bears a strong affinity to the work of Henri Lefebvre (1996) and his concept of a "right to the city."

2. The Cases: Comparing São Paulo and Johannesburg

1. Race and class are closely correlated in settlement patterns and access to public goods in São Paulo (see França 2015).

2. A "São Paulo school" of urban sociology, which has gone untranslated in English, emerged in the 1970s as Brazilian researchers began to document dimensions of extreme segregation and differentiation in the city. The titles of the most prominent works from this period tell the tale: "Critique of Dualist Reason" (Oliveira 1972), *São Paulo 1975: Growth and Poverty* (Camargo et al. 1976), and *Urban Plunder* (Kowarick 1980).

3. Antonio Luiz Marchioni (Padre Ticão), interview with the author, October 10, 2017.

4. Ibid.

5. As would become clear the following year, with the election of Jair Bolsonaro, this historical role for the Catholic Church was much diminished. Evangelical Christian affiliations would later become much more dominant in the city's peripheries (Richmond 2020).

6. Evaniza Rodrigues, interview with the author, May 8, 2017.

7. At the time of completing this book in March 2024, contemporaneous polling suggested that the ANC was at risk of falling below a 50 percent vote share in upcoming national elections in 2024.

8. This number accounts for the three main social welfare grants: pension, disability, and child support.

3. Housing: Subaltern Rights and Elite Resistance

1. Graça Xavier, interview with the author, June 27, 2016.

2. Erminia Maricato, interview with the author, June 21, 2016.

3. Juncal would go on to be the president of the municipal housing company, Metropolitan Housing Company of São Paulo, under the third PT mayoral administration of Fernando Haddad (2013–16).

4. Geraldo Juncal, interview with the author, May 24, 2017.

5. Claudio Bernardes, interview with the author, July 11, 2016. The reference to Erundina as "a northeasterner" was clearly intended as a pejorative. Brazil's northeast is the country's poorest region and, historically, the dominant source of migrants to cities in the country's wealthier south, such as São Paulo.

6. Evaniza Rodrigues, interview with the author, June 6, 2017.

7. Bernardes, interview with the author, July 11, 2016.

8. Frente da Luta por Moradia (Front for the Housing Struggle), group interview with the author, June 5, 2017.

9. Municipal decree number 44.667, April 26, 2004.

10. Dito Barbosa, interview with the author, July 6, 2016.

11. Eduardo Della Mana, interview with the author, September 29, 2017.

12. Frente da Luta por Moradia (Front for the Housing Struggle), group interview with the author, June 5, 2017.

13. Ricardo Pereira, interview with the author, May 4, 2017.

14. Elisabete França, interview with the author, July 4, 2016; Maria Teresa Diniz, interview with the author, October 17, 2017.

15. França, interview with the author, July 4, 2016. Methodologically, readers should not necessarily take these comments at face value (see Jerolmack and Khan 2014). The salient point here is that the fact that this was such a consistent form of articulation among bureaucrats in center-right governments in São Paulo suggests that they were operating in a context where their work had to be framed in these terms. The hard outcomes documented in chapter 2 speak for themselves.

16. Rodrigues, interview with the author, May 8, 2017.

17. Afonso Silva, interview with the author, June 12, 2017. I made multiple visits to two different MTST occupations and spoke with local leaders of those occupations.

18. Ricardo Yazbek, interview with the author, December 6, 2017.

19. Fernando Haddad, interview with the author, June 5, 2017.

20. Ronaldo Cury, interview with the author, June 6, 2017.

21. Transvaal was the name of the province including Johannesburg.

22. Erky Wood, interview with the author, July 7, 2015.

23. Trevor Ngwane, interview with the author, July 20, 2015.

24. Anne Stephny, interview with the author, July 20, 2015.

25. Ibid.

26. Ibid.

27. Gerald Olitzky, interview with the author, June 11, 2015.

28. Ibid.

29. David Savage, interview with the author, August 11, 2017.

30. Parks Tau, interview with the author, August 10, 2017.

31. Kenny Fihla, interview with the author, July 15, 2015.

32. Johannesburg was running an annual expenditure of R8.5 billion.

33. Fihla, interview with the author, July 15, 2015.

34. Ibid.

35. Anthony Orelowitz, interview with the author, June 18, 2015. *Robot* is a commonly used term in South Africa for a traffic light.

36. A senior advisor to Tau who claimed to have coined the term told me that "corridors of freedom" was not initially a stand-alone plan but, rather, a new slogan to encompass existing spatial and budgetary plans.

37. Herman Pienaar, interview with the author, July 21, 2015.

38. Tau, interview with the author, August 10, 2017.

39. Herman Pienaar, interview with the author, August 8, 2017.

40. Lloyd Druce, interview with the author, July 22, 2015.

41. This was reported to me by private developers and planners, as well as city officials.

42. Gina Zanti, interview with the author, July 7, 2015.

43. Charl Fitzgerald, interview with the author, June 26, 2015.

44. Zanti, interview with the author, July 7, 2015.

45. Savage, interview with the author, August 11, 2017.

46. There is an irony here. While officials were describing this as a new plan, the speechwriter of Mayor Parks Tau's inaugural address, in which he coined the term, suggested to me that the term was not initially deployed to describe a fleshed-out plan. Rather, it was a rhetorical device that—after it was well received—led to an insistence for a plan to substantiate the slogan.

47. Yondela Silimela, interview with the author, July 6, 2015.

4. Transportation: Institutions versus Technology

1. Almost all business sectors in Brazil are organized in "syndicates" that represent their collective interests. This is a legacy of the "corporatist" economic reforms during the presidencies of Getúlio Vargas in the 1930s and 1940s (Skidmore 1967).

2. Francisco Christovam, interview with the author, April 26, 2017.

3. Municipal Law 11.037/1991, gazetted July 25, 1991.

4. Paulo Sandroni, interview with the author, May 11, 2017.

5. Municipal Decree 31.347, gazetted March 20, 1992; Municipal Decree 33.593, gazetted August 12, 1993; Municipal Decree 37.347, gazetted February 20, 1998. For more, see Campos 2016.

6. Nivaldo Azevedo, interview with the author, December 14, 2017.

7. Ibid.

8. Municipal Law 13.241, gazetted December 12, 2001.

9. Vanderley Pezzotta, interview with the author, October 3, 2017. This number appears to conflict with that cited above by a former perueiro and current bus cooperative representative for 1997, which was 23,000. Other municipal officials cited fifteen thousand. It is possible that the massive expansion in the late 1990s led to some consolidation of unprofitable routes in later years due to the very thin profit margins characteristic of the sector.

10. Ibid.

11. Azevedo, interview with the author, December 14, 2017.

12. Municipal Decree 42.184, gazetted July 11, 2002.

13. Azevedo, interview with the author, December 14, 2017.

14. Jilmar Tatto, interview with the author, December 12, 2017.

15. Tatto has faced persistent rumors of connections to organized crime in the South Zone in the city. I was unable to confirm these allegations independently. Whether they are true or not, I understood them to reveal a general sense that Tatto's activist history had rooted him in both the formal and informal organizational life of the South Zone of the city. See Zanini and Linhares 2020.

16. Ana Odila, interview with the author, April 21, 2017.

17. Christovam, interview with the author, April 26, 2017.

18. Frederico Bussinger, interview with the author, November 13, 2017.

19. Ibid.

20. Odila, interview with the author, April 21, 2017.

21. In 2022, *classe C* was defined as monthly household income between $833 and $2,083.

22. Haddad, interview with the author, June 5, 2017.

23. Tatto, interview with the author, December 12, 2017.

24. Ciro Biderman, interview with the author, June 8, 2017.

25. Tatto, interview with the author, December 12, 2017.

26. Darko Skrbinsek, interview with the author, July 18, 2017.

27. Eric Motshwane, interview with the author, July 25, 2017.

28. Ibid.

29. Bob Stanway, interview with the author, July 18, 2017.

30. Ibid.

31. Ibid.

32. Rehana Moosajee, interview with the author, July 9, 2015.

33. Rehana Moosajee, interview with the author, July 12, 2017.

34. Darko Skrbinsek, interview with the author, July 21, 2017.

35. Lisa Seftel, interview with the author, June 25, 2015.

36. Eric Motshwane, interview with the author, July 18, 2017.

37. Seftel, interview with the author, June 25, 2015.

38. Yolisa Kani, interview with the author, July 25, 2017.

39. Skrbinsek, interview with the author, July 21, 2017.

40. Motshwane, interview with the author, July 25, 2017.

41. Sojane Modise, interview with the author, August 24, 2017.

42. Tau, interview with the author, August 10, 2017.

43. Ibid.

5. Sanitation: Cohesion versus Competition

1. Mário Reali, interview with the author, October 4, 2017.

2. Ibid.

3. Amir Khair, interview with the author, June 9, 2017.

4. Hélio Castro, interview with the author, May 2, 2017.

5. Maria Teresa Diniz, interview with the author, October 17, 2017.

6. Sandra Gianella, interview with the author, June 7, 2017.

7. "Apresentação Nucleo Gestor," slideshow, February 2017, internal document provided to the author.

8. Denise Lopez de Souza, interview with the author, September 26, 2017.

9. Ibid.

10. Castro, interview with the author, May 2, 2017; emphasis added.

11. Ibid.; emphasis added.

12. Jay Bhagwan, interview with the author, July 27, 2017.

13. Abri Vermulen, interview with the author, August 16, 2017.

14. Kathy Eales, interview with the author, June 22, 2018.

15. Roland Hunter, interview with the author, July 28, 2017.

16. Savage, interview with the author, August 11, 2017.

17. Pascal Moloi, interview with the author, August 4, 2017.

18. Jean-Pierre Mas, interview with the author, August 28, 2017.

19. Eales, interview with the author, June 22, 2018.

20. Ibid.

21. Ibid.

22. Hunter, interview with the author, July 28, 2017.

23. Mas, interview with the author, August 28, 2017.

24. Anthony Still, interview with the author, August 28, 2017.

25. Moloi, interview with the author, August 4, 2017.

26. To be clear, I am not in a position to independently assess these claims of corruption. What we can do is assess that there was a widespread sense among those within the bureaucracy that corruption shaped bureaucratic action. What I am reporting as evidence is that this attitude existed and that it shaped how key actors within bureaucratic agencies behaved.

27. Eales, interview with the author, June 22, 2018.

28. Ibid.

29. Ibid.

30. Savage, interview with the author, August 11, 2017.

31. Ibid.

32. Samantha Naidoo, interview with the author, July 20, 2015.

Abiko, Alex K., and Leandro Oliveira Coelho. 2004. "Procedimentos De Gestão De Mutirão Habitacional Para População De Baixa Renda." *Ambiente Construido* 4 (1): 7–20.

Adebayo, Pauline. 2011. "Post-Apartheid Housing Policy and a Somewhat Altered State Role: Does Incremental Housing Still Have a Place in South Africa?" *Built and Human Environment Review* 4 (2): 3–16.

Agbiboa, Daniel. 2022. *They Eat Our Sweat: Transport Labor, Corruption and Everyday Survival in Urban Nigeria.* Oxford: Oxford University Press.

Aldana Cohen, Daniel. 2016. "The Rationed City: The Politics of Water, Housing, and Land Use in Drought-Parched São Paulo." *Public Culture* 28 (2), 79: 261–89.

Alexander, Peter, Carin Runciman, Trevor Ngwane, Boikanyo Moloto, Kgothatso Mokgele, and Nicole Van Staden. 2018. "Frequency and Turmoil: South Africa's Community Protests, 2005–2017." *South African Crime Quarterly* 63: 27–42.

Alonso, Angela, and Ann Mische. 2016. "Changing Repertoires and Partisan Ambivalence in the New Brazilian Protests." *Bulletin of Latin American Research* 36 (2), March 16: 144–59.

Alvim, Angélica A. T. Benatti, Eunice Helena Sguizzardi Abascal, and Luís Gustavo Sayão de Moraes. 2011. "Projeto Urbano E Operação Urbana Consorciada Em São Paulo: Limites, Desafios E Perspectivas." *Cadernos Metrópole* 13 (25): 213–33.

Amenta, Edwin. 2014. "How to Analyze the Influence of Social Movements." *Contemporary Sociology* 43 (1): 16–29.

Amenta, Edwin, Neal Caren, Elizabeth Chiarello, and Yang Su. 2010. "The Political Consequences of Social Movements." *Annual Review of Sociology* 36 (1): 287–307.

Amsden, Alice H. 1989. *Asia's Next Giant: South Korea and Late Industrialization.* Oxford: Oxford University Press.

Anria, Santiago. 2018. *When Movements Become Parties: The Bolivian MAS in Comparative Perspective.* Cambridge: Cambridge University Press.

Armstrong, Elizabeth A., and Mary Bernstein. 2008. "Culture, Power, and Institutions: A Multi-institutional Politics Approach to Social Movements." *Sociological Theory* 26 (1), February 1: 74–99.

Arretche, Marta T. S. 1999. "Políticas sociais no Brasil: Descentralização em um Estado federativo." *Revista Brasileira de Ciências Sociais* 14 (40): 111–41.

Auerbach, Adam. 2020. *Demanding Development: The Politics of Public Goods Provision in India's Urban Slums.* Cambridge: Cambridge University Press.

Avritzer, Leonardo. 2002. *Democracy and the Public Space in Latin America.* Princeton, NJ: Princeton University Press.

Avritzer, Leonardo. 2007. *Urban Reform, Participation, and the Right to the City in Brazil.* Sussex, UK: Institute of Development Studies.

Baiocchi, Gianpaolo, Einar Braathen, and Ana Claudia Teixeira. 2012. "Transformation Institutionalized? Making Sense of Participatory Democracy in the Lula Era." In *Democratization in the Global South: The Importance of Transformative Politics*, ed. C. Stokke and O. Thornquist, 217–39. London: Palgrave Macmillan.

Baiocchi, Gianpaolo, Patrick Heller, and Marcelo K. Silva. 2011. *Bootstrapping Democracy: Experiments in Urban Governance in Brazil*. Stanford, CA: Stanford University Press.

Ball, M. 1986. "The Built Environment and the Urban Question." *Environment and Planning D: Society and Space* 4 (4): 447–64.

Bassett, Carolyn. 2008. "South Africa: Revisiting Capital's 'Formative Action.'" *Review of African Political Economy* 35 (116): 185–202.

Beall, Jo, Owen Crankshaw, and Sue Parnell. 2002. *Uniting a Divided City*. London: Earthscan Publications.

Bellah, Robert. 1958. "Religious Aspects of Modernization in Turkey and Japan." *American Journal of Sociology* 64 (1): 1–5.

Bhardwaj, Gaurav, Thomas Esch, Somik V. Lall, Mattia Marconcini, Maria Edisa Soppelsa, and Sameh Wahba. 2020. "Cities, Crowding, and the Coronavirus: Predicting Contagion Risk Hotspots." Washington, DC: World Bank. https://openknowledge.worldbank.org/server /api/core/bitstreams/a155c5ae-cd99-5635-a9de-4b86905f402f/content.

Bond, Patrick. 2005. *Elite Transition: From Apartheid to Neoliberalism in South Africa*. London: Pluto.

Bonduki, Nabil. 1994. "Crise da habitação e luta pela moradia no pós-guerra." In *As Lutas Sociais e a Cidade—São Paulo: Passado e Presente*, ed. Lúcio Kowarick. São Paulo, Brazil: Editora Paz e Terra.

Bonner, Philip, and Lauren Segal. 1998. *Soweto: A History*. Cape Town, South Africa: Maskew Miller Longman.

Bradlow, Benjamin H. 2021. "Weapons of the Strong: Elite Resistance and the Neo-Apartheid City." *City and Community* 20 (3): 191–211.

Bradlow, Benjamin H. 2022. "Embeddedness and Cohesion: Regimes of Urban Public Goods Distribution." *Theory and Society* 51 (1): 117–44.

Bradlow, Benjamin H. 2024. "Urban Social Movements and Local State Capacity." *World Development* 173: 106415.

Bradlow, Benjamin, Joel Bolnick, and Clifford Shearing. 2011. "Housing, Institutions and Money: The Failures and Promise of Human Settlements Policy and Practice in South Africa." *Environment and Urbanization* 23 (1): 267–75.

Brenner, Neil, and Nik Theodore. 2002. "Cities and the Geographies of 'Actually Existing Neoliberalism.'" *Antipode* 34: 349–79.

Burawoy, Michael. 1989. "Two Methods in Search of Science: Skocpol versus Trotsky." *Theory and Society* 18 (6): 759–805.

Burdick, John. 1996. *Looking for God in Brazil: The Progressive Catholic Church in Urban Brazil's Religious Arena*. Oakland: University of California Press.

Burgess, Ernest. 1982. "The Growth of the American City: An Introduction to a Research Project." In *Urban Patterns: Studies in Human Ecology*, ed. George Theodorson, 34–41. University Park: Pennsylvania State University Press.

Burra, Sundar, Sheela Patel, and Thomas Kerr. 2003. "Community-Designed, Built and Managed Toilet Blocks in Indian Cities." *Environment and Urbanization* 15 (2): 11–32.

Caldeira, Teresa P. 2017. "Peripheral Urbanization: Autoconstruction, Transversal Logics, and Politics in Cities of the Global South." *Environment and Planning D: Society and Space* 35 (1): 3–20.

Caldeira, Teresa, and James Holston. 2015. "Participatory Urban Planning in Brazil." *Urban Studies* 52 (11): 2001–17.

Camargo, Candido Procopio Ferreira, Fernando Henrique Cardoso, Frederico Mazzucchelli, José Álvaro Moisés, Lúcio Kowarick, Maria Herminia Tavares de Almeida, Paul Israel Singer, and Vinicius Caldeira Brant. 1976. *São Paulo 1975: Crescimento e Pobreza*. São Paulo, Brazil: Edições Loyola.

Campos, Marcos. 2016. "O Mercado de Viagens e as Disputas em Torno das Linhas de Ônibus." *Novos Estudos* 105: 35–53.

Campos, Marcos. 2018. "Public Policy Instruments and Their Impact: From Analogue to Electronic Government in the Bus Services of São Paulo." *Brazilian Political Science Review* 12 (1): 1–26.

Carolini, Gabriella, and Prasana Raman. 2021. "Why Detailing Spatial Equity Matters in Water and Sanitation Evaluations." *Journal of the American Planning Association* 87 (1): 101–7.

Chaskalson, Matthew, Karen Jochelson, and Jeremy Seekings. 1987. "Rent Boycotts, the State, and the Transformation of the Urban Political Economy in South Africa." *Review of African Political Economy* 14 (40): 47–64.

Chibber, Vivek. 2002. "Bureaucratic Rationality and the Developmental State." *American Journal of Sociology* 107 (4): 951–89.

Cities Alliance. 2004. *Integrating the Poor: Urban Upgrading and Land Tenure Regularization in the City of São Paulo*. São Paulo, Brazil: Cities Alliance.

Clarno, Andy. 2017. *Neoliberal Apartheid: Palestine/Israel and South Africa after 1994*. Chicago: University of Chicago Press.

Clavel, Pierre, and Wim Wiewel. 1991. "Introduction." In *Harold Washington and the Neighborhoods*, ed. Pierre Clavel and Wim Wiewel. New Brunswick, NJ: Rutgers University Press.

Couto, Cláudio Gonçalves. 1995. *O desafio de ser governo: O PT na prefeitura de São Paulo (1989–1992)*. São Paulo, Brazil: Editora Paz e Terra.

Cox, Anna. 2011. "Goodbye Oxford Rd, Hello Louis Botha. . . ." *The Star*, November 1. Retrieved from https://www.iol.co.za/motoring/industry-news/goodbye-oxford-rd-hello-louis-botha -1168965 (accessed June 23, 2020).

Crankshaw, Owen. 2008. "Race, Space and the Post-Fordist Spatial Order of Johannesburg." *Urban Studies* 45 (8): 1692–711.

Crankshaw, Owen. 2022. *Urban Inequality: Theory, Evidence and Method in Johannesburg*. London: Zed Books.

Crankshaw, Owen, and Caroline White. 1995. "Racial Desegregation and Inner City Decay in Johannesburg." *International Journal of Urban and Regional Research* 19 (4): 622–38.

Cruxen, Isadora. 2022. "The Limits of Insulation: The Long-Term Political Dynamics of Public-Private Service Delivery." *International Development Planning Review* 44 (3): 317–43.

Cunha Linke, Clarisse, and Roberto Andrés. 2022. "Teresina está sem ônibus. Sua cidade pode ser a próxima." *Intercept Brasil*, April 29. https://theintercept.com/2022/04/29/teresina-onibus -crise-transporte-publico/.

Davies, Jonathan S. 2002. "Urban Regime Theory: A Normative-Empirical Critique." *Journal of Urban Affairs* 24: 1–17.

Davis, Mike. 2006. *Planet of Slums*. New York: Verso Books.

Department of Housing. 1994. "White Paper: A New Housing Policy and Strategy for South Africa." https://www.dhs.gov.za/sites/default/files/legislation/Policies_Housing_White _Paper.pdf.

Diwakar, Rekha. 2016. "Local Contest, National Impact: Understanding the Success of India's Aam Aadmi Party in 2015 Delhi Assembly Election." *Representation: Journal of Representative Democracy* 52 (1): 71–80.

Dreger, Christian, Tongsan Wang, and Yanqun Zhang. 2015. "Understanding Chinese Consumption: The Impact of *Hukou*." *Development and Change* 46 (6): 1331–44.

du Plessis, Anja. 2023. "Johannesburg Has Been Hit by Severe Water Shortages: New Plan to Manage the Crisis Isn't the Answer." *The Conversation*, October 5. https://theconversation

.com/johannesburg-has-been-hit-by-severe-water-shortages-new-plan-to-manage-the-crisis
-isnt-the-answer-214975.

Dugard, Jackie. 2001. "From Low-Intensity War to Mafia War: Taxi Violence in South Africa, 1987–2000." Violence and Transition Series, vol. 4. Johannesburg, South Africa: Centre for the Study of Violence and Reconciliation.

Dyson, Tim. 2011. "The Role of the Demographic Transition in the Process of Urbanization." *Population and Development Review* 37: 34–54.

Earle, Lucy. 2012. "From Insurgent to Transgressive Citizenship: Housing, Social Movement and the Politics of Rights in Sao Paulo." *Journal of Latin American Studies* 44 (1): 97–126.

Ebrahim, Zohra. 1991. "Civics: Meeting the Challenges of South Africa." Report prepared for the National General Council of the United Democratic Front, Johannesburg, South Africa, March 1–3.

Esping-Andersen, Gøsta. 1990. *The Three Worlds of Welfare Capitalism*. Princeton, NJ: Princeton University Press.

Estado de São Paulo. 1990. "Erundina quer ônibus de graça em SP." September 20.

Estado de São Paulo. 2009. "Conheça a vida e os escândalos de Celso Pitta." November 21. https://www.estadao.com.br/politica/conheca-a-vida-e-os-escandalos-de-celso-pitta/.

Evans, Peter. 1995. *Embedded Autonomy: States and Industrial Transformation*. Princeton, NJ: Princeton University Press.

Evans, Peter, and Patrick Heller. 2015. "Human Development, State Transformation, and the Politics of the Developmental State." In *The Oxford Handbook of Transformations of the State*, ed. Stephan Leibfried, Evelyne Huber, Matthew Lange, Jonah D. Levy, Frank Nullmeier, and John D. Stephens, 691–713. Oxford: Oxford University Press.

Evans, Peter, Evelyne Huber, and John D. Stephens. 2017. "The Political Foundations of State Effectiveness." In *State Building in the Developing World*, ed. M. Centeno, A. Kohli, and D. Yashar, 380–408. Princeton, NJ: Princeton University Press.

Evans, Peter, Dietrich Rueschemeyer, and Theda Skocpol. 1985. "On the Road toward a More Adequate Understanding of the State." In *Bringing the State Back In*, ed. Peter Evans, Dietrich Rueschemeyer, and Theda Skocpol, 347–66. Cambridge: Cambridge University Press.

Fahlberg, Anjuli. 2023. *Activism under Fire: The Politics of Non-violence in Rio de Janeiro's Gang Territories*. Oxford: Oxford University Press.

Fainstein, Susan. 2010. *The Just City*. Ithaca, NY: Cornell University Press.

Faletti, Tulia, and James Mahoney. 2015. "The Comparative Sequential Method." In *Advances in Comparative-Historical Analysis*, ed. James Mahoney and Kathleen Thelen, 211–39. Cambridge: Cambridge University Press.

Fang, Wanli, and Sameh Wahba. 2020. "Urban Density Is Not an Enemy in the Coronavirus Fight: Evidence from China." *Sustainable Cities*, April 20. https://blogs.worldbank.org/sustainablecities/urban-density-not-enemy-coronavirus-fight-evidence-china.

Faoro, Raymundo. 1958. *Os donos do poder: Formação do patronato político brasileiro*. São Paulo, Brazil: Editora Globo.

Fasenfest, David. 2017. "A Neoliberal Response to an Urban Crisis: Emergency Management in Flint, MI." *Critical Sociology* 45 (1): 33–47.

Fernandes, Edésio. 2007. "Implementing the Urban Reform Agenda in Brazil." *Environment and Urbanization* 19 (1): 177–89.

Fine, Ben, and Zavareh Rustomjee. 1996. *The Political Economy of South Africa: From Minerals-Energy Complex to Industrialisation*. Boulder, CO: Westview Press.

Fix, Mariana. 2007. *São Paulo cidade global*. São Paulo, Brazil: Boitempo Editorial.

Folha de São Paulo. 1996. "Mutirão versus Cingapura." November 14. https://www1.folha.uol.com.br/fsp/1996/11/14/caderno_especial/50.html.

Folha de São Paulo. 1998. "Catraca eletrônica está atrasada." September 15. https://www1.folha
.uol.com.br/fsp/cotidian/ff15099830.htm (accessed April 14, 2020).

Folha de São Paulo. 1999. "Cingapura foi maior destaque." March 30. https://www1.folha.uol.com
.br/fsp/cotidian/ff30039902.htm.

Folha de São Paulo. 2000. "Aliança com novatos seria decisiva para PT." December 26. https://
www1.folha.uol.com.br/fsp/cotidian/ff2612200013.htm.

França, Danilo. 2015. "Desigualdades e segregação residencial por raça e clase na RMSP
(2000–2010)." In *A metropole de São Paulo no século XXI*, ed. Eduardo Marques, 223–54.
São Paulo, Brazil: Editora Unesp.

Franco, Marielle. 2018. "After the Take-Over: Mobilizing the Political Creativity of Brazil's Favelas."
New Left Review 110, March–April: 135–40. https://newleftreview.org/issues/ii110/articles
/marielle-franco-after-the-take-over.pdf.

Friedman, Eli. 2022. *The Urbanization of People: The Politics of Development, Labor Markets, and
Schooling in the Chinese City*. New York: Columbia University Press.

Friendly, Abigail. 2017. "Urban Policy, Social Movements, and the Right to the City in Brazil."
Latin American Perspectives 44 (2): 132–48.

Fung, Archon, and Erik O. Wright. 2001. "Deepening Democracy: Innovations in Empowered
Participatory Governance." *Politics and Society* 29 (1): 5–41.

Garcia, Diego. 2020. "Quase metade dos domicílios brasileiros não tem acesso a rede de esgoto."
Folha de São Paulo, July 22. https://www1.folha.uol.com.br/mercado/2020/07/quase-metade
-dos-domicilios-brasileiros-nao-tem-acesso-a-rede-de-esgoto.shtml (accessed July 23, 2020).

Garrido, Marco. 2019. *The Patchwork City: Class, Space, and Politics in Metro Manila*. Chicago:
University of Chicago Press.

Garrido, Marco, Xuefei Ren, and Liza Weinstein. 2021. "Toward a Global Urban Sociology: Key-
words." *City and Community* 20 (1): 4–12.

Gelb, Stephen. 1987. "Making Sense of the Crisis." *Transformation: Critical Perspectives on Southern
Africa* 5: 33–50.

Gentile, Rogério. 1999. "Maluf chama Pitta de traidor e pede desculpas por tê-lo indicado." *Folha
de São Paulo*, April 24. https://www1.folha.uol.com.br/fsp/cotidian/ff24049901.htm.

Gentile, Rogério, and Gonzalo Navarrete. 1999. "Pitta esquece Maluf e adota 'linha Erundina.'"
Folha de São Paulo, May 25. https://www1.folha.uol.com.br/fsp/cotidian/ff25059904.htm.

Germani, Gino. 1969. "Stages of Modernization." *International Journal* 24 (3): 463–85.

Gibson, Christopher L. 2018. "Programmatic Configurations for the Twenty-first-Century Developmental State in Urban Brazil." *Sociology of Development* 4 (2): 169–90.

Gibson, Christopher L. 2019. *Movement-Driven Development: The Politics of Health and Democracy
in Brazil*. Palo Alto, CA: Stanford University Press.

Globalization and World Cities Research Network. 2020. "The World according to GaWC." https://
www.lboro.ac.uk/microsites/geography/gawc/gawcworlds.html (accessed March 5, 2020).

Gollin, Doulglas, Remi Jedwab, and Dietrich Vollrath. 2016. "Urbanization with and without
Industrialization." *Journal of Economic Growth* 21: 35–70.

Götz, Graeme, Chris Wray, and Brian Mubiwa. 2014. "The 'Thin Oil of Urbanisation'? Spatial
Change in Johannesburg and the Gauteng City-Region." In *Changing Space, Changing City:
Johannesburg after Apartheid*, ed. Philip Harrison, Graeme Götz, Alison Todes, and Chris
Wray, 42–62. Johannesburg, South Africa: Wits University Press.

Granovetter, Mark. 1985. "Economic Action and Social Structure: The Problem of Embeddedness." *American Journal of Sociology* 91 (3): 481–510.

Gregori, Lúcio, Mauro Zilbovicius, and José Jairo Varoli. 2001. "Um novo desafio no transporte público." *Folha de São Paulo*, August 31. https://www1.folha.uol.com.br/fsp/opiniao
/fz3108200110.htm.

Gulyani, Sumila, and Ellen M. Bassett. 2007. "Retrieving the Baby from the Bathwater: Slum Upgrading in Sub-Saharan Africa." *Environment and Planning C: Government and Policy* 25 (4): 486–515.

Haddad, Fernando. 2017. "Vivi na pele o que aprendi nos livros: Um encontro com o patrimonialismo brasileiro." *Revista Piauí* 129: 28–37. https://piaui.folha.uol.com.br/materia/vivi-na -pele-o-que-aprendi-nos-livros/.

Harber, Anton. 2011. *Diepsloot.* Johannesburg, South Africa: Jonathan Ball.

Harber, Jesse, and M. Bryer. 2020. "Governing the GCR Series: Unrealistic Expectations, Unrealised—Bus Rapid Transit in Johannesburg." GCRO Provocation 7. Johannesburg, South Africa: Gauteng City-Region Observatory. https://www.gcro.ac.za/outputs/provocations /detail/governing-the-gcr-series-unrealistic-expectations-unrealised-bus-rapid-transit-in -johannesburg/.

Harris, Peter. 2010. *Birth: The Conspiracy to Stop the '94 Election.* Johannesburg: Penguin Random House South Africa.

Harrison, Philip, Graeme Götz, Alison Todes, and Chris Wray. 2014. "Materialities, Subjectivities and Spatial Transformation in Johannesburg." In *Changing Space, Changing City: Johannesburg after Apartheid*, ed. P. Harrison, G. Götz, A. Todes, and C. Wray, 2–41. Johannesburg, South Africa: Wits University Press.

Hart, Gillian. 2014. *Rethinking the South African Crisis: Nationalism, Populism, Hegemony.* Athens: University of Georgia Press.

Harvey, David. 1989. "From Managerialism to Entrepreneurialism: The Transformation in Urban Governance in Late Capitalism." *Geografiska Annaler. Series B, Human Geography* 71 (1): 3–17.

Heller, Patrick. 1999. *The Labor of Development: Workers and the Transformation of Capitalism in Kerala, India.* Ithaca, NY: Cornell University Press.

Heller, Patrick. 2001. "Moving the State: The Politics of Democratic Decentralization in Kerala, South Africa, and Porto Alegre." *Politics and Society* 29 (1): 131–63.

Herrera, Veronica, and Alison E. Post. 2014. "Can Developing Countries Both Decentralize and Depoliticize Urban Water Services? Evaluating the Legacy of the 1990s Reform Wave." *World Development* 64, December: 621–41.

Hill, Matthew. 2009. "More Pain before Gain." *Business Day*, September 11. https://www .businesslive.co.za/archive/2009-09-11-more-pain-before-gain/ (accessed June 21, 2020).

Hirata, Daniel Veloso. 2011. "Produção da desordem e gestão da ordem: Notas para uma história recente do transporte clandestino em São Paulo." *Dilemas—Revista de Estudos de Conflito e Controle Social* 4 (3): 441–65.

Hirsch, Alan. 2015. "How Compromises and Mistakes Made in the Mandela Era Hobbled South Africa's Economy." *The Conversation*, December 23. https://theconversation.com/how -compromises-and-mistakes-made-in-the-mandela-era-hobbled-south-africas-economy-52156.

Hirschman, Albert. 1971. *A Bias for Hope: Essays on Development and Latin America.* New Haven, CT: Yale University Press.

Hockett, Robert. 2017. "Putting Distribution First." *Theoretical Inquiries in Law* 18: 157–225.

Hockett, Robert. 2020. "The InvestAmerica Plan—Reconstruction with or without Senate Help." *Forbes*, November 9. https://www.forbes.com/sites/rhockett/2020/11/09/the-investamerica -planreconstruction-with-or-without-senate-help/?sh=2ead636e78f2.

Holston, James. 2008. *Insurgent Citizenship: Disjunctions of Democracy and Modernity in Brazil.* Princeton, NJ: Princeton University Press.

Huber, Evelyne, and John D. Stephens. 2012. *Democracy and the Left: Social Policy and Inequality in Latin America.* Chicago: University of Chicago Press.

Imparato, Ivo, and Jeff Ruster. 2003. *Slum Upgrading and Participation: Lessons from Latin America.* Directions in Development. Washington, DC: World Bank.

Inkeles, Alex. 1969. "Making Men Modern: On the Causes and Consequences of Individual Change in Six Developing Countries." *American Journal of Sociology* 75 (2): 208–25.

International Panel on Climate Change. 2014. *Climate Change 2014: Synthesis Report. Contribution of Working Groups I, II and III to the Fifth Assessment Report of the Intergovernmental Panel on Climate Change.* Core Writing Team. Ed. R. K. Pachauri and L. A. Meyer. Geneva, Switzerland: International Panel on Climate Change.

Jacobs, Jane. 1961. *The Death and Life of Great American Cities.* New York: Vintage Books.

Jerolmack, Colin, and Shamus Khan. 2014. "Talk Is Cheap: Ethnography and the Attitudinal Fallacy." *Sociological Methods and Research* 43 (2): 178–209.

Johnson, Reed, and Rogerio Jelmayer. 2015. "Mayor Fernando Haddad's Pro-Bike Push Polarizes São Paulo." *Wall Street Journal*, September 23. https://www.wsj.com/articles/mayor-fernando -haddads-pro-bike-push-polarizes-sao-paulo-1443031374 (accessed May 28, 2020).

Kaboolian, Linda. 1998. "The New Public Management: Challenging the Boundaries of the Management vs. Administration Debate." *Public Administration Review* 58 (3): 189–93.

Kerstenetzky, Celia Lessa. 2014. "The Brazilian Social Developmental State: A Progressive Agenda in a (Still) Conservative Political Society." In *The End of the Developmental State?* ed. Michelle Williams, 172–96. New York: Routledge.

Kfouri, Antonio Carlos. 1995. "SOS—Mananciais." *Folha de São Paulo*, February 9. https://www1 .folha.uol.com.br/fsp/1995/2/09/cotidiano/12.html.

Klink, Jeroen, and Rosana Denaldi. 2016. "On Urban Reform, Rights and Planning Challenges in the Brazilian Metropolis." *Planning Theory* 15 (4): 402–17.

Kowarick, Lúcio. 1980. *A espoliação urbana.* São Paulo, Brazil: Editora Paz e Terra.

Kracker Selzer, Amy, and Patrick Heller. 2010. "The Spatial Dynamics of Middle-Class Formation in Postapartheid South Africa: Enclavization and Fragmentation in Johannesburg." *Political Power and Social Theory* 21: 171–208.

Lee, Cheol-Sung. 2012. "Associational Networks and Welfare States in Argentina, Brazil, South Korea, and Taiwan." *World Politics* 64 (3): 507–54.

Lefebvre, Henri. 1996 [1968]. *Right to the City.* In *Writings on Cities: Henri Lefebvre*, ed. and trans. E. Kofman and E. Lebas, 61–181. Oxford: Blackwell Publishing.

Lei, Ya-Wen. 2023. *Technology, Development, and State Capitalism in China.* Princeton, NJ: Princeton University Press.

Leite, Carlos, Claudia Acosta, Tereza Herling, Ligia Barrozo, and Paulo Saldiva. 2019. "Indicadores de desigualdade para financiamento urbano de cidades saudáveis." *Estudos Avançados* 33 (97): 37–60.

Lerner, Daniel. 1958. *Passing of Traditional Society: Modernizing the Middle East.* New York: Free Press.

Levenson, Zachary. 2022. *Delivery as Dispossession: Land Occupation and Eviction in the Postapartheid City.* Oxford: Oxford University Press.

Logan, John, and Harvey Molotch. 1987. *Urban Fortunes: The Political Economy of Place.* Berkeley: University of California Press.

Macaulay, Fiona. 1996. "'Governing for Everyone': The Workers' Party Administration in São Paulo, 1989–1992." *Bulletin of Latin American Research* 15 (2): 211–29.

Mackay, C. J. 2007. "The Development of Housing Policy in South Africa in the Post-Apartheid Period." *Housing Studies* 11 (1): 133–46.

Madlingozi, Tsepho. 2007. "Post-Apartheid Social Movements and the Quest for the Elusive 'New' South Africa." *Journal of Law and Society* 34 (1): 77–98.

Mann, Michael. 1984. "The Autonomous Power of the State: Its Origins, Mechanisms and Results." *European Journal of Sociology* 25 (2): 185–213.

Marais, Hein. 2011. *South Africa Pushed to the Limit: The Political Economy of Change.* London: Zed.

Marques, Eduardo. 2014. "Estrutura Social e Segregação em São Paulo: Transformações na Década de 2000." *DADOS—Revista de Ciências Sociais* 57 (3): 675–710.

Marques, Eduardo, ed. 2015. *A metrópole de São Paulo no século XXI, Espaços, Heterogeneidades e Desigualdades*. São Paulo, Brazil: University of São Paulo Press.

Marques, Eduardo. 2017. "A Rede Dos Gestores Locais Em São Paulo." *Dados* 60 (2): 437–72.

Marques, Eduardo. 2021. "Introduction." In *The Politics of Incremental Progressivism: Governments, Governances, and Urban Policy Changes in São Paulo*, ed. Eduardo Marques, 1–42. London: Wiley-Blackwell.

Marques, Eduardo. 2023. "Continuity and Change of Urban Policies in São Paulo: Resilience, Latency, and Reanimation." *Urban Affairs Review* 59 (2): 337–71.

Marques, Eduardo, and Camila Saraiva. 2017. "Urban Integration or Reconfigured Inequalities? Analyzing Housing Precarity in Sao Paulo, Brazil." *Habitat International* 69: 18–26.

Martin, Isaac. 2001. "Dawn of the Living Wage: The Diffusion of a Redistributive Municipal Policy." *Urban Affairs Review* 36 (4): 470–96.

Marwell, Nicole P., and Shannon L. Morrissey. 2020. "Organizations and the Governance of Urban Poverty." *Annual Review of Sociology* 46 (18). https://doi.org/10.1146/annurev-soc-121919-054708.

Mayekiso, Mzwanele. 1996. *Township Politics: Civic Struggles for a New South Africa*. New York: Monthly Review Press.

McAdam, D., J. McCarthy, and M. Zald, eds. 1996. *Comparative Perspectives on Social Movements*. Cambridge: Cambridge University Press.

McCaull, Colleen. 1990. *No Easy Ride: The Rise and Future of the Black Taxi Industry*. Johannesburg: South African Institute of Race Relations.

McDonnell, Erin Metz. 2017. "Patchwork Leviathan: How Pockets of Bureaucratic Governance Flourish within Institutionally Diverse Developing States." *American Sociological Review* 82 (3): 476–510.

Mckenzie, R. D. 1924. "The Ecological Approach to the Study of the Human Community." *American Journal of Sociology* 30: 287–301.

Millington, Nate. 2018. "Producing Water Scarcity in São Paulo, Brazil: The 2014–2015 Water Crisis and the Binding Politics of Infrastructure." *Political Geography* 65: 26–34.

Millington, Nate, and Suraya Scheba. 2021. "Day Zero and the Infrastructures of Climate Change: Water Governance, Inequality, and Infrastructural Politics in Cape Town's Water Crisis." *International Journal of Urban and Regional Research* 45 (1): 116–32.

Mitlin, Diana, and David Satterthwaite. 2012. *Urban Poverty in the Global South: Scale and Nature*. London: Routledge.

Mkandawire, Thandika. 2009. "Institutional Monocropping and Monotasking in Africa." Democracy, Governance and Well-Being Programme Paper 1. U.N. Research Institute for Social Development. https://digitallibrary.un.org/record/662977?ln=en.

Morgan, Kimberly, and Ann Orloff. 2017. "Introduction." In *The Many Hands of the State: Theorizing Political Authority and Social Control*, ed. Kimberly Morgan and Ann Orloff, 1–32. Cambridge: Cambridge University Press.

Mosselson, Aidan. 2017. "'Joburg Has Its Own Momentum': Towards a Vernacular Theorisation of Urban Change." *Urban Studies* 54 (5): 1280–96.

Municipality of São Paulo. 2010. *Plano Municipal de Saneamento Básico de São Paulo*. https://smastr20.blob.core.windows.net/conesan/Sao%20Paulo_AE_DU_RS_2010.pdf.

Municipality of São Paulo Municipal Housing Secretariat. 2013. "Em seis meses, Fundo de Saneamento investe 36 milhões em obras em Heliópolis." September 2. https://www.prefeitura.sp.gov.br/cidade/secretarias/habitacao/noticias/?p=155716 (accessed July 27, 2020).

Municipality of São Paulo Secretariat of Urban Development. 2019. "O que mudou na mobilidade no município de São Paulo entre 2007 e 2017?" *Informes Urbanos* 40, October.

Murray, Martin J. 2011. *City of Extremes: The Spatial Politics of Johannesburg.* Durham, NC: Duke University Press.

Murray, Martin J. 2015. "Waterfall City (Johannesburg): Privatized Urbanism In Extremis." *Environment and Planning A: Economy and Space* 47 (3): 503–20.

Mutongi, Kenda. 2017. *Matatu: A History of Popular Transportation in Nairobi.* Chicago: University of Chicago Press.

Offe, Claus, and Helmut Wiesenthal. 1985. "Two Logics of Collective Action: Theoretical Notes on Social Class and Organizational Form." *Political Power and Social Theory* 1: 67–115.

Oliveira, Francisco de. 1972. "A economia brasileira: Crítica à razão dualista." *Estudos Cebrap* 2: 4–82.

Organisation for Economic Co-operation and Development, African Tax Administration Forum, and African Union Commission. 2018. *Revenue Statistics in Africa 2018.* Organisation for Economic Co-operation and Development. https://doi.org/10.1787/9789264305885-en-fr.

Ostrom, Elinor. 1990. *Governing the Commons: The Evolution of Institutions for Collective Action.* Cambridge: Cambridge University Press.

Paller, Jeffrey. 2019. *Democracy in Ghana: Everyday Politics in Urban Africa.* Cambridge: Cambridge University Press.

Palocci, Antonio, Celso Daniel, Cezar Alvarez, Cristovam Buarque, Delúbio Soares, Edmilson Rodrigues, Gilberto Carvalho, Luiz Dulci, Luiz Sérgio Nóbrega, Marco Aurélio Garcia, Maria do Carmo, Olívio Dutra, Patrus Ananias, Raul Pont, and Tarso Genro. 1997. *Desafios do governo local: O modo petista de governar.* São Paulo, Brazil: Fundação Perseu Abramo.

Paret, Marcel. 2018. "The Community Strike: From Precarity to Militant Organizing." *International Journal of Comparative Sociology* 61 (2–3): 159–77.

Paret, Marcel. 2022. *Fractured Militancy: Precarious Resistance in South Africa after Racial Inclusion.* Ithaca, NY: Cornell University Press.

Park, Robert E. 1936. "Human Ecology." *American Journal of Sociology* 62 (1): 1–15.

Parnell, Susan, and Jennifer Robinson. 2012. "(Re)Theorizing Cities from the Global South: Looking beyond Neoliberalism." *Urban Geography* 33 (4): 593–617.

Patarra, Ivo. 1996. *O governo Luiza Erundina.* São Paulo, Brazil: Geração Editorial.

Peck, Jamie, Neil Brenner, and Nik Theodore. 2018. "Actually Existing Neoliberalism." In *The SAGE Handbook of Neoliberalism,* ed. Damien Cahill, Melinda Cooper, Martijn Konings, and David Primrose, 3–15. London: SAGE Publications.

Pereira, Rafael H. M., Tim Schwanen, and David Banister. 2017. "Distributive Justice and Equity in Transportation." *Transport Reviews* 37 (2): 170–91.

Pereira, Tatiana, and Léo Heller. 2015. "Planos municipais de saneamento básico: Avaliação de 18 casos brasileiros." *Engenharia Sanitaria e Ambiental* 20 (3): 395–404.

Petersen, Paul. 1981. *City Limits.* Chicago: University of Chicago Press.

Pieterse, Edgar. 2019. "Urban Governance and Spatial Transformation Ambitions in Johannesburg." *Journal of Urban Affairs* 41 (1): 20–38.

Pithouse, Richard. 2008. "A Politics of the Poor: Shack Dwellers' Struggles in Durban." *Journal of Asian and African Studies* 43 (1): 63–94.

Polanyi, Karl. 1944. *The Great Transformation.* Boston: Beacon Press.

Portes, Alejandro. 1976. "On the Sociology of National Development: Theories and Issues." *American Journal of Sociology* 82 (1): 55–85.

Puls, Maurício. 2000. *O malufismo.* São Paulo, Brazil: Publifolha.

Purdy, Sean. 2017. "Brazil's June Days of 2013: Mass Protest, Class, and the Left." *Latin American Perspectives* 22 (2): 1–22.

Pzeworski, Adam. 1985. *Capitalism and Social Democracy*. Cambridge: Cambridge University Press.

Ren, Xuefei. 2018. "From Chicago to China and India: Studying the City in the Twenty-First Century." *Annual Review of Sociology* 44 (1): 497–513.

Ren, Xuefei. 2020. *Governing the Urban in China and India: Land Grabs, Slum Clearance, and the War on Air Pollution*. Princeton, NJ: Princeton University Press.

Republic of South Africa Department of Human Settlements. 2009. *National Housing Code, 2009*. https://www.dhs.gov.za/content/national-housing-code-2009.

Republic of South Africa Department of Water Affairs and Forestry. 1994. "Water Supply and Sanitation Policy: White Paper." https://www.gov.za/sites/default/files/gcis_document/201409/wssp.pdf.

Rich, Jessica. 2019. *State-Sponsored Activism: Bureaucrats and Social Movements in Democratic Brazil*. Cambridge: Cambridge University Press.

Richmond, Matthew A. 2020. "Narratives of Crisis in the Periphery of São Paulo: Place and Political Articulation during Brazil's Rightward Turn." *Journal of Latin American Studies* 52: 241–67.

Rigaud, Kumari Kanta, Alex de Sherbinin, Bryan Jones, Jonas Bergmann, Viviane Clement, Kayly Ober, Jacob Schewe, Susana Adamo, Brent McCusker, Silke Heuser, and Amelia Midgley. 2018. *Groundswell: Preparing for Internal Climate Migration*. Washington, DC: World Bank. https://openknowledge.worldbank.org/entities/publication/2be91c76-d023-5809-9c94-d41b71c25635.

Robinson, Jennifer. 2022. *Comparative Urbanism: Tactics for Global Urban Studies*. London: Wiley.

Rocha de Barros, Celso. 2022. *PT, Uma História*. São Paulo, Brazil: Companhia Das Letras.

Rolnik, Raquel. 2015. *Guerra dos Lugares: A colonização da terra e da moradia na era das finanças*. São Paulo, Brazil: Boitempo Editorial.

Rolnik, Raquel, Lúcio Kowarick, and Nadia Somekh, eds. 1990. *São Paulo: Crise e Mudança*. São Paulo, Brazil: Editora Brasiliense.

Rossouw, Jannie. 2017. "Why Social Grants Matter in South Africa: They Support 33% of the Nation." *The Conversation*, February 16. https://theconversation.com/why-social-grants-matter-in-south-africa-they-support-33-of-the-nation-73087.

Rostow, W. W. 1959. "Stages of Economic Growth." *Economic History Review* 12 (1): 1–16.

Roy, Ananya. 2009. "Why India Cannot Plan Its Cities: Informality, Insurgence and the Idiom of Urbanization." *Planning Theory* 8 (1): 76–87.

Roy, Arundhati. 2020. "The Pandemic Is a Portal." *Financial Times*, April 3.

Rueschemeyer, Dietrich, Evelyne Huber Stephens, and John D. Stephens. 1992. *Capitalist Development and Democracy*. Chicago: University of Chicago Press.

Runciman, Carin. 2015. "The Decline of the Anti-privatisation Forum in the Midst of South Africa's 'Rebellion of the Poor.'" *Current Sociology* 63 (7): 961–79.

Rust, Kecia, and Sue Rubinstein. 1996. *A Mandate to Build: Developing Consensus around a National Housing Policy in South Africa*. Johannesburg, South Africa: Ravan Press.

Santini, Daniel. 2023. "Só a Tarifa Zero não basta." *Revista Rosa (Rosa Luxemburg Foundation)* 7 (3). https://revistarosa.com/7/so-a-tarifa-zero-nao-basta.

Sassen, Saskia. 1991. *The Global City: New York, London, Tokyo*. Princeton, NJ: Princeton University Press.

Saule Júnior, Nelson. 2001. "Estatuto da Cidade: Instrumento de Reforma Urbana." In *Estatuto da Cidade: Perspectivas para a reforma urbana*, ed. Nelson Saule Júnior and Raquel Rolnik, 10–36. São Paulo, Brazil: Instituto Pólis.

Scruggs, Gregory. 2016. "'We Managed to Kick Off a Paradigm Shift in São Paulo,' Mayor Says on Leaving Office." *Citiscope*.

Seekings, Jeremy. 2000. *The UDF: A History of the United Democratic Front in South Africa, 1983–1991.* Cape Town, South Africa: David Philip; Oxford: James Currey; and Athens: Ohio University Press.

Seidman, Gay. 1994. *Manufacturing Militance: Workers Movements in Brazil and South Africa, 1970–1985.* Berkeley: University of California Press.

Seippel, Ørnulf. 2001. "From Mobilization to Institutionalization? The Case of Norwegian Environmentalism." *Acta Sociologica* 44 (2): 105–89.

Sekhonyane, Makubetse, and Jackie Dugard. 2004. "A Violent Legacy: The Taxi Industry and Government at Loggerheads." *South African Crime Quarterly* 10: 13–18.

Sen, Amartya. 1999. *Development as Freedom.* New York: Anchor Books.

Sewell, William H. 2010. *Logics of History: Social Theory and Social Transformation.* Chicago: University of Chicago Press.

Singer, Paul. 1995. *Um governo de esquerda para todos: Luiza Erundina na prefeitura de São Paulo (1989–1992).* São Paulo, Brazil: Editora Brasiliense.

Skidmore, Thomas. 1967. *Politics in Brazil 1930–1964: An Experiment in Democracy.* Oxford: Oxford University Press.

Small, Mario Luis, and Jessica McCrory Calarco. 2022. *Qualitative Literacy: A Guide to Evaluating Ethnographic and Interview Research.* Oakland: University of California Press.

Snyder, Richard. 2001. "Scaling Down: The Subnational Comparative Method." *Studies in Comparative International Development* 36: 93–110.

The Star. 1999. "iGoli 2002: Unions Take to Streets." October 25. https://www.iol.co.za/news/south-africa/igoli-2002-unions-take-to-streets-17474.

Stoker, G., and K. Mossberger. 1994. "Urban Regime Theory in Comparative Perspective." *Environment and Planning C: Government and Policy* 12 (2): 195–212.

Stone, Clarence N. 1989. *Regime Politics.* Lawrence: University Press of Kansas.

Stone, Clarence N. 1993. "Urban Regimes and the Capacity to Govern: A Political Economy Approach." *Journal of Urban Affairs* 15 (1): 1–28.

Tarrow, Sidney. 1994. *Power in Movement: Social Movements, Collective Action and Politics.* Cambridge: Cambridge University Press.

Tatagiba, Luciana, Stella Zagatto Paterniani, and Thiago Apaecido Trindade. 2012. "Ocupar, reivindicar, participar: Sobre o repertório de ação do movimento de moradia de São Paulo." *Opinião Pública* 18 (2): 399–426.

Thompson, James Philip. 2006. *Double Trouble: Black Mayors, Black Communities and the Call for Deep Democracy.* New York: Oxford University Press.

Tissington, Kate. 2011. *A Resource Guide to Housing in South Africa 1994–2010: Legislation, Policy, Programmes and Practice.* Socio-economic Rights Institute of South Africa. https://www.seri-sa.org/images/stories/SERI_Housing_Resource_Guide_Feb11.pdf.

Todes, Alison. 2014. "The Impact of Policy and Strategic Spatial Planning." In *Changing Space, Changing City: Johannesburg after Apartheid,* edited by P. Harrison, G. Götz, A. Todes, and C. Wray, 83–100. Johannesburg, South Africa: Wits University Press.

Tomlinson, Mary R. 2006. "From 'Quantity' to 'Quality': Restructuring South Africa's Housing Policy Ten Years After." *International Development Planning Review* 28 (1): 85–104.

Tomlinson, Richard. 1999. "From Exclusion to Inclusion: Rethinking Johannesburg's Central City." *Environment and Planning A: Economy and Space* 31 (9): 1655–78.

Tomlinson, Richard, Robert Beauregard, Lindsay Bremmer, and Xolela Mangcu, eds. 2003. *Emerging Johannesburg: Perspectives on the Postapartheid City.* New York: Routledge.

Transaction Capital. 2019. *Integrated Annual Report.* https://www.sharedata.co.za/Data/014202/pdfs/TRANSCAP_ar_sep19.pdf.

Turok, Ivan. 2014. "The Resilience of South African Cities a Decade after Local Democracy." *Environment and Planning A: Economy and Space* 46 (4): 749–69.

Van Onselen, Charles. 1982. *Studies in the Social and Economic History of Witwatersrand, 1886–1914*. Johannesburg, South Africa: Ravan Press.

Venter, Irma. 2016. "Rea Vaya to Reach Sandton Central by 2018." *Engineering News*, July 18. https://www.engineeringnews.co.za/article/rea-vaya-to-reach-sandton-central-by-2018-2016 -07-18 (accessed June 23, 2020).

Vince, Gaia. 2022. *Nomad Century: How Climate Migration Will Reshape Our World*. New York: Flatiron Books.

Wacquant, Loïc. 2008. *Urban Outcasts: A Comparative Sociology of Advanced Marginality*. Cambridge: Polity.

Wade, Robert. 1990. *Governing the Market*. Princeton, NJ: Princeton University Press.

Wahba, Sameh, Maimunah Mohd Sharif, Mami Mizutori, and Lauren Sorkin. 2020. "Cities Are on the Front Lines of COVID-19." *Sustainable Cities*, May 12. https://blogs.worldbank.org /sustainablecities/cities-are-front-lines-covid-19 (accessed August 10, 2020).

Wampler, Brian. 2008. "When Does Participatory Democracy Deepen the Quality of Democracy? Lessons from Brazil." *Comparative Politics* 41 (1): 61–81.

Water and Sanitation Program. 2011. "Water Supply and Sanitation in South Africa: Turning Finance into Services for 2015 and Beyond." An African Ministers Council on Water Country Status Overview, 69923. World Bank. https://documents1.worldbank.org/curated/fr /330331468007268303/pdf/6992300REPLACE0LIC00CSO0SouthAfrica.pdf.

Weinstein, Barbara. 1996. *For Social Peace in Brazil: Industrialists and the Remaking of the Working Class in São Paulo, 1920–1964*. Chapel Hill: University of North Carolina Press.

Weinstein, Liza. 2014. *The Durable Slum*. Minneapolis: University of Minnesota Press.

Whitaker Ferreira, João Sette, Eduardo Rojas, Higor R. De Souza Carvalho, Carolina Rago Frignani, and Ligia Santi Lupo. 2020. "Housing Policies and the Roles of Local Governments in Latin America: Recent Experiences." *Environment and Urbanization* 32 (2). https://doi.org /10.1177/0956247820935699.

Wines, Michael. 2006. "Cartels Battle for Supremacy in South Africa's Taxi Wars." *New York Times*, September 17. https://www.nytimes.com/2006/09/17/world/africa/17africa.html (accessed June 17, 2020).

Wirth, Louis. 1938. "Urbanism as a Way of Life." *American Journal of Sociology* 44: 1–24.

Wolpe, Harold. 1972. "Capitalism and Cheap Labour-Power in South Africa: From Segregation to Apartheid." *Economy and Society* 1 (4): 425–56.

World Bank. 2014. "Changing Commuters' Choices Helps São Paulo Reduce Traffic Congestion." May 1. https://www.worldbank.org/en/news/feature/2014/05/01/changing-commuter -choices-helps-sao-paulo-reduce-traffic-congestion.

Zanini, Fábio, and Carolina Linhares. 2020. "Cargos, festas e verba pública impulsionam 'Tattolândia,' reduto do candidato do PT em SP." *Folha de São Paulo*, May 24. https://www1.folha .uol.com.br/poder/2020/05/cargos-festas-e-verba-publica-impulsionam-tattolandia-reduto -do-candidato-do-pt-em-sp.shtml (accessed June 1, 2020).

A NOTE ON THE TYPE

This book has been composed in Adobe Text and Gotham.
Adobe Text, designed by Robert Slimbach for Adobe,
bridges the gap between fifteenth- and sixteenth-century
calligraphic and eighteenth-century Modern styles.
Gotham, inspired by New York street signs, was designed
by Tobias Frere-Jones for Hoefler & Co.

Printed in the USA
CPSIA information can be obtained
at www.ICGtesting.com
JSHW020438250924
70303JS00001B/1

9 780691 237121